Critical Muslim 5
Love and Death

Editors: Ziauddin Sardar and Robin Yassin-Kassab
Deputy Editor: Samia Rahman
Senior Editors: Aamer Hussein, Ehsan Masood
Publisher: Michael Dwyer
Managing Editor: (Hurst Publishers) Daisy Leitch
Cover Design: Fatima Jamadar

Associate Editors: Abdulwahhab El-Affendi, Muhammad Idrees Ahmad, Iqbal
Asaria, Vinay Lal, Hassan Mahamdallie
Contributing Editors: Alev Adil, Merryl Wyn Davies, Nader Hashemi,
Boyd Tonkin, Iftikhar Malik, Parvez Manzoor

International Advisory Board: Waqar Ahmad, Karen Armstrong, William Dal-
rymple, Farid Esack, Anwar Ibrahim, Bruce Lawrence, Ebrahim Moosa, Ashish
Nandy, Ruth Padel, Bhikhu Parekh
Critical Muslim is published quarterly by C. Hurst & Co (Publishers) Ltd on behalf
of and in conjunction with Critical Muslim Ltd and the Muslim Institute, London.

All correspondence to Muslim Institute, CAN Mezzanine, 49–51 East Road,
London N1 6AH, United Kingdom
e-mail for editorial: editorial@criticalmuslim.com

The editors do not necessarily agree with the opinions expressed by the
contributors. We reserve the right to make such editorial changes as may be
necessary to make submissions to Critical Muslim suitable for publication.

C. Hurst & Co (Publishers) Ltd.,
41 Great Russell Street, London WC1B 3PL

ISBN: 978-1-84904-307-6
ISSN: 2048-8475

To subscribe or place an order by credit/debit card or cheque (pounds ster-
ling only) please contact Kathleen May at the Hurst address above or email
kathleen@hurstpub.co.uk
Tel: 020 7255 2201
A one year subscription, inclusive of postage (four issues), costs £50 (UK), £65
(Europe) and £75 (rest of the world).

A Cataloguing-in-Publication data record for this book is available from the
British Library.

The British Museum

Discover the Islamic World

From early scientific instruments to contemporary art, explore how Islam has shaped our world through objects for centuries

Great Russell Street,
London WC1B 3DG
⊖ Tottenham Court Road,
Holborn, Russell Square
britishmuseum.org

Mosque lamp. Enamelled glass.
Syria, c. AD 1330–1345.

OUR MISSION

Critical Muslim is a quarterly magazine of ideas and issues showcasing ground-breaking thinking on Islam and what it means to be a Muslim in a rapidly changing, increasingly interconnected world.

We will be devoted to examining issues within Islam, and Muslim societies, providing a Muslim perspective on the great debates of contemporary times, and promoting dialogue, cooperation and collaboration between 'Islam' and other cultures, including 'the West'. We aim to be innovative, thought-provoking and forward-looking, a space for debate between Muslims and between Muslims and others, on religious, social, cultural and political issues concerning the Muslim world and Muslims in the world.

What does 'Critical Muslim' mean? We are proud of our strong Muslim identity, but we do not see 'Islam' as a set of pieties and taboos. We aim to challenge traditionalist, modernist, fundamentalist and apologetic versions of Islam, and will attempt to set out new readings of religion and culture with the potential for social, cultural and political transformation of the Muslim world. Our writers may define their Muslim belonging religiously, culturally or civilisationally, and some will not 'belong' to Islam at all. *Critical Muslim* will sometimes invite writers of opposing viewpoints to debate controversial issues.

We aim to appeal to both academic and non-academic readerships; to emphasise intellectual rigour, the challenge of ideas, and original thinking.

In these times of change and peaceful revolutions, we choose not to be a lake or a meandering river. But to be an ocean. We embrace the world with all its diversity and pluralism, complexity and chaos. We aim to explore everything on our interconnected, shrinking planet — from religion and politics, to science, technology and culture, art and literature, philosophy and ethics, and histories and futures — and seek to move forward despite deep uncertainty and contradictions. We stand for open and critical engagement in the best tradition of Muslim intellectual inquiry.

Wider Concerns of Halal

You think you know what is *halal*?

It's not just about '*halal* meat' and '*halal* food'.

In fact, *halal* is one of the most sophisticated concepts of Islam. It is best translated as 'praiseworthy' and has a direct relationship to public interest, environment, business ethics and moral behaviour. During the 'Golden Age of Islam', the concept of *halal* was used to generate policy and legislation for city planning, protection of flora and fauna, trade and commerce and was a driving force behind social and cultural productions of Muslim civilisation.

We aim to advance a more holistic understanding of what is *halal* and what it means to lead an ethical, socially responsible life in the twenty-first century.

Look out for our workshops, seminars and school visits.

Halal Food Foundation is a charitable arm of Halal Food Authority.

Halal Food Foundation
109 Fulham Palace Road, London W6 8JA, UK
Registered Charity Number: 1139457
Website: www.halalfoodauthority.com
E-mail: info@halalfoodauthority.com

CM5

January–March 2013

CONTENTS

LOVE AND DEATH

THE CULMINATION OF LOVE

Aamer Hussein

I love you with a double love: I love you passionately, and I love you for
yourself.
Loving you passionately has put me off others.
I love you for yourself so you would drop your shutters and let me see you.
I am not the one to be thanked, all thanks must go to you.

Rabia of Basra lived in twelfth-century Iraq. She wrote in Arabic, but her
exemplary piety made her a saint who is venerated all over the Muslim
world. In her era, the mystical tradition of Islam was growing, even burgeoning. In contrast to the crippling orthodoxy, which emphasised the fear
of God, and the rise of materialism in her society, the advocate of mysticism
focused on love. The mystics preferred an intimate relationship with God
rather than many of the barren rituals of formal worship. 'This was the
period', says the German scholar Anne-Marie Schimmel, 'when early
Islamic mysticism, with its austere and world-detesting outlook, began to
turn into love-mysticism.' And Rabia took the lead. Schimmel thinks that
the absoluteness of devotion Rabia displays in her verses is 'stronger than
her art'. Artistic or not, such poetic intimacies, as Rabia's twentieth-century
biographer, Widad Sakkakini, points out, were seen by many as transgres-
sive. To address one's maker as if He were her lover?

Another saintly figure took transgression even further. The tenth-century
Iraqi poet Mansur al-Hallaj, whose seemingly blasphemous declarations of
love and of identification with God led him to be executed in public by the
authorities, became both metaphor and heroic subject for generations of his
successors. His famous utterance, '*ana al-haq*' ('I am the absolute truth')
echoes through the languages of the Muslim world as the limit of transgres-
sive devotion: it seems to point to self-identification with the Creator. But
other verses cast a different light on his immersion in the object of his love:

I saw my lord with the eye of the heart
and said: Who are you? He answered: You.

or:

I am He whom I love, and He whom I love is I.

If Rabia abides in the Muslim imagination as a symbol of love in its purest
and most disembodied form, which leads to peaceful reconciliation with a
world that was formerly renounced, Hallaj occupies another corner, that of
death in pursuit of the Beloved. Such all-encompassing love is, however,
difficult to maintain in its earthly form, especially when harnessed to the
writer's craft.

By the time the centre of Sufi literary activity moved to Persia, several
other strategies of expressing love had become common to its poets – just
as the *ghazal*, love lyric, had become a popular form of self-expression. The
ghazal, as Robert Irwin notes, evolved from the pre-Islamic Arabian *qasida*,
or ode. Irwin beautifully chronicles the origin and development of *ghazal*
and shows how it spread far and wide throughout the Muslim world – to
Andalusia, Persia and the Indian Subcontinent.

Sufi poets too turned to tales of benighted lovers from every country they
had lived or travelled in. Popular among these were Solomon and Sheba and
Joseph and Potiphar's wife from the Qur'an, Vis and Ramin, and Shirin and
Khusrau from the annals of Persian legend. Entire cycles of romances were
retold by the great poets; allegories of love unrequited or passion betrayed
were reinvented to convey subtle moral truths. The *masnavi*, formed of
rhyming couplets, was their favoured vehicle. The twelfth-century poet
Nizami of Ganja's *Haft Peykar*, for example, is an exquisite cycle of seven
love stories, in each of which the vagaries and hazards of love and desire are
recounted. These stories have contemporary echoes: in her story 'Akhit
Jadoo', Fahmida Riaz, one of the finest living Urdu poets, turns to these
pre-Islamic Persian sources for her searing parable of sacred and profane
modes of being and loving.

Nizami is the architect for what is arguably the greatest and most influen-
tial of metaphysical reinventions of love stories derived from extant sources:
the reclaiming of the obscure Bedouin poet Qais, known as Majnun (the

mad), from the annals of Bedouin history and folklore. In his masterpiece, a quasi-realistic retelling of the story of Laila and Majnun, Nizami reshapes the legend to portray Majnun as an ideal lover. Just one sideways glance from Laila bewitches him and he starts dancing around her like a dervish. Ostensibly, Majnun is a fool who is totally broken by his love for Laila, a man to be pitied or derided. But as Rudolph Gelpke says in the introduction to his translation, 'Nizami understands the three aspects of the traditional Majnun – his love, his insanity, and his poetic genius – as three aspects of one, indivisible unity. Only when he is driven out of the paradise of his earthly love does Majnun become both insane and a poet. Insanity and genius are two expressions of the same state of mind, a soul estranged in the world of men.'

Nizami, turning the secular and abject into the spiritually transcendent, gives poetic form to the yearning that, even in solitude and separation, unites the lover with the beloved, in a series of compelling images – for example, Majnun wasting away at his beloved's grave, where he dies alone. Such metaphors would be elaborated upon by many of his successors. The ill-starred lovers of seventh-century Arabia continue to appear in both *ghazal* and *masnavi*. One of the most beautiful recapitulations of the legend is a short text by the twelfth-century poet Fariduddin Attar, in which someone asks Majnun how he loves Laila. 'I no longer love her', Majnun says. His friend asks him why he spends his nights and days weeping, composing verses, without eating or sleeping: is this not, then, love? 'All that is over', Majnun responds: 'At present, Laila has become Majnun; Majnun has become Laila. They are drowned in each other, no longer two but one'. Attar's near-contemporary, Maulana Jalaluddin of Balkh, gives us Majnun in the sandy wastes, writing, over and over again, a name in the sand with his fingertip. When asked by a passing traveller to explain this redundant action, he responds that in Laila's absence he is playing the game of love with the letters of her name.

Maulana Jalaluddin flourished in Konya in the thirteenth century. He was born in what is now Afghanistan but moved in his youth to Turkey. It is with Turkey, and the appellation Rumi by which he is now known, that his life and work are now identified. He continued, however, to write in Persian, producing the allegories, fables, and poems which have made him the most famous writer ever to emerge from the Muslim world. His poetry adds another dimension to adoration for his mentor Shams of Tabriz, to whom he devoted a divan, and in whose name he sang:

> Love for you has seized my rosary and given me verses and song –
> I very often said *la haul* and *tauba* but the heart didn't listen
> Through love's hand I became a ghazal singer, hand-clapping;
> Your love burnt honour and shame....

Rumi has inspired generations of writers. Numerous festivals are held to honour his memory. While in Turkey during 2009, I was asked if I knew of a festival which, to my Persianised ear, sounded like *shab-e-arus*, the 'Night of the Wedding'. This is, in fact, the celebration of Rumi's passing from the world. Like Rabia and unlike his mentor who was probably murdered, Rumi lived to be very old, and saw his own departure from this world of matter as merely one more stage of his journey towards the divine reality. Every year, on 17 December, over a million people attend the Whirling Dervishes Festival in Konya. The American Sufi orders hold the Rumi Festival in early September in Chapel Hill and Carrboro, North Carolina, where thousands of people gather to read his poetry and sing and dance in spiritual ecstasy. A very contemporary continuation of his anecdotal technique, with its stories within stories, can be seen in the Turkish Cypriot poet Alev Adil's surreal feminist collage of tales and texts, 'Night of Destiny', included in this issue of *Critical Muslim*, with their fiery evocation of love and death-as-sacrifice.

Like Rumi, several other poets had a spiritual mentor or guide, who served as their platonic beloved and surrogate object of their affections. For the fourteenth-century Indian poet Amir Khusrau, the saint Nizamuddin Auliya, who was his near contemporary, was the doorway to the contemplation of the divine. Inspired by his guide, Khusrau wrote:

> I am a pagan and a worshipper of love: Islam I do not need
> Every vein of mine has become taut like a wire, the pagan's girdle I do not need....
> The people of the world say that Khusrau worships idols.
> So what? He does: the people and the world he does not need.

Blasphemy and faith, as Hallaj had earlier proclaimed, differ only in name: both are given by the Creator. But to assimilate such formulations requires sophistication on the part of the reader and listener. For some, excessive veneration for a living teacher can, of course, be anathema, especially to those who erase the boundary between subject and object to see such poetry as disguised erotic effusion.

In contrast, commentators desperate to prove that that all poetry written by mystics stems solely from their longing for divine love, say that women and the Beloved are merely embodiments of the divine, which seems unfair to both poet and subject. As Christopher Shackle shows in his essay, which explores the themes of love and death in Punjabi Muslim poetry, the famine is both subject and object of love. Shackle examines how the great love stories of Hir and Ranjha, Sohni and Mahinval, and Sassi and Punnum have been turned into epic poems by mystical poets such as Bulleh Shah, Varis Shah, Shah Abdul Latif, Khwaja Farid and Mian Muhammad. These mystical renderings are not devoid of the erotic. In some cases, the poets themselves were inspired by their attachment to a girl. Khwaja Farid's Sassi story, for example, 'is closely associated with his own attachment to the local Rohi desert of Bahawalpur, where he spent much time and where he formed a romantic attachment to a girl from one of the desert tribes'. *Masnavis*, given their length and often epic scope, can juxtapose the erotic with the metaphysical, moving from rapt lyricism to the aphoristic dryness of moral stricture, slanting emphases to suit individual talents and purposes.

More vexed, however, is the question of when a seemingly profane celebration of love demands a spiritual interpretation. To what extent do some of the ghazals of the fourteenth-century Persian poet Hafiz, synonymous with mastery of the form, gain a deeper significance when read as metaphysical allegories? Is the beloved always divine? Is red wine always the symbol of spiritual ecstasy? Are narcissus eyes and curling locks always expressions of a higher reality? Do the nightingale and the rose always echo the despair of the human soul separated from God? One answer is that aspects of the sacred and the profane, the existential and the spiritual, blend perfectly in Hafiz's verses:

Love is where the glory falls
Of thy face: on convent walls

or on tavern floors the same
unextinguished flame.
Where the turbaned anchorite chanteth Allah day and night
church bells ring the call to prayer
and the cross of Christ is there.

In such poems, love is figured as universal and all-pervading, the subject of
its own contemplation, to be found within the heart. It is both the pilgrimage and its goal, the gateway to the divine, with no need of intercession.

With the fifteenth-century Persian Jami, who spent much of his life in
Herat in what is now Afghanistan, the mystic tradition in the Persian *masnavi*
reached its apogee. Jami wrote his acknowledged masterpiece, *Yusuf and
Zulaikha*, at the age of seventy, in 1483. The sketchy narrative of Joseph and
Potiphar's wife in the Old Testament was elaborated in the Qur'an (Surah
Yusuf, Chapter 12) but over the centuries the Muslim imagination has transformed it into a complex exploration of the nature of love, betrayal and
loyalty. In Jami's version we see, for a change, the lover embodied as a
woman, and the beloved as a man, where all too often the woman in earlier
narratives was presented as the obscure object of an ardent male lover's
desire. Interpolated in the richly detailed account, we find passages on the
nature of God and love:

'As soon as God chooses a being, and raises him to the place of honour in
his love, he closes to him all avenues of help, and will not allow him to
depend on anyone else. He draws his attention exclusively to Himself, and
severs all other attachments. He does not wish that any others should share
his spoils, nor that the chosen one should need anyone else but him. He
does not wish to be involved with any other person. The captive caught in
His net is His, and His alone.'

The romantic and the erotic thus acquired metaphysical significance; but
the narrative element in the poems of Nizami, Jami and other great poets
adds to the abstractions of love and death the dimension of character.
Though by Western standards this dimension may appear idealised and flat,
we can see in these narratives the roots of the secular fictions that would
emerge in the twentieth century, ostensibly under the influence of Western
literature but also, in their poetic diction and romantic agony, shaped by
sensibilities steeped in classical syntax, for example The Blind Owl by Sadiq

Hidayat and Simin Danishvar's novella Sutra. An exacerbated romantic sensibility, secularised and commercialised, also crept into popular films, television drama and women's magazines all over Asia. And the shift in social norms gradually replaced the inevitability of the death of romantic love with the possibility of a happy ending.

Both Martin Rose, who was held in Baghdad as a human shield by Saddam Hussain, and Ramin Jehanbegloo, who was framed for promoting 'soft overthrow' and held in solitary confinement 'Inside Evin' by the Iranian regime, under constant threat of torture and execution, met happy endings. Both survived their harrowing ordeals. The real threat of death they faced was not a product of unconditional romantic love – but of more worldly concerns. As 'A Veronica on the Eve of War' demonstrates, Rose has an infectious love for Muslim cultures. There is nothing he likes more than to live and work in a Muslim city; and Baghdad, with all its historic romantic connotations, seemed like a wonderful place to immerse oneself in things Islamic. As a philosopher, Jehanbegloo is motivated by truth. His writings on non-violence and association with Western academics and intellectuals were seen as a threat by the Islamic regime. Pitted against both was an unconditional love of deathly ideologies that echoed al-Hallaj: 'I am the absolute truth'. But while al-Hallaj's utterance was aimed at the annihilation of his ego, the pronouncements of Ba'athist Iraq and theocratic Iran are aimed solely at earthly power and worldly gains.

Sufi poets did not altogether ignore earthly concerns. Even in Jami's times, Persian poets were turning to more worldly matters. Sufism was spreading fast among the semi-literate and unlettered in the lands where Persian was the language of courtiers and the elite, while the vast majority spoke their vernaculars. In India, which was to enter a long period of poetic excellence, Urdu would eventually supplant Persian as the favoured language of poets, but in the period of *interregnum* more and more poets turned to humbler vernaculars to tell their tales. A good example is *Madhumalati*, the sixteenth-century verse romance by the Sufi teacher, Mir Sayyid Manjhan. It uses an eastern dialect of Hindavi or Hindi, and the rich local colour and earthy myths of its local settings. The hero and heroine are Hindu, rather than Muslim, Jewish or Zoroastrian. The lessons of the Persian *masnavi* have been well-learnt and then adapted to indigenous needs; this Hindu

tale is set within the Sufi framework of eulogy, theophany and praise of the
Holy Prophet. Characteristically, love is elevated above all:

Love is the costliest jewel in existence
the man whose soul knows love is blessed.
God made the world only for love.
Through God, love itself is manifest.
Love's radiance lights up all of creation.
No rival to love exists anywhere.

In other local dialects and languages, Sufism was creating new and syncretic
traditions. As the Ottoman empire gained cultural confidence, Turkish poets
created their own distinctive idiom, and in the Indonesian and Malaysian
archipelago, poetic and musical forms like the impassioned *asmaradana* and
the graceful *pantun* respectively portrayed the pains of love. In the lands of
the Indus – Sind and Punjab – the greatest poets would emerge from about
the seventeenth century onwards. Steeped in the doctrines and practices of
conventional as well as heterodox Islam, these poets would draw largely on
their own vernacular traditions, weaving parables from local stories that often
pre-dated the rise of Islam. In Sindh, as Shackle shows, the great Shah Abdul
Latif, born at the end of the seventeenth century, took seven folk heroines of
the sort known as death brides as the mouthpieces of his reflections of love
and death, the former always doomed and the latter often violent.

The creators of the profane or secularised *masnavi* in Urdu-speaking
Northern India, including Mir Hassan, Mir Taqi Mir, Dagh and Shauq,
chronicled the punishable excesses of love in their own segregated society,
with only a passing nod to the mandatory inclusion of the sacred sanctioned
by the poetic tradition. However, in these resolutely modern narratives
madness and death in the name of love still evoke the image of the Sufi lover-
as-martyr, with love itself staged as a social and even a moral transgression,
reminding us again of the bedouin lover Qais and the original Arab notion of
his *junun* which gave him his immortal appellation, *Majnun*. Today, though,
the madness of the lovelorn in a segregated society can be replaced, with
more than a touch of humour, by the incursion of the text and the email,
which facilitate communication without the help of friends, carrier pigeons
or magical messengers. And those seeking love, as Samia Rahman discovers,

can access the tools of high technology such as Facebook and match-making websites, and become a node in highly tailored 'Networks of Love'.

As romantic poets grew more complacent, a nascent form was to be revitalised to express the public agony of the time. In the hands of the nineteenth-century poets Mir Anis and Mirza Dabir, emerged the *marsia* or elegy, recounting the Battle of Karbala. As Imranali Panjwani notes, the martyrdom of Imam Husain, the grandson of Prophet Muhammad, on 10 October 680, is 'a central event in Islamic history'. Yazid, the reigning Umayyad caliph at the time, wanted Husain to accept him as his king and give him his unconditional allegiance. Husain saw Yazid as a tyrant. 'In the end', writes Panjwani, 'al-Husayn and his small band of men, women and children (including al-Husayn's six-month-old infant son by the name of 'Abdallah) were deprived of water for several days. The commander of the Umayyad army abandoned the convention of one-to-one combat, surrounded al-Husayn, and ordered his vastly larger and superior army to kill him. Al-Husayn was butchered; the few remaining women and children were tortured and enslaved.' A generation of poets have portrayed these events in vivid detail in formal verse as a moral triumph against the evil of the despot Yazid.

Like Panjwani, the feminist and socialist novelist Ismat Chughtai sees Karbala as a human rights issue. In the 1960s, in a brief preface to her *Ek qatra-i-khun* (A Drop of Blood), a retelling of the Karbala chronicles, she writes of 'those superior people who, in the service of human rights, battled with imperial forces. This story, fourteen hundred years old, is the story of today, for today too man's worst enemy is man. And the flag bearer of humanity is man. And when, in any corner, a Yazid arises, Husain advances to restrain him, and today too light still tries to break through the darkness.' (My literal translation)

Thus Chughtai interprets the verses of Anis, and through them the tragedy of Karbala, as a testament of the war between man's love for man (and by extension, the divine) and inhumanity and barbarism. This Karbala narrative, in its varied forms, has influenced generations of writers, both Shia and Sunni. In the Lebanon and Iran, for example, where the portrayal or personification of saints is allowed, dramatised enactments of the Karbala passion, in the sacred month of Muharram, were witnessed in their childhood by writers Hanan al-Shaykh and Shusha Guppy, shaping their view of war and conflict. It is impossible to read the tragic accounts of war, death and collective disaster from the regions familiar with this grand epic of Islam without hearing overtones, conscious or unconscious, of the laments ritually recited during Muharram, and the hope that somewhere, in Afghanistan, Iran, Palestine, or Iraq, light and its harbingers will prevail against the enveloping darkness of conflict, sectarian strife and imperial ambition. The long and protracted conflict between India and Pakistan is also in dire need of history lessons. As Sabita Manian's account of the movement that aims to bring love and harmony between the two neighbours, *Aman ki Asha*, shows, both sides have to contend with right wing bigots intoxicated with nationalism and their own perceptions of truths. The blind love of the nation and the sense of superiority it engenders can be a toxic mix. The distance between absolute conviction of one's own moral superiority and evil, as Jalees Rahman demonstrates in his account of Nazi doctors who felt no moral compulsion in doing deathly experiments on Jews, is no distance at all.

The tragedy of Karbala is a constant and continuous reminder, not just for Muslims but the whole of humanity, of the perils of self-love. The innovative retelling of the sacred story by Aniswas was to influence no less great a figure than the twentieth century poet-philosopher Muhammad Iqbal. Anis's *marsias* are regarded as the model in Urdu of narrative-lyrical-dramatic poetry both in the technical scope of their epic sweep, and their lyrical elevation of collective love and sacrifice as duty. Iqbal, rejecting the traditional and outmoded idiom of a love poetry that was increasingly declared 'decadent' by the Muslim modernists and reformers of the Raj, extended the potential offered by Anis. Boundaries between muhabbat and ishq, or agape and eros, were erased. Serving people meant serving, and loving, God.

Iqbal was born in 1870 in what is now Pakistan and was then imperial India. He lived until 1938 in one of the most decisive periods of his country's and the world's history. Trained as a philosopher in England and Germany, Iqbal was exposed to the ideas of Hegel, Bergson, and Nietzsche. Yet the lens through which he studied Western (and also Vedantic) philosophy was the once-glorious and now-declining heritage of Islam. Denouncing the world-denying quietism of his predecessors, he called for a passionate mysticism of action and activity in the real world, based on an intimate, though at times antagonistic, relationship with God. And the strength of the bond was love:

> Love is Gabriel's breath, love is Muhammad's strong heart.
> Love is the envoy of God, love the utterance of God,
> Love is a new-pressed wine, love is the goblet of kings,
> Love the priest, love the commander of hosts,
> Love the son of the road, counting a thousand homes,
> Love is the plectrum that draws music from life's strings.
> Love is the warmth of life, love is the radiance of life.

Despite his pervasive influence, Iqbal did not establish a school of thought. But in other parts of the world, his contemporaries were thinking in parallel modes, improvising and meditating on the theme of love as universal salvation. The Malian sage Tierno Bokar, technically illiterate, passed on his beliefs about love, charity and brotherhood without boundaries to his sophisticated francophone student Amadou Hampate Ba. Ba would immortalise his teacher's words in his most famous work, *Le Sage de Bandiagara* (1957): 'may our love not be centred on ourselves! May this love not incite us to love only those who are like us or to espouse ideas that are similar to our own! Only to love that which resembles us is to love oneself; this is not how to love'.

In Istanbul, towards the end of a richly productive life, the renowned novelist and essayist Samiha Ayverdi paid tribute to her mentor, the Bulgarian-born Kenan Rifai, in her book *Dost* (The Friend) (1980). In her work, as in Ba's, the love and devotion to a mentor echoes Rumi's devotion to Shams, but is firmly placed not in the world of the mind but in the realm of contemporary realities and of brotherly love. Quoting Rifai, Ayverdi writes: 'love people. You have within you the potential for forgiveness, mercy and tolerance. Cultivate these....If you desire an element of virtue or an act of beauty for yourself, desire it just as much for others, too. That is the culmination of love'.

THE GHAZAL

Robert Irwin

> Very deep is the well of the past. Should we not call it bottomless?
> Thomas Mann, *Joseph and His Brothers*.

The *ghazal*, or love lyric, evolved out of the pre-Islamic Arabian *qasida*, or ode, and the origins of the qasida go back to a time before Arabic became a written language. The *qasida*, which was originally orally transmitted and which was conventionally divided into three parts, began with a *nasib*, a lament for lost love, before proceeding on to the *rihla*, a journey which often involved hard riding. This second section was likely to include praise of the poet's horse or camel, as well as vivid evocations of landscape and perhaps also desert storms in which lightning featured prominently. Finally, it was traditional to end with a *madih*, a panegyric addressed to a patron from whom the poet hoped to receive a reward. It is the *nasib* which concerns us here, for this was an amatory prelude, in which the poet, contemplating the deserted campsite, reflected on a past sexual encounter and, implicitly at least, on lost youth. The amatory prelude was always in the retrospective mode and dealt with youthful love. *Tashbib* (a noun form which derives from the verb *shabba*, to become a young man) means youthfulness, but it is also an alternative word for the love lyric.

Imru'l-Qays, who died around 540, was and is the most widely admired of the pre-Islamic or Jahili poets. Here is an extract from the *nasib* of his *Mu'allaqa*, (a poem which was honoured by being suspended in the enclosure of the Ka'ba):

Oh yes, many a fine day I've dallied with the white ladies,
And especially I call to mind a day at Dara Julul,

And the day I slaughtered for the virgins my riding-beast
(and how marvellous was the dividing of its loaded saddle),
And the virgins went on tossing its hacked flesh about
And the frilly fat like fringes of twisted silk.
Yes and the day I entered the litter where Unaiza was
And she cried, 'Out on you! Will you make me walk on my feet?'
She was saying, while the canopy swayed with the pair of us,
'There now, you've hocked my camel, Imr al-Kais. Down with you!'
But I said, 'Ride on, and slacken the beast's reins,
And oh, don't drive me away from your refreshing fruit.
Many's the pregnant woman like you, aye, and the nursing mother
I've night-visited, and made her forget her amuleted one-year-old,
Whenever he whimpered behind her, she turned to him
With half her body, her other half unshifted under me . . .
[AJ Arberry, *The Seven Odes*]

A little further on in the *nasib*, Imru'l-Qays provides a somewhat atomis-
tic evocation of the woman's beauty:

I twisted her side-tresses to me, and she leaned over me;
slender-waisted she was, and tenderly plump her ankles,
shapely and taut her belly, white fleshed, not the least flabby,
polished the lie of her breast-bones, smooth as a burnished mirror.
She turns away, to show a soft cheek, and wards me off
with the glance of a wild deer of Wajra, a shy gazelle with its fawn;
she shows me a throat like the throat of an antelope, not ungainly
when she lifts it upwards, neither naked of ornament;
she shows me her thick black tresses, a dark embellishment
clustering down her back like bunches of a laden date tree –
twisted upwards meanwhile are the locks that ring her brow,
the knots cunningly lost in the plaited and loosened strands;
she shows me a waist slender and slight as a camel's nose-rein,
and a smooth shank like the reed of a watered, bent papyrus.
[Arberry]

Imru'l-Qays was a boastful amatory predator and a truly great poet. We
are to understand that he won the lady's favours with a gift of the meat of
his riding-camel. Jahili poets scorned unfulfilled or platonic love and looked
back on fleshly couplings. As Hugh Kennedy has noted, Jahili poets did not
see lost or unattainable love as spiritually improving: 'It was bad news'.
Jahili sex was always contemplated in retrospect, for love is irretrievably
lost, and *dahr*, or fate, has separated the poet from his beloved and often he
laments his grey hairs. If the woman can return, it is only as a *tayf al-khayal*,
a ghost. There can be no real consolation for lost love and the finest *qasidas*
are intensely bleak. (A later poet of the Umayyad period, Waddah, contra-
posed the composition of love poetry and the fear of death.)

The art historian Richard Ettinghausen, drawing upon his reading of early
Arabic *ghazals*, was able to construct a composite portrait of the ideal
woman: 'In these love lyrics one reads that the ideal Arab woman must be
so stout that she nearly falls asleep: that she must be clumsy when rising and
lose her breath when moving quickly; that her breasts should be full and
rounded, her waist slender and graceful, her belly lean, her hips sloping and
her buttocks so fleshy as to impede her passage through a door . . . her eyes
are those of a gazelle'. (The Arabic root GH. Z. L. generates words that
denote not only dalliance and love poetry, but also spinning and gazelle. It
was common for a poet to compare his beloved to a gazelle.) The literary
scholar Andras Hamori noted that the Jahili ideal was 'always the same
woman; all pampered softness, languor, plenitude'. The ninth-century
essayist al-Jahiz, in one of his pieces, noted of one woman that she had two
of the attributes of Paradise, 'width and coolness'.

Early in the Islamic period the Caliph 'Umar I issued a ban on the composition and recitation of love poetry, but he might just as well have legis-
lated against the tides of the sea. The *ghazal*, emancipated from the *qasida*,
emerged as an independent lyric in the Umayyad period (661-750). Though
Jahili poetry continued to furnish formal models for the poets who came
after, there was a sea-change in sensibility. After 661 power moved from the
Hejaz to Syria and to the political capital of the Umayyads, Damascus.
Medina, though now a political backwater, became for some decades the
pleasure capital of the expanding Caliphate. It was there that moneyed
idlers who had been politically sidelined went to find singers, dancers and
transvestite performers and perhaps also attend drinking parties and have

affairs. It was in this environment that Hijazi *ghazals* were produced, often composed to be sung at parties. In contrast to the Jahili love poems, the Hijazi ones were more flirtatious; they were vaguer about the physical attributes of the beloved; and they were no longer presented as nostalgic retrospection, for the poets now lived in hope of future amorous conquests.

Though one gets the impression that the ideal woman of the Umayyad era was more slender than her pre-Islamic ancestor, nevertheless descriptions of the ideal woman in Umayyad poetry remain conventional and generalised, so that one would never be able to pick out the subject in a crowd.

'Umar ibn Abi Rabi'a (644-712 or 721) was the most famous of the Hijazi love poets. According to R.A. Nicholson, 'his poetry was so seductive that it was regarded by devout Muslims as "the greatest crime ever committed against God"'. 'Umar was as boastful as Imru'l-Qays, but his poems were lighter, more flirtatious.

'I reached for her and she swayed towards me
like a bough moved by the breeze.
After a quarrel she let me taste her sweetness
like honey mixed with pure wine
and then her body like a shirt touched
the skin of her suffering, passionate lover.
Panting she complained that her sash was tight
And cast off her veil towards me . . .
[Lewis, *Music of a Distant Drum*]

Some of 'Umar's poems celebrated the beauty of women who had arrived on the hajj and his assignations with them. There were many more than one woman and his poems are as much in praise of himself and his conquests as they are of the women. In this period love was too grand a thing to be expressed in prose. But sometimes the Medinese *ghazal* seems like a literary game and it is even uncertain whether the poem in question was actually addressed to a real woman or whether it was just an exercise in wordplay, the literary display of fine sentiment. Love has to be learnt and poetry teaches how to love. (The Duc de la Rochefoucauld once remarked that 'No one would ever have fallen in love unless he had first read about it'.)

'Udhrite poets also flourished in the Hijaz at roughly the same time as the Medinese school, but, whereas the latter were urban poets who celebrated sexual delight which either had been experienced or soon would be, the 'Udhrites, 'a people who when they love, die', produced mournful poems about loved ones who were forever unattainable. They were desert poets and their name derives from two poets of the Yemeni tribe of Banu 'Udhra. For an 'Udhrite poet falling in love has proved to be a disaster, but yet it is a disaster that he can never wish to be without. Death was the ultimate metaphor for unattainable love. A *hadith* circulated to the effect that, 'He who loves and remains chaste and conceals his secret and dies, dies a martyr'. Passionate love (*'ishq*) was presented as a sickness, or, more precisely, a form of madness. (Socrates once remarked that the male libido 'was like being chained to a lunatic'.) The semi-legendary 'Udhrite poet Qays ibn Mulawwah al-Majnun (the mad) may have lived in the seventh century. It was recorded that Qays, thwarted in his love for Layla, a woman of another tribe, went mad and dwelt with the beasts of the desert. In the desert he composed verses about Layla's beauty and his abjection.

Jamil ibn Ma'mar (d.701) was perhaps the most famous of the historical 'Udhrite poets. He is said to have fallen desperately in love with a woman called Buthyna, but she rejected him because he had dishonoured her by naming her in his verses and she married someone else. Nevertheless he continued to pursue her until the scandal grew so great and Buthyna's family were so hostile that he was forced to flee the Hijaz and find refuge in Egypt.

> Oh, might it flower anew, that youthful prime,
> And restore to us, Buthayna, the bygone time!
> And might we again be blest as we were wont to be,
> When thy folk were nigh and grudged what thou gavest me!

> Shall I ever meet Buthayna alone again,
> Each of us as full of love as a cloud of rain?
> Fast in her net was I when a lad, and till
> This day my love is growing and waxing still.

> I have spent my lifetime, waiting for her to speak,
> And the blossom of youth is faded from off my cheek;

But I will not suffer that she my suit deny,
My love remains undying, though all things die!
[Nicholson]

Much later, in the fourteenth century, Mughulta'i, a religious scholar
based in Egypt, produced a dictionary of those deemed to have become
martyrs for love.
Under the 'Abbasids Baghdad, founded in 762, became the political capital. The love poet al-'Abbas ibn al-Ahnaf flourished under the patronage of
the Caliph Harun al-Rashid in Baghdad. Many of 'Abbas's poems were
addressed to a certain Fauz ('Success'). She seems to have been a lady of
tender sensibilities.

Fauz is beaming on the castle.
When she walks amongst her maids of honour
you would think that she is walking upon eggs and green bottles.
Somebody told me that she cried for help
on beholding a lion engraved upon a signet ring.
[JC Burgel, in *Society and the Sexes in Medieval Islam*]

Perhaps Fauz was a lady of the court who was too grand to be given her
real name by the humble poet. She was also known to al-'Abbas as Zalum
('Tyrant'), but perhaps she was not really known at all, perhaps she was just
a made-up woman, designed to be the object of elegant poetry.
Though Baghdad was the centre of government of the 'Abbasids, Basra
was the literary capital. By the beginning of the second century AH Medina
had lost its dissolute glitter and the *jeunesse dorée* and the singers moved on
to Basra which became the base for pleasure expeditions into the desert.
The powerful and wealthy dynasty of Barmecide administrators, who pos-
sessed property in the region, were leading literary patrons. In the 'Abbasid
period Basra produced or at least nourished hundreds, or more likely thousands of poets. Bashshar ibn Burd (c.718-784) was a Persian born in Basra.
He was blind from birth, so he was never able to see how spectacularly ugly
he was. (He was also known as *al-Mara'ath*, 'the Wattled'.) He was rude and
arrogant and his rudeness and arrogance fuelled his invectives and satires,
but still women found him sexy. He was a pioneer of *badi'*, the ornate,

metaphor-heavy, modern style of poetry that came fully into fashion a little
later in the ninth century.

> God help me, see my weakness against this self-assured evildoer.
> He grabbed at my bracelet and crushed it. He is strong, overpowering.
> He pushed his beard against me rough and black, like needles.
> He came upon me when my kinsfolk were absent
> But he would overbear them even were they present.
> [Lewis, *Music of a Distant Drum*]

Bashshar was an expert in making enemies and the licentiousness of his
verse attracted a lot of criticism from the pious, but it was a political satire
that led to Bashshar's being tortured and then sewn into a sack that was
dumped in the Tigris.

Abu Nuwas, born in Ahwaz around 755, was half Persian (on his mother's
side). He spent his youth in Basra and apparently it was there that he fell in
love with Janan, a slave-singing girl. Singing girls were an important feature
of high society in Iraq, the best of them were educated like geishas and sang
from a repertoire of Arabic poetry that was commonly accompanied on the
lute. Abu Nuwas went to Baghdad in search of patronage and eventually
became the cup companion of the Caliph al-'Amin. Later, he served as the
cup companion of Harun al-Rashid (and as such features in several of the
tales of *The Thousand and One Nights*). Abu Nuwas composed wine poems,
hunting poetry, satire, homosexual love poetry, heterosexual love poetry,
satires and ascetic poetry. He is best known for the wine poetry that shaded
into erotic poetry, as the carousing poet often found himself fancying the
bearer of the wine, or the singer in the background or one or other of his
cup companions. It is surprisingly difficult in the 'Abbasid period to differ-
entiate the homosexual poetry from the heterosexual, because of the conventions regarding pronouns in medieval poetry. Moreover, sometimes
poets used male pronouns to refer to women, perhaps in order to protect
their honour. Besides writing homosexual poetry, Abu Nuwas wrote in
praise of *ghulumiyyat*, young women who dressed as men. By the time Abu
Nuwas set up his stall, the *ghazal* had acquired its fixed cast of characters -
the blamer, the jealous watcher, the go-between, and a few others. Abu

Nuwas delighted in parodying the stale conventions of the *ghazal* and he also produced *mujuniyya* (verses that were outright obscene).

Andalusia was something of a cultural backwater and its poets always trailed some distance behind eastern Islamic literary fashions. The heyday of the Andalusian love lyric was in the eleventh and twelfth centuries. *The Dove's Neck Ring: On Love and Lovers* by Ibn Hazm (994-1064) is one of the most delightful masterpieces of Arabic literature. (A dove was often used to carry messages between lovers; while in poetry the cooing of a dove signified loss.) Ibn Hazm's treatise dealt with the signs of love, falling in love in a dream, falling in love with the description of a woman, love at first sight, flirtation, messages, secrecy, obedience to the beloved, the watcher, the slanderer, separation, death and the supreme virtue of continence. In order to illustrate these topics he drew on his own experience and those of his acquaintances. In particular he looked back on his greatest passion, which was for a slave girl called Nu'm. But there were other affairs, apparently always with blondes. Besides the reminiscences of his love affairs and those of his friends, Ibn Hazm's arguments were illustrated with love lyrics, mostly of his own composition and, unfortunately, these are less interesting than his prose. 'Love begins in joking, but it always ends in seriousness.' Underlying all the concerns with flirtation and other matters of the heart in *The Dove's Neck Ring*, there was a strain of sadness and an implicit lament for the collapse of the Umayyad Caliphate, the destruction of the palace of Madinat al-Zahra and the sack of Cordova in 1013. Ibn Hazm was a strange man and in one of his other treatises he denounced the production of love poetry as something that led the soul to dissipation, pleasure, deceit and the disparagement of religion.

Ibn Zaydun (1003-70) is among the most famous poets of love in Arabic literature. An aristocrat and ultimately a failed politician, Ibn Zaydun had an ill-fated affair with Wallada. Red-haired, blue eyed and free-spoken, she was the daughter of a former caliph of Cordova, and a poet in her own right with two of her own verses embroidered on the hems of her robe:

I am by God fit for high positions,
And am going my way with pride!

And:

Forsooth, I allow my lover to touch my cheek,
And bestow my kiss on him who craves it!
[Nykl, *Hispano-Arabic Poetry*]

For a while Ibn Zaydun and Wallada met in secret and could imagine that
their love was mutual, but she soon turned against him and preferred to
marry an intellectually inferior, wealthy mediocrity called Ibn 'Abdus. She
then went on to denounce Ibn Zaydun as a thief and a sodomite. Ibn Zaydun
composed a *qasida* in which he looked back on their assignations. Its first
lines are as follows:

Morning came – the separation –
substitute for the love we shared,
for the fragrance of our coming together,
falling away . . .

We poured for one another
the wine of love. Our enemies seethed
and called for us to choke
– and fate said let it be.

The knot our two souls tied
came undone,
and what our hands joined
was broken.
[Devin J Stewart]

Love for another woman or man is a portal which may lead one to God,
as earthly love may segue into divine love. As EJW Gibb wrote in *A History
of Ottoman Poetry*:

And how is the Self to be conquered? By Love. By Love and by Love alone, can the
dark shadow of Not-being be done away; by Love and by Love alone, can the soul
of man win back to its Divine source and find its ultimate goal in reunion with the

Truth. And the first lessons of this Love, which is the keynote of Sufism and of all the literature it has inspired, may be, nay, must be learned through a merely human passion. Than true love 'there is no subtler master under heaven'.

So it is necessary for the soul to be first awakened by earthly love. Andalusia's most famous Sufi Muhyi al-Din ibn al-'Arabi set out on the hajj in 1201. His pilgrimage inspired *Tarjuman al-Ashwaq* (The Interpreter of Desires). This last consisted of a series of poems that was inspired by his encounter with 'Ayn al-Shams Nizam, a Persian lady from a family of Sufis from Isfahan, who was noted for her beauty, asceticism and intelligence. Since the poems in the *Tarjuman* had an overt erotic content, this attracted criticism from Ibn al-'Arabi's numerous enemies and consequently he was driven to produce a commentary on the poems that explained their true mystical meaning. The following verses overtly deal with lost human loves:

> I wonder whether they really knew
> What kind of heart they did subdue:
> And my heart would like to know
> To what country they went hence!
> I wonder whether they are safe
> Or whether they perished there?
> People in love became confused
> Because of love and rode away!
> [Nykl]

In the commentary 'they' turn out not to be women, but Divine Ideas. By 'heart' the perfect Muslim heart is meant. And so on. The poem turns out to be really about the obstacles on a person's way to be united with God. Doris Behrens Abouseif, in *Beauty in Arabic Culture*, summarises Ibn al-'Arabi's views on love in the following terms: 'Beauty is powerful and attracts love and desire; the sympathy between humanity and the universe is based upon love (*'ishq*)'. Beauty is 'a theophany, a manifestation of God'.

Whether Ibn al-'Arabi was writing poetry or prose, he expressed himself most obscurely. The Egyptian Sufi poet Ibn al-Farid (1181-1235), known as the 'Sultan of lovers', was more popular though hardly less controversial, for the question whether his poems dealt with earthly or divine love was regularly debated. Certainly he wrote some of his love poetry before he became a Sufi sheikh and perhaps it was love and poetry that led him to Sufism. Some of his shorter poems seem to have been composed to be sung at Sufi gatherings. He composed verses that conformed precisely to the conventions and imagery of the pre-Islamic *qasida*, with the abandoned campsite in the desert, the retrospect on lost love, the ride across the desert and the concluding panegyric. However, these poems were intended to be decoded and read for their latent spiritual content as the poet laments his separation from God and gives an account of his journey to find him once more. One of his most famous poems begins as follows:

> Did Layla's fire shine
> at Dhu Salam
> or did lightning flash
> at al-Zawra and al-Alam?
> [Homerin]

Here Layla is a woman's name and, in legend at least also the name of Qays ibn Mullawah al-Majunun's beloved, but *layla* is also the Arabic for 'night' and hence 'Layla' is perhaps here a metaphor for a Sufi 'dark night of the soul'. Layla frequently appears in Sufi poetry, though the significance of the name may vary. For example a poem by the twentieth-century Sufi Sheikh Ahmad al-'Alawi opens with these lines:

> Full near I came unto where dwelleth
> Layla, when I heard her call.
> That voice, would I might ever hear it!
> She favoured me, drew me to her,
> Took me into her precinct,
> With discourse intimate addressed me.
> She sat me by her, then came closer,
> Raised the cloak that hid her from me,
> Made me marvel to distraction,
> Bewildered me with all her beauty.
> [Lings]

Though the form and imagery of the *ghazal* originated in Arabic culture, the *ghazal* is not restricted to Arabic, for it pervades Islamic culture and one finds many examples in Persian, Turkish, Urdu and other languages. Persian *ghazals* were mostly composed by courtiers and, overtly at least, they were usually homoerotic. In some cases this may have arisen from discretion, from the wish not to risk identifying the lady who is the true object of the poet's passion, but in other cases references to such things as the beginning of a beard seem to leave no doubt that the beloved who is being addressed is a male. One sometimes has the impression that the court poet's true object of love was not a living breathing woman, but courtliness itself. It was axiomatic that lower-class people could not fall in love, since they lacked the capacity for refined sentiment. Love, like poetry, was something that had to be learned. As Hafiz of Shiraz put it:

'Only the bird of dawn can interpret the book of the rose;
For not all who read a page can understand its subtle sense.'

In the Persian *ghazal* each couplet is independent, so that the poem as a whole does not contain a developing argument but rather resembles a string of differently coloured beads. The Persian garden replaced the Arabian desert and the imagery of the Persian poems was softer and more luxuriant. Persian poets worked with a set of stock symbols, including the mole on the cheek, tresses of hair, the cypress tree, the narcissus, the tavern, the wine seller, the cup bearer, the nightingale and the rose. In the case of the nightingale and the rose, the bird stands in for the poet who sings of his hopeless love for the rose and the rose, in full bloom, is complacently aware of her beauty, but ignorant of the fact that this will fade.

Muhammad Iqbal (1873-1938), the philosopher and political leader who wrote poetry in Urdu and Persian, criticised the traditional Persian *ghazal* in these terms:

The butterfly imagination of the Persian flies half inebriated, as it were, from flower to flower and seems to be incapable of reviewing the garden as a whole. For this reason his deepest thought and emotions find expression in disconnected verses, *ghazal*, which reveal all the subtlety of his artistic soul.

Rather than commemorate sexual conquests, Persian *ghazals* express yearning and their address to the beloved is customarily humble. Though overtly amorous in content, the verses are fraught with ambiguity and often carry Sufi or political messages. Hafiz of Shiraz (1315?-1389?) is the most famous Persian composer of *ghazals* and remains the most popular.

> Last night she brought me wine, and sat beside my pillow;
> Her hair hung loose, her dress was torn, her face perspired —
> She smiled and sang of love, with mischief in her eyes,
> And whispering in my ear, she drunkenly inquired:
>
> "My ancient lover, can it be that you're asleep?
> The true initiate, when offered wine at night,
> Would be a heretic of love if he refused
> To take the draught he's given, and drink it with delight."

Though there are no gender markers in Persian, in the translation given above, the distinguished scholar and translator Dick Davis has chosen to present the nocturnal visitor as 'she', though the visitor may just as well have been a 'he', or, much less likely, a robotic 'it'. (Though Hafiz was married, his wife never appears in his verses.) Wine features frequently in the poetry of Hafiz and others. In many cases the intoxication that 'wine' brings should be read as a figure for Sufi ecstasy and many expert commentators on the verses of Hafiz have consistently interpreted them as Sufi allegories in which the Beloved is God, drunkenness is mystical ecstasy and so forth. But others are more doubtful. Dick Davis in his introduction to Faces of Love, a selection of translations of fourteenth-century Shirazi poetry, asked the question, 'How would a poem that talked about wine and a lover look if it actually was about wine and a lover?' Elsewhere, Davis has questioned the automatic interpretation of the poet's drunkenness as an evocation of a mystical state and he has quoted Freud to the effect that 'sometimes a cigar is just a cigar'. In some cases it does seem fairly clear that the poet is writing about earthly love and the sort of wine that one can obtain in an off licence. But whether one chooses to read the poems of Hafiz and others in a mystical or a non-mystical sense, one should eschew trying to read anything autobiographical in their verses. One will get nowhere if one tries to construct the life of a saintly Hafiz or a dipsomaniac Hafiz from his verses. In many cases he and less talented poets were merely playing with accepted conventions and timeworn imagery. Incidentally,

Ayatollah Khomeini wrote erotic poetry in the manner of Hafiz (and naturally Khomeini was adamant that Hafiz composed only mystical verses). The *ghazal* is also a genre in Urdu and Punjabi literature. *Ghazals* are commonly composed to be sung with a musical accompaniment. Qawwali (deriving from the Arabic *qawwal*, a reciter) designates *ghazals* which carry a mystical meaning and which are sung at Sufi reunions, though qawwali songs are not restricted to the love themes of the *ghazal*, and, for example there may be songs in praise of the Prophet or songs about annihilation in the Divine. Qawwali is particularly associated with the Chisti order in the Indian subcontinent. In recent decades Bombay film music has drawn heavily on the themes and tunes of the Urdu *ghazal* as performed in qawwali, though the film music ignores any mystical message that may be latent in the love lyric.

In Naguib Mahfouz's marvellous, dark novel *Al-Liss wa'l-kilab* (1961, English translation, *The Thief and the Dogs*, 1984), Sa'id Mahran, a thief just released from jail, seeks bloody revenge on his associates who put him there. But then, having murdered two of the wrong people, he is on the run from the police. He holes up for a short while in a Sufi *zawiya* in Cairo. He is awoken from his rest by the chanting of a *dhikr* ceremony and then the recitation of verses:

> My time in vain is gone
> And I have not succeeded.
> For a meeting how I long,
> But hope of peace is ended
> When life is two days long;
> One day of vexation
> And one of separation
>
> Love enough to lay me down enthralled:
> My passion before me, my fate behind.'

The lines are those of Ibn al-Farid and their melancholy theme prefigures Sa'id Mahran's imminent bloody end.

In modern times the themes of 'Udhrite and of Sufi love poetry have crossed over to the novel. The Turkish word *hüzün* can be translated as 'melancholy' or as 'nostalgia for what has been lost'. In *Istanbul: Memories of a City* Orhan Pamuk has written about how the Sufi follower is suffused with *hüzün*, since 'he suffers from grief, emptiness and inadequacy because he can never be close enough to Allah, because his apprehension of Allah is not deep enough'. In *The Museum of Innocence*, Pamuk's long novel which is effectively the fictional companion to the non-fiction book, Kemal, a young and wealthy businessman, becomes erotically obsessed with a shop girl called Füsun (Magic). Enslaved by passion, he steals everything he can that has been touched by her or is otherwise associated with her: cigarette butts, film posters, olive pits, handkerchiefs, ice cream cones . . . The resulting collection is at once a visual encyclopedia of everyday life in 1970s Istanbul and a chronicle of Kemal's erotic abjection, as he loves and serves a woman who has married someone else. Kemal, deranged by love, is a modern Majnun, but, since he succeeds in accumulating a vast collection of erotically charged everyday objects, we have come a long way from the bleak desert inhabited by the first of the great madmen for love, Qays ibn Muwallah.

Al-Andalus Rediscovered

Iberia's New Muslims

MARVINE HOWE

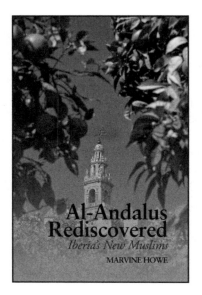

Iberia is a special place of colliding myths over its Islamic past and the Christian reconquista, the Inquisition and massive expulsion of Muslims and Jews some five centuries ago. Long a land of emigrants and explorers, it has now become home to Europe's latest, rapidly growing Muslim communities.

9781849042031 / November 2012
£24.99 / Hardback / 224pp

Al-Andalus Rediscovered focuses on Iberia's new Muslims, and their lives in a largely Roman Catholic region. Also featured are the Spanish and Portuguese officials, academics, NGOs and ordinary citizens who are trying to find better ways to integrate Muslims and other immigrants, despite domestic and European pressures for tougher counter-measures.

This book seeks to answer the basic questions: whether an Iberian model of a humane immigration policy is possible in 'fortress' Europe and whether the partisans of the Andalusian spirit of tolerance and diversity can prevail at this time of economic hardship and heightened radicalism in both the Islamic World and the West.

'A superb and remarkably comprehensive account of the recent transformation of Spain and Portugal into "immigrant-receiving" countries — with a particular emphasis on Muslim immigrants. [...] This is the first book-length analysis of the contemporary resonance of Moorish Iberia in Spanish and Portuguese society, and the different responses of both countries to that historical legacy in the context of a new era of Muslim immigration.' — Matthew Carr, author of *Blood and Faith: The Purging of Muslim Spain*

www.hurstpublishers.com/book/al-andalus-rediscovered

41 GREAT RUSSELL ST, LONDON WC1B 3
WWW.HURSTPUBLISHERS.COM
WWW.FBOOK.COM/HURSTPUBLISHERS
020 7255 2201

SACRED LOVE, LYRICAL DEATH

Christopher Shackle

If it is death that determines the limits of life, it is love which offers the promise of overcoming those limits. Between these two great defining factors of human existence there is a necessarily complex relationship, which in one way or another involves just about every aspect of what it means to be truly human. Every society therefore has to evolve its own ways of understanding how that relationship is ideally to be managed. These various ways are typically best expressed in the finest creations of its artists and thinkers, which in turn help form the values and attitudes of the society at large. In the modern world, where no society lives in isolation from another, it is through the study of their different creative legacies that we can hope to understand how societies other than our own have formulated their own understandings of love and death, and that we may perhaps come to distinguish between socially conditioned norms and truly universal values.

Love and Death in Traditional Society

Punjabi Muslim society, which as the largest element in Pakistani society to a considerable extent determines the character of the nation, has a long and complex cultural history. From the time of the Muslim conquests initiated by Mahmud of Ghazna in around 1000, the Punjab was a crucial bridge between the Muslim societies of Western Asia and the very different cultural and religious world of India. The region was variously subjected over time to different imperial powers, variously based in Ghazna and Kabul or in Delhi and Agra, and traditional Punjabi society evolved as a not always stable combination of different elements. Besides the not always easy coexistence of the religious communities of Muslims, Sikhs, and Hindus, each with their own religious specialists, there were the divisions created by caste groupings and by the distinctions between indigenous inhabitants and immigrants from

31

Western Asia, as well as by the rivalries between the tribes of pastoralists and agriculturalists for the control of the all-important resources of the land. And within this very large area, there were also of course sub-regional variations, marked by differences of ecology and dialect. As in other parts of South Asia, the period of British rule brought about major changes to that traditional society. The massive extension of canal irrigation greatly extended agriculture at the expense of the pastoral way of life, the new education system replaced Persian with Urdu and English, and a new publishing industry helped spread entirely new kinds of literature and distinctively modernist understandings of Islam. Above all, the increasing bitterness of communal rivalry led eventually to the Partition of 1947, when ethnic cleansings and enforced population transfers saw the temporary triumph of death over love, and resulted in the different Muslim society of Pakistan Punjab today.

Throughout the long pre-British period, Persian was the language used for most kinds of writing, so the Persian poetry written by literate Punjabi Muslims was as closely based on the styles first developed in Iran as contemporary Pakistani writing in English is shaped by Western aesthetic models. While Punjabi was the vehicle of a vigorous folk literature, this was largely an oral tradition which was only reduced to writing in quite recent times. Of the few books written in Punjabi, many were popular treatments of topics of Islamic law composed in rhyming doggerel, with plenty to repeat from the old legal textbooks about rules of inheritance or the regulations governing dowry and the marriage contract, but virtually nothing to say about the meaning of death or love.

Since Islam was introduced into the Punjab by outside forces, the formal scheme of religious values taught by the religious specialists was superimposed on the sometimes very different sets of indigenous social values which were maintained by most social groups after their formal conversion to the new religion. In the tribal society of the western Punjab, these values were based upon a strictly enforced code of loyalty to the *izzat* or honour of the kin-group, with its heroic emphasis on male bravery and generosity, underpinned by and underpinning the absolute power invested in senior males to determine their daughters' marriage partners. This code can allow no place to the rival claims of love and mutual attraction to decide who marries whom, and the conflict between the two sets of values can be resolved only by death, in the form of the 'honour killings' which are still carried out both in Pakistan itself and among the Pakistani diaspora in Britain.

This traditionally sanctioned use of death as a penalty for love is repeatedly explored in the traditional poetry. Several popular stories tell of famous pairs of lovers whose illicit love brought about their death by the girl's kinsfolk. The starkest illustration of this tragic theme is in the story of Mirza and Sahiban, already the subject of two narrative poems composed in the seventeenth century. Set among the Jat pastoralists of the western Punjab around the river Chenab, this tells how Mirza fell in love with his young cousin Sahiban. She was, however, betrothed to another, so Mirza came to carry her away from her wedding. The speed of his horse at first allowed the pair to escape their pursuers, but when Mirza stopped to rest Sahiban hung up his bow out of reach so that he would not be able to kill her brothers. Thus unarmed, Mirza could not defend himself and the lovers were killed to expunge the disgrace of Sahiban's family.

Sufi Ideas of Love and Death

Although Mirza and Sahiban first met in a mosque school, their story has little to say about Islam. But, as in many pre-modern Muslim societies, the rules of the mullahs and *qazis*, who were notoriously subservient to the wealthy and powerful, were counterbalanced by the larger understandings of the Sufis, and it is the Punjabi Sufi poets who have much to say about love. The very first Punjabi verses which have come down to us, as a result of the accident of their preservation in the Sikh scriptures, are those composed by the great Sufi saint Shaikh Farid Shakarganj (d. 1265). Here we already find a keen sense of the simultaneous presence of death whose coming is inevitable and of love which gives life its precious meaning:

People always speak of love, and love's pain rules us all. Farid, the body which lacks love is dead as any cemetery.

But, beautiful as many of Farid's verses are, they are too fragmentary to offer more than glimpses of an overall poetic and spiritual vision. For this we have to turn to the better preserved poetry of much later poets who date from the first half of the eighteenth century when Mughal authority in

Punjab was coming to an end amidst the chaos simultaneously caused by invasions from Afghanistan and internal uprisings by the Sikhs. The greatest of all these Punjabi Sufi poets is Bulleh Shah (d. 1758), whose passionate lyrics express a powerfully articulated understanding of the rival forces of death and love.

Although they may not be so appealing as his evocations of love to modern readers, it is an important characteristic of Bulleh Shah that many of his poems are designed to arouse a very Islamic sense of the inevitability of death and of the need to prepare for this rapidly approaching end by the performance of meritorious deeds. This is typically expressed with metaphorical reference to the lifecycle of a girl who grows up in the security of her parental home, but who must dutifully spin the thread which will go to make up the clothes she will need to take with her as dowry after she has been married and must go away to live with her husband's family:

Get up, wake up, and do not snore. This sleeping is no good for you.
One day you must leave the world and go to be interred in the grave. The worms will eat your flesh. Be aware and do not forget death.
The day appointed for your wedding has drawn near, have you had the clothes for your dowry dyed? Why have you ruined yourself? Heedless one, have you no awareness?
You have wasted your life in sleep, now your moment has come. You have not even started spinning. You have no dowry prepared, so what will you do?

Just as the observance of the requirements of Islamic law is regarded by most Sufis as a necessary but insufficient pre-requisite for the spiritual discipline which is their main object, so too does this didactic aspect of Bulleh Shah's poetry underpin the mystical vision which is its principal theme. The core expression of this vision is again a very Islamic one, relying upon the repeated citation of a number of Quranic phrases and other sacred sayings in their original Arabic wording to convey an overwhelming sense of the absolute unity of the divine presence in all things, as is confirmed by its revelation in scripture. For Bulleh Shah, as for so many Sufis, the primary reason for creation was God's desire to be loved, and the primal compact between God and man means that man must recognise God as the lord of his devotion who is present in all things, but especially so within man as the noblest of his creatures. A particular role is accorded to the Prophet Muhammad, whose other name Ahmad symbolises his intimate connection with Ahad, or God the One, and whose ethnic title of 'Arab' can be shortened to *rab* 'the Lord':

> Oh girlfriends, now I have found you, beloved. You are contained in each and every thing.
> You recited the song of *I am Ahad the One*. Then you decreed *I am Ahmad*. Then you explained *I am an Arab without the A*. Then you took the name of the Apostle.
> Becoming manifest you called yourself light. You made it present through Ahmad. You displayed being from not-being. You proclaimed *And we breathed into him*.

In continually repeated verses, Bulleh Shah proclaims the need to recognise this mystery of God being universally present despite the apparently contrary evidence of superficial differences of appearance. Memorably, he often speaks of this as the divine 'peeping out' of the human. And it is his central perception of the meaninglessness of outward diversity that inspire those memorable poems on the essential unity of 'Turk' and 'Hindu' which have acquired such a special reference in modern South Asia, with its long history of intensely pursued communal bigotry:

> Behold, God is openly revealed, whatever the Brahmin may then proclaim from the Veda.
> If you focus your attention, he is not an unbeliever, no matter whether he is called Hindu or Turk.
> Whenever I look, only he, only he exists. Bulleh, the lord is contained in every colour.

Bulleh Shah's mystical perception of the unity of all things in the divine is not a merely intellectual one. It is a dynamic process which is pursued through love, the source of both man's greatest delights and his most acute emotional suffering. In keeping with the Sufi doctrine of a disciple's self-obliteration in his Shaikh, the most important focus of Bulleh Shah's love is his spiritual guide Shah Inayat, who is so frequently named in the concluding verses of his lyrics, now as the present source of his joy, now as the absent cause of his pain.

The extraordinary richness of the dynamic of love is conveyed by Bulleh Shah's remarkable range of poetic reference. This extends beyond the Islamic tradition to include occasional references to figures from the Hindu world, but the sacred history of the past is mainly conceived as the story of a succession of martyrs to the divine power of love, starting with the scriptural figures regarded as prophets in Islam like Ibrahim, Sulaiman, Ayub or Zakariya, who were all painfully tested in the their turn by God. Then there are the great Sufi saints, especially the great martyr Mansur, who was executed for daring to proclaim the mystery of identity with the divine in his famous saying *ana 'l-haq* 'I am the Real, that is, God'. To the prophets and the saints are added, both in incidental references and in long lists of those who have suffered in the name of love, the famous pairs of lovers of Islamic legend whose stories formed the core themes of the Persian romance, like Yusuf who was loved by Zulaikha in Egypt, or Laila who was madly adored by Majnun in Arabia:

> They put Yusuf in the well, then sold him in the bazaar. He was paid for in full with a hank of yarn. You will be priced at a cowrie.
>
> Zulaikha fell in love and bought him. Lovers are writhing in agony over there. Majnun says 'Ah, ah, ah!' What will you bring back from over there?
>
> Over there some like Shams have their skins flayed, some like Zakariya are cut up with saws, others like Mansur are seized and put on the gallows. You too will get your head cut off over there.

Besides these invocations of the glorious lovers and martyrs of the past, this long story of the eternal power of love is at the same time brought home through Bulleh Shah's frequent allusions to the local legends of the Indus valley. The standard convention of Indian lyric poetry which makes the poet take on the persona of a female lover, is given added resonance by his assumption of the role of one of local romantic heroines.

The Story of Hir

The greatest of these heroines is Hir, whose story is best known through the famous narrative poem written by Bulleh Shah's younger contemporary Varis Shah, which he finished in 1766. Written in the genre termed *qissa*, this is generally regarded as the greatest work of Punjabi literature. It tells the full story of how Dhido, known by his tribal name of Ranjha, leaves his family home in Takht Hazara to come to Jhang, in search of Hir the daughter of Chuchak, a chieftain of the Sial tribe (to which Sahiban's family also belonged). Hir persuades her father to hire Ranjha as a herdsman, allowing her the chance to meet him in the river-glades beside the Chenab where he brings the buffaloes to graze. When their love is discovered, Hir's parents marry her off by force to a man from the Khera tribe, with all her objections being overruled by the complicit local qazi. In order to win her back, Ranjha goes off to the great yogi Gorakhnath for initiation, and having already lost his original tribal status when he took on the menial job of herdsman he now abandons all outward ties to society by becoming a yogi. Thus radically transformed, he returns to win back Hir from her huband's home. The two elope to a local ruler who orders that Hir should be divorced from the Khera and married to Ranjha. But when her family conspire to poison her instead, Ranjha dies of grief.

Bulleh Shah does not tell the whole story in his lyrics, but instead focuses on key aspects of the heroine's experience of love, in the same way as his great Sindhi contemporary Shah Abdul Latif (d. 1752) dealt with the romantic legends known to him. For Bulleh Shah, Hir's love for Ranjha is an unambiguous image for the passionate mystical apprehension of the divine which is universally present behind the shifting shapes of material creation. So it is not the lovers' tragic fate but the wonder evoked by the beloved's transformations which excites Hir's expressions of love. So when Ranjha appears transformed from a herdsman into a yogi, Hir vows to leave with him, having turned herself into a yogini:

I will go with the yogi, having put a mark on my forehead.
I will go, I will not be stopped from leaving. Who is going to turn me
back me as I go? It has become impossible for me to turn back, now that
I have experienced reproaches for being in love.

He is not a yogi, but my heart's beloved. I have forgotten why I fell in love. I lost all control, once I gained a sight of him. What did this yogi do to me? He put his hooks in my heart. He cast the net of love, when he uttered his sweet talk.

While the story of Hir makes some appearance in the earlier Punjabi Sufi poetry of Shah Husain, it is Bulleh Shah who properly exploits the rich potential for mystical allegory inherent in the relationship between Hir and her beloved. Although Ranjha the chieftain's son from Takht Hazara assumes different appearances, whether as a yogi or as a flute-playing herdsman who recalls the divine figure of Krishna, the mystery ultimately lies in his being fundamentally identical with Hir. Many of Bulleh Shah's most memorable lyrics express this sweet yet painful contradiction:

Through repeating 'Ranjha, Ranjha,' I have now myself become Ranjha. Call me Dhido Ranjha, let no one call me Hir.
Ranjha is in me, and I am in Ranjha, this is my only thought. There is no me, there is only him, and he is the one who pays attention to himself.
Whoever dwells within us determines who we are. I have become identical with the one I love.
With a staff in my hand and a rough blanket round my shoulders, I drive the buffaloes before me. Take me to Takht Hazara, Bulleh, I can find no refuge with the Sials.

In short and apparently simple Sufi lyrics such as these, the unambiguous expression is very different from the elaborate equivocations between human divine love which are typical of the *ghazal* first invented in Persian, then taken up in the elite literature of other languages like Ottoman Turkish and Urdu. In these poems Bulleh Shah shows the identity of the lover and the beloved, in that real world of true reality which lies behind the screen of apparent diversity, and which quite transcends death through its appeal at several levels to so many of the deepest of human aspirations to a universal understanding of the meaning of human existence in a divine world.

The Stories of Sohni and Saiful Muluk

Since the power of love is omnipresent, all love stories are in principle amenable to be interpreted as examples of this Sufi vision. In practice, however, the conflicts induced by social realities are less easily idealised away in some cases than in others. So the Mirza-Sahiban story, for example, in which the abduction of Sahiban from her wedding is such a brutally explicit challenge to social norms, never really proved as amenable to Sufi allegorising as did other local romances.

The most popular of the Punjabi romantic legends after the Hir-Ranjha story is that of Sohni and Mahinval (literally, 'Beauty and the Buffalo-herd'). Similarly set in the golden age of great Mughals, it tells how Izzat Beg, the son of a wealthy Bukharan merchant comes to India on a business trip. On his return from Delhi, he stops at the town of Gujrat where the Grand Trunk Road back to Kabul crosses the river Chenab, which is not for nothing known as 'the lovers' river'. He learns of the exceptional beauty of Sohni, the daughter of a local potter, and goes to her father's shop. Falling completely in love, he returns to buy more and more pots to keep having the chance to see her. Eventually all his money is gone, and he gets Sohni's father to hire him to herd his buffaloes. Now that his status is reduced from lordly Izzat Beg to mere Mahinval, he at last wins Sohni's love. But their secret is discovered as Sohni is married off to a husband from the potter caste. Mahinval becomes a *fakir*, living in a hut across the Chenab, and secretly swims to Sohni by night, bringing fish kebabs for her to eat. When a storm means no fish is available, he slices the flesh from his thigh to give her this instead. When she tastes the difference, Sohni realises his suffering and decides that she will now be the one to cross the river to him. She uses an earthenware pot as a float to help her, and hides this in the bushes on the riverbank on her return. Her sister-in-law discovers what she is doing and replaces Sohni's pot with an unfired one. On the next dark and stormy night, Sohni takes this pot with her, but when it dissolves she is drowned. Mahinval hears her cries and plunges into the river himself, there to join her in death.

While the social backgrounds of the protagonists are very different, there are many obvious similarities with the Hir-Ranjha story. The ending of the Hir story is, however, almost incidental; indeed, several earlier versions avoid the tragic end described by Varis Shah and have the lovers departing for Mecca and a happy marriage. But the Sohni story can end only in the tragedy of death. The focus of the Sufi poets is, therefore, on the image of Sohni poised between love and death as she stands on the riverbank on the eve of her fatal journey, as in these poignant verses by Bulleh Shah:

On the other side of the Chenab there are jungles and thickets, where cruel tigers and panthers roam. May the lord bring me quickly to my beloved. This anxiety is killing me.

It is the middle of the night and the stars are waning. Some have already waned, others are about to do so. I got up and come to the river-bank. Now I am standing here waiting to cross.

I cannot swim and do not have a clue what to do. I have no pole or oar, and my raft is old. There are whirlpools and no crossing-place is marked. I weep and wring my hands.

Only later did the Sohni story become a favourite subject for narrative qissa poems. The best known of these is the *Sohni Mahinval* by the Lahore poet Fazal Shah (d. 1890), which he completed as a very young man in 1848, but its popularity is due to its exploitation of superficial verbal effects of word-plays, assonance and alliteration, and any nuancing of the narrative is rejected in favour of maximum rhetorical effect, so that for instance not just one but some dozen stanzas describe Sohni's last laments as she drowns in the river. A much finer version of the story was written in 1857 by Mian Muhammad Bakhsh (d. 1907), the greatest Punjabi Sufi to write narrative poems, as opposed to lyrical verse. The first part of the poem dwells on the hero's progressive loss of pride and possessions as he pays the price of love, until it is at last reciprocated by Sohni too late to avoid her enforced marriage to another. Mian Muhammad's exalted view of the demands of love is then exemplified by Sohni's courageous decision to be true to her love for Mahinval and to brave the perilous river crossing. The poem ends with a reflection on how death is the ultimate fate of us all, including even the greatest of lovers.

This theme of the courage and determination required by true love is more fully developed in Mian Muhammad's greatest poem, *The Story of Saiful Muluk*, which is revered in the north-western Punjab and adjacent districts of Azad Kashmir as the supreme literary and spiritual masterpiece of the region, fully on a par with the way in which Varis Shah's *Hir* is regarded in the central Punjab. The long story, which is found in *The Thousand and One Nights*, opens with the grief caused by his childlessness to the aged king of Egypt, and the wonderful birth to him of a son called Saiful Muluk at the same time as that of the vizier's son who is to be his faithful companion. As a youth, Saiful Muluk is given two gifts once presented to his father by the great king Sulaiman himself, a ring and a picture wrapped in cloth. That night he unwraps the cloth and sees the likeness of a beautiful woman with which he falls madly in love. It is a picture of Badiul Jamal, daughter of the mighty king of the peris of the Garden of Iram. The desperate Saiful Muluk takes leave of his father to lead an expedition in search of her.

He first reaches China, but is directed from there to Constantinople to search for further clues. The middle section of the story describes the perils which befall Saiful Muluk during his quest, starting with a shipwreck which separates him from his companion. As he voyages for many years from island to island, he has many dangerous encounters of the kind described in the story of Sindbad as he escapes from an Old Man of the Sea, an island of Ghouls, and captivity by a negro king whose hideous daughter tries to seduce him. All these episodes, particularly the hero's grotesque plight in the last, afford wonderful scope for the imagination of story-tellers and poets and are fully exploited by Mian Muhammad. From an island filled with giant apes he reaches a mysterious castle where he finds a princess who has been confined there by a jinni. She tells him she is the daughter of king Tajul Muluk of India. When Saiful Muluk tells her his own story, she reveals that Badiul Jamal is her foster-sister and she can arrange their meeting if first he frees her from the jinni's power. He accomplishes this by conjuring up from the ocean depths the chests in which the jinni's soul has been hidden and destroying it with the aid of Sulaiman's ring.

In the final part of the story Saiful Muluk and the princess reach her father's capital, the fabled city of Sarandip. There he is reunited with his companion, who reports his own adventures. Besides the usual Old Men of the Sea and Ghouls, these adventures of the side-hero include an encounter with a Polyphemus-like figure whom he has to blind before escaping from his cave. When a meeting with Badiul Jamal is at last arranged, she at first resists, but then tells Saiful Muluk to go to Iram and persuade her grandmother to intercede with her father, king Shahpal son of Shahrukh, who will certainly oppose a marriage between a man and a peri. The grandmother agrees to help, but Saiful Muluk is captured by the Blue King of Qulzum, the father of the jinni whose soul he destroyed. Initially reluctant to take sides in support of a human, the peri king finally orders his forces to attack and they are finally victorious after a fierce battle which allows Mian Muhammad to display his skill in describing martial scenes before he proceeds to a rich evocation of the subsequent royal festivities as Shahpal's victory is followed by the double marriage of Saiful Muluk to Badiul Jamal and of his companion to the princess. Happiness is theirs at last, as they spend many years partly in Egypt and partly in Sarandip, until they are finally 'visited by the terminator of delights and the separator of companions.'

It can immediately be seen that this is a quite different kind of narrative from the tragic local romantic legends, being a fairy-story quest of the kind so popular in courtly Persian and Urdu verse narratives, with a human prince falling in love with the picture of a fairy princess and embarking on a long series of dangerous adventures before he eventually wins her as his bride and they live happily ever after. But whereas the courtly poems are typically composed as elaborate pieces of entertainment, Mian Muhammad's poem, which he called *Safar ul Ishq* 'The Journey of Love', is immensely serious in conception and is far more deserving of good translation to bring it to the notice of a wider audience. Like all Sufis, Mian Muhammad describes love as the most significant force in life, one which makes supreme demands on the lovers who alone amongst humanity can be called truly human. Since the focus of his poem is on a male hero, the conception of the ideal lover is conveyed in distinctively masculine terms, as in these verses from the prologue to the poem:

If you are a true man, do not lose your resolve, in case you should be called unmanly. When you set to a task with resolve, you will die achieving your desire.
So long as you draw breath do not despair, let your breath be lost before your hope. Do not draw back from your quest, for if you do you will be laughed at.

Endure what you must and do not lose your resolve, for one day things will change. If someone goes out to beg, Muhammad, his bowl will eventually be filled.

The incidents of the following long narrative, however excitingly told, are thus important only as representations of a higher spiritual reality. Passages of teaching such as these, often including memorable and easily quoted rhyming verses, are continually woven into the story. Mian Muhammad's great poem thereby powerfully reinforces the ideal of a resolute attachment to love which is to be pursued at all costs, even if death is the necessary price to be paid.

The Story of Sassi

The role which Mian Muhammad's *Saiful Muluk* plays in the north-western Punjab as a supreme poetic masterpiece containing within itself all the lessons which Sufi tradition has to teach about love and death is occupied in the south-western parts of the region by his great contemporary Khwaja Ghulam Farid (d. 1901), who composed a large number of lyrics in the distinctive local language called Siraiki. Like Bulleh Shah, Khwaja Farid refers to a number of local legends, but he displays a particular attachment to the figure of Sassi. Her story is of Sindhi origin and she also plays the chief part in the classic Sufi lyrical poetry of the great Shah Abdul Latif, but it had also long been popular in the Punjab alongside the indigenous romantic legends.

The most popular narrative treatment of the Sassi story in Punjabi was the poem *Sassi Punnun* composed sometime in the late eighteenth century by Hasham Shah (d. 1823). According to this account, Sassi is born as the daughter of a king. When she is predicted to bring disgrace upon her family, she is put as an infant into a chest filled with treasure and cast adrift on the river. She is found by a washerman in the city of Bhambore who uses the treasure to bring her up in style as his own daughter. But when the time comes for her betrothal, Sassi shrinks from the prospect of being married off to a washerman. A wealthy merchant in Bhambhore has a collection of portraits in which Sassi one day sees and falls in love with a picture of Punnun, son of the chief of the Hot tribe of Baloch whose capital is at Kech in the Thal desert. When some Baloch traders come to Bhambhore, Sassi detains them, sending messengers requiring Punnun to come to her. When he arrives, the two fall in love and she refuses to let him leave. Tribesmen are sent by Punnun's father to get him back, and they ply the prince with drink until he becomes unconscious, enabling them to snatch him from Sassi's side and take him away on their swift camels. When Sassi wakes up to find herself abandoned she is distraught. After an altercation with her adoptive mother who urges her to be sensible and settle for a washerman, she races out into the terrible desert of the Maru Thal. There at last, after much wandering she finds a camel's footprint which she believes must be Punnun's. Mad with thirst and grief, she dies over it lamenting her lost beloved. She is found by a shepherd who buries her. When Punnun finally realises how he has been abducted he races back to find Sassi but discovers only her grave, which opens to allow him to die by her side.

As this outline shows, this is another story of a very similar type to the legend of Sohni and Mahinval. The geographical and social setting may be different, but this too is a narrative whose weight lies in the tragedy of its ending, when the ill-matched lovers are united in death. For Khwaja Farid, whose magnificent poetry marks the end of the local Sufi tradition, the parallels between the fate of all these lovers are repeatedly alluded to. Sometimes this is done in order to point out the ultimate evanescence of the joys of human love, however great, since death must come to all:

> Where are Laila and Majnun, where are Sohni and Mahinval?
> Where are Ranjh, where are the Kheras, where is Hir the Sial?
> Where are Sassi and Punnun? Where are their griefs and troubles?
> Where are Saiful and the fairies? Where is that separation and that union?

More often, it is as one who has himself experienced the pains of love that the poet counts himself as one of the timeless company of lovers:

> I am not alone in this company. Thousands travel in this group, Farid. The heart drowns some and makes others wander lost. There are so many Sohnis, Sassis and Hirs.

It is, however, with Sassi that Khwaja Farid particularly identifies himself, and many of his most poignant verses describe the sufferings which Sassi experiences at her two most painful experiences of separation, when she wakes up to find Punnun gone from her side, and when she vainly searches for him in the burning desert:

> Punnun the Hot did not stay to say goodbye. He abandoned me and set out for Kech. My fair beloved deliberately set me wandering, using the feeble excuse that I was asleep.
> You left me alone and helpless, and prepared to leave for Kech. Alas, what injustice that was, my beloved.
> My dear Hot has left me burning, melting, and wringing my hands. As I pine and suffer, the pebbles smitten by the hot wind turn to coals.
> My companion Punnun, without whom I cannot endure for an instant, left me far behind. Wandering through the mountains and over the passes, I have entered the earth, overwhelmed by love.

The particular significance of the Sassi story to Khwaja Farid is closely associated with his own attachment to the local Rohi desert of Bahawalpur, where he spent much time and where he formed a romantic attachment to a girl from one of the desert tribes. Both the burning heat of the desert sands in the hot season, and their delightfully changed appearance when the rains bring the vegetation to life are evoked with a vivid appreciation of natural beauty unusual in the pre-modern poetry:

> Where the desert and its grasses lie, menace is ever present, my love.
> See the fair ruined cities, the dunes and sandhills, and the graceful pebbles and stones. When the gullies, tanks, hollows and soft patches of ground are filled with rain, then grief vanishes, my love.
> The desert seems like tidings of pure joy. Although we be killed and destroyed we shall never fear. Through fear of the cruel one's heart, we are filled with agitation night and day, my love.
> Since the day that Hot removed his camp terribly far from the city of Bhambhore, Sassi's food has been the lumps and gobbets of her heart's flesh.

A yet further meaning for Khwaja Farid of the desert setting of the Sassi story emerges from the memorable poems which were inspired by his performance of the Haj in 1875. The desert is now the sands of the Hijaz, and

the poet's beloved is now the Prophet himself. So when he sees the transport available to the pilgrims at Jeddah he expresses his joy in these words:

> Today the camel-litters, single and double, delight me. They must surely
> come from dear Punnun's land.

When he leaves for home and has to the converse pain of separation from
his Beloved, it is again the Sassi story which provides the emotional framework for his grief:

> Holy Arabia has gone, alas. The scent of Sindh and the Punjab has reached me.
> These eyes weep without Arabia, and with their weeping they thread a
> garland of tears. My face is bathed with the water of my tears, and grief
> makes my heart suffer agony.
> Without you, my dark beloved, in my home I am surely embarked on a
> cruel journey. In the desert of the Maru Thal and the desolate wilderness
> I suffer greater torment each day.

The End of the Tradition

With the deaths of Mian Muhammad and Khwaja Farid at the beginning of
the twentieth century, the great tradition of Punjabi Muslim poetry effectively came to an end. For at least two centuries of recorded literary history, the lyrics and narratives created by its greatest practitioners had
provided powerfully articulated treatments of the fundamental experiences
of love and death. But the great changes in Punjabi Muslim society over the
last hundred years have yet to be reflected in normative poetry of remotely
comparable significance. The great romantic legends which underpinned
the old poetry are now part of a world which is past, so that Sassi and Sohni
can be seen simply as figures whose complementary sufferings can be
neatly ticked off against one another, as in the quite elegant poem called
The Full Sisters by the twentieth century Punjabi poet Pir Fazal Gujrati,
which begins:

> Sassi and Sohni are full sisters, both born in the house of painful love.
> Separate fates were ordained for each of them, as written from the start.

The sand of the river-bank was far from the grasp of one, the other experienced the desert's sand. One died desperate for lack of water, water caused the other's death.

As so often happens when classic works of literature no longer have the full appeal to adults which they once enjoyed, the Punjabi tales of love and death are nowadays frequently recycled as stories suitable for children, with simplified English versions archly updated to suit the supposed taste of a contemporary readership. In such a changed environment, Khwaja Farid's once natural association between Sassi's beloved and the Prophet might seem incongruous at best, even blasphemous at worst.

While it is one of the paradoxes of the peculiar Pakistani education system, with its strong emphasis on English and Urdu as the languages of instruction, that rather few Punjabis find it natural to read the classic texts written in their mother tongue, the heritage of the great poets lives on through music, since the Sufi lyrics of Bulleh Shah and Khwaja Farid continue to be sung and Varis Shah's *Hir* and Mian Muhammad's *Saiful Muluk* continue to be recited to their special melodies. In the course of time, the artwork of the future which will reinterpret their message in a vitally new way will doubtless emerge, but since that will necessarily be an original creation of genius it is impossible to predict its shape. Who, after all, a century and a half ago could have foretold that a couple of medieval German narrative poems would be radically reshaped to form Richard Wagner's magnificent music drama *Tristan and Isolde*, one of the very greatest Western expressions of the universally mysterious relationship between love and death?

DEMYSTIFYING THE CALIPHATE

Edited by Madawi Al-Rasheed, Carool Kersten and Marat Shterin

9781849042284 / January 2013
£25.00 / Paperback / 356pp

In Western popular imagination, the Caliphate often conjures up an array of negative images, while rallies organised in support of resurrecting the Caliphate are treated with a mixture of apprehension and disdain, as if they were the first steps towards usurping democracy. Yet these images and perceptions have little to do with reality. While some Muslims may be nostalgic for the Caliphate, only very few today seek to make that dream come true. Yet the Caliphate can be evoked as a powerful rallying call and a symbol that draws on an imagined past and longing for reproducing or emulating it as an ideal Islamic polity. The Caliphate today is a contested concept among many actors in the Muslim world, Europe and beyond, the reinvention and imagining of which may appear puzzling to most of us. Demystifying the Caliphate sheds light on both the historical debates following the demise of the last Ottoman Caliphate and controversies surrounding recent calls to resurrect it, transcending alarmist agendas to answer fundamental questions about why the memory of the Caliphate lingers on among diverse Muslims. From London to the Caucasus, to Jakarta, Istanbul, and Baghdad, the contributors explore the concept of the Caliphate and the re-imagining of the Muslim ummah as a diverse multi-ethnic community.

'This is a book of exceptional scope and erudition that is nevertheless accessible and very timely. By bringing together such a wealth of regional expertise it succeeds admirably in living up to the promise of its title. More than that, these essays throw new light on the many ways in which even a mythical caliphate can exercise a powerful hold on contemporary political imaginations.'
— Charles Tripp, School of Oriental and African Studies, University of London

www.hurstpublishers.com/book/demystifying-the-caliphate

41 GREAT RUSSELL ST, LONDON WC1B
WWW.HURSTPUBLISHERS.COM
WWW.FBOOK.COM/HURSTPUBLISHERS
020 7255 2201

THE MASSACRE OF KARBALA

Imranali Panjwani

The massacre at Karbala is a central event in Islamic history. Its significance can be judged by the fact that the very mention of Karbala evokes strong emotions amongst Muslims, particularly the Shi'a. On 10 October 680, corresponding to the Islamic date 10 Muharram 61, the grandson of Prophet Muhammad, Husayn b. 'Ali (referred to as 'al-Husayn') along with his family and companions, was brutally martyred. The army of Yazid b. Mu'awiyah, the reigning Umayyad caliph at the time, hunted down al-Husayn and showed no remorse in killing children and abusing the women in his camp. The literature describing the martyrdom (both in Shi'i and Sunni sources), ranging from narrations to poetry, has propelled the event into a cathartic tragedy which is remembered and re-enacted every year by Shi'i Muslims worldwide on 10 Muharram, known as the Day of 'Ashura. The event is normally described as a 'battle' or a 'tragedy', giving the misleading implication that the martyrdom of al-Husayn was some kind of evenly matched battle or that the event should only be remembered as a tragedy and nothing more. This has unfortunately played a paradoxical role in the minds of Shi'i Muslims because whilst it is important to remember Karbala and mourn its victims, it has by and large only remained as an emotional event. It would be more accurate to describe it as a massacre, which not only depicts the severity of the event but also focuses our attention on the human rights violations which took place.

Al-Husayn's martyrdom has not been translated into practical terms. It is not a means by which Shi'i Muslims can channel their emotions to construct frameworks to combat injustices around the world, to reform theological outlooks in Muslim scholarship and heighten awareness for moral duties in society. The love Shi'i Muslims have for al-Husayn does not ignite the consciences of scholars, leaders and community members to inform interpretations of Islam and make intellectual contributions to humanity. Rather, al-Husayn's martyrdom is contained within the four walls of a mosque and the tears for his death are not felt by the rest of humanity. Yet the massacre of Karbala can shape ethics, theology and culture and lay the seeds for further developments in these areas.

What was the event all about? Al-Husayn, son of 'Ali b. Abi Talib (the cousin and son-in-law of Prophet Muhammad) refused to give allegiance to Yazid bin Mu'awiyah. Yazid's reign as caliph in Arabia had resulted in civil strife, instability, indignity and corruption. He demanded unquestioning allegiance from the people and that they accept him as their king. Al-Husayn, his family, relatives, and a few followers (numbering approximately seventy-two) refused. They saw Yazid as a tyrant manipulating the notions of good and evil. Yazid decided to force al-Husayn to accept his allegiance. In the end, al-Husayn and his small band of men, women and children (including al-Husayn's six month old infant son by the name of 'Abdallah) were deprived of water for several days. The commander of the Umayyad army abandoned the convention of one-to-one combat, surrounded al-Husayn, and ordered his vastly larger and superior army to kill him. Al-Husayn was butchered; the few remaining women and children were tortured and enslaved.

The classical eighth-century Shi'i historian, Abu Mikhnaf, describes the martyrdom of al-Husayn in the following words: 'Shimr gave out a call to the people, "Woe to you! What are you waiting for? May your mothers be deprived of you". Then they launched an attack from all sides. Zur'ah b. Sharik Tamimi struck Husayn on his left hand and shoulder. They kept a distance from him as he fell upon his face. In this state, Sinan b. Anas struck him with a spear. He did not allow anyone to approach Husayn out of fear that he might lose Husayn's head. Finally, he sat upon Husayn's body and severed his head, which he handed over to Khawali b. Yazid. Items that were on Husayn's body were plundered. Qays b. Ash'ath grabbed Husayn's cloak and Ishaq b. Haywah took his shirt. A man from Banu Nashal robbed the sword and a member from Aswad grabbed the sandals. Bahr b. Ka'b took his trousers. Husayn's body lay bare on the sands of Kerbala'.

The massacre has become etched in people's memory as an indescribably callous incident, not least because it has been the subject of many poems such as the one below by Qaani, the nineteenth-century Iranian poet:

What is raining? Blood.
Who? The eyes.

How? Day and night.
Why? From grief.
Grief for whom?
Grief for the king of Karbala.

But the language and discourse on Karbala has been viewed through one
lens only – commemoration. Literature, at least in English, has focused more
on the ritual aspects of the various martyrdoms. Books such as *The Martyrs of
Karbala: Shi'i Symbols and Rituals in Modern Iran* by Kamran Scot Aghaie (2004),
The Shi'ites: Ritual and Popular Piety in a Muslim Community by David Pinault
(1992) and *Ta'ziyeh: Ritual and Drama in Iran* by Peter Chelkowski (1979)
emphasise the ritualistic, symbolic and ceremonial aspects of Shi'i commemo-
rations. Arguably the only work to intellectualise the tragedy is the seldom
cited 1984 conference published in a book by the Muhammadi Trust entitled,
Al-Serat: Imam Hussain – Conference. Additionally, the late Iranian political scientist, Hamid Enayat, has dealt with the need to broaden the massacre of
Karbala from its commemorative to its practical aspects in his seminal work,
Modern Islamic Political Thought (2005).

But Karbala is still not seen as an intellectual paradigm for Muslim scholarship and humanity. Why do Shi'i Muslims only look at the event as an emotional symbol? And why does the wider Muslim community (even though all
Muslims have a basic respect for the family of Prophet Muhammad) and the
world as a whole not recognise the martyrdom of al-Husayn as a seminal,
universal event? The answer, I would argue, lies in the inability of Shi'i Muslim
scholars to contextualise Karbala for society's problems, and draw upon the
intellectual implications of al-Husayn's vision, ethics and decision-making.
They are mostly carried away by the emotive dimensions of the massacre.

The ethical dimension to al-Husayn's martyrdom is the most significant.
Why al-Husayn refused to give his allegiance to Yazid is made clear in a letter
to his brother, Muhammad b. Hanafiyyah: 'I have not risen against Yazid in
order to create corruption or discord, nor to elevate myself in the eyes of the
people, nor to oppress. I have only risen to rectify the affairs of the Ummah
of my grandfather and the affairs of the Shi'ah of my father 'Ali ibn Abi Talib. I
wish to exhort good and reprimand evil. Whosoever accepts my position will
be on the side of Allah and the side of righteousness. Whosoever rejects me,
may Allah be the final judge between them and me. He is the best judge. Oh

my brother! Indeed success is from Allah. Upon Him do I rely and unto Him do I return'.

Al-Husayn's prime motivation in refusing to give allegiance was 'commanding that which is befitting' (*amr bil ma'roof*) and 'prohibiting that which is detestable' (*nahy anil munkar*) – two foundational principles of universal morality that run throughout the Qur'an. For him, it was a matter of upholding justice and not allowing an immoral leader to govern a society. Far from engaging in a political war, al-Husayn never wanted any political gain. If political gain was the goal, why would he take his family members and young children with him on his journey? Al-Husayn's humility in allowing God to judge his own actions is astounding, despite the explicitness of Yazid's tyranny.

In Western academia, the sources of the massacre of Karbala have not been properly investigated; and the motivations and ethical implications of al-Husayn's martyrdom are overlooked. It is incorrectly described as a 'second *fitna*' (upheaval) and Yazid is given a rather vague treatment in that he was both 'grossly dissolute and oppressive' as well as 'skilled and capable' in undergraduate textbooks such as *Introducing Islam* by William Shepard. However, classical Muslim historians, Sunni and Shi'i, unanimously agree that Yazid was a hypocrite, oppressor and drunkard. The celebrated fourteenth century Sunni historian ibn Kathir states that 'Yazid loved worldly vices, would drink, listen to music, kept the company of boys with no facial hair, played drums, kept dogs and made frogs, bears and monkeys fight. Every morning he used to be intoxicated and used to bind a monkey with the saddle of a horse and make the horse run'.

The question we must ask is why the massacre of Karbala, an event exemplifying what we call today a 'human rights issue', has been treated politically? There is huge potential for the event to inform our understanding of justice in society, the way we implement human rights, the spirit of legal and jurisprudential frameworks and the extent that Muslim scholars and politicians should go to in speaking against injustice in the world. The universal appeal of Karbala is self-evident but its discourse remains one of emotiveness and political history.

As an example of how literature on Karbala can be contextualised, consider this passage from the tenth century Sh'i scholar, Shaykh al-Saduq, who reports that al-Husayn's descendent, 'Ali b. Musa al-Ridha (the eighth Shi'i Imam) stated: 'O Ibn Shabib! Muharram is the month in which the people of the Age of Ignorance had forbidden committing any oppression and fighting in. However, this nation did not recognize the honour of this month or the honour of their own Prophet. In this month, they killed the Prophet's offspring, they enslaved the women and took their belongings as booty. God will never forgive them. O Ibn Shabib! If you wish to cry, then cry for Husayn who was slaughtered like a sheep and was killed along with the members of this household. Eighteen people were martyred along with al-Husayn who had no equal on earth. The seven heavens and the earths mourned for his martyrdom. Four thousand angels descended to the earth to assist him. They will remain at this shrine with wrinkled hair until the Riser (al-Mahdi) rises. Then they will be among those who will assist him. Their slogan will be 'Revenge for al-Husayn!'

Significantly, the language of 'Ali b. Musa al-Ridha is graphic both in its meaning and the sound of the Arabic exemplifying the absolute inhumanity of the martyrdom and his own grief. For example, in Arabic the words 'he was slaughtered like a sheep' (*dhubiha kama yudhbahu al-kabsh*), combine simile, alliteration, and imagery to create a horrific picture of al-Husayn's martyrdom. He also says, 'Revenge for al-Husayn' (*ya li tharat al-Husayn*). The plainness and directness of the language used here shows his cry for justice. Yet it is not just a cry; it is also a demand for justice and recognition of human rights violations of the highest order. For example, the treatment of al-Husayn and his companions is an infringement of article 1 of the Universal Declaration of Human Rights 1948 which states, 'all human beings are born free and equal in dignity and rights. They are endowed with reason and conscience and should act towards one another in a spirit of brotherhood'. Clearly, their dignity was not respected and there was a spirit of oppression, not brotherhood. The massacre itself is an infringement of article 3 which guarantees the 'right to life, liberty and security of the person'. The torturing of the women and children violates article 5 which prohibits 'torture, cruel, inhuman or degrading treatment or punishment'. The fact that al-Husayn was not allowed to express his own thought or conscience is an infringement of article 18 which emphasises the right to 'freedom of thought, conscience and religion'. This is connected to article 20 which guarantees the 'right to freedom of peaceful assembly and association and no one may be compelled to belong to an association'. Al-Husayn's pacifist approach in refusing to give allegiance, constantly providing opportunities for the opposing side and even his own army to change their minds, and only fighting when compelled, is an infringement of this article. Finally, the fact that al-Husayn was not given a fair trial violates article 10 which states 'everyone is entitled in full equality to a fair and public hearing by an independent and impartial tribunal'.

What is desperately needed is to use Karbala literature in a practical manner to connect the martyrdom of al-Husayn to our notions of justice and normative ethics. The science of the principles of jurisprudence (*Ilm al-usul al-fiqh*) remains a hermeneutic exercise for both Shi'i and Sunni scholars where traditions and narrations are used as specification (*takhsis*) of the Qur'an in order to clarify verses and derive laws but they are seldom used to create norms concerning dignity, rights and freedoms. This separation between jurisprudence and ethics is constantly widening. That's precisely why basic questions about what gives a person human dignity in Islam, or what constitutes justice, or how laws are derived in relation to the human person are seldom properly answered. And this is why Muslim reformist scholars, such as Abdullahi an-Na'im and Mohsen Kadivar continue to speak about the conflict between Western and Islamic conceptions of rights. Although one has to be aware of Eurocentrism as a tool which constricts the human rights discourse in accordance with the European experience of rights, the debate itself demonstrates the need to create a paradigm shift in Islamic law which is currently centred more on textual and legal injunctions, rather than ethical norms. The massacre of Karbala can offer this ethical paradigm and help Muslim scholars develop the subject of political philosophy, rather than be perpetually trapped in classical seminary sciences.

One of the most intriguing aspects of al-Husayn's martyrdom is the way in which he dealt with al-Hurr bin Yazid al-Riyahi, a general of the Umayyad army who later changed sides and supported al-Husayn. Al-Hurr's own thoughts in wanting to support al-Husayn are also interesting. He was asked by the men on the side of Yazid when he would start to fight al-Husayn. Al-Hurr, who it should be noted was not a Muslim, hesitated with his answer. He reflected on al-Husayn's call to the people, 'is there any helper who will help us?' Yazid's army thought he was going to leave the battle but was unwilling to be seen when he left. The rest of the story is related by the tenth-century Shi'i scholar, Shaykh al-Mufid:

'What do you want, Ibn Yazid?', asked Muhajir bin Aws, but he did not answer. (Instead) a great shudder came over him. 'Your behaviour is suspicious', said Muhajir. 'By God, I have never seen you act like this before. If I was asked who was the bravest of the (tribe of) Kufans, I would not neglect to mention you. What is this I see in you?'

'By God, I am giving my soul the choice between Heaven and the fire (of Hell)', answered al-Hurr. 'By God, I will not choose anything before Heaven, even though I am cut to pieces and burnt.' He whipped his horse and (galloped over) and joined al-Husayn, peace be on him. 'May I be your ransom, son of the Apostle of God?' he said. 'I was your companion who stopped you from returning. I accompanied you along the road and made you stop in this place. But I did not think that the people would refuse to respond to what you have offered them and that they would ever come to this position (which they have now come to) with regard to you. By God, if I had known that they would finish up (by doing) what I am seeing (them do) to you, I would not have committed what I have committed against you. I repent to God for what I have done. Will you accept my repentance?' 'Yes', replied al-Husayn, peace be on him, 'God will forgive you. So get down'.

What is significant about this incident is that al-Hurr is regarded as one of the greatest martyrs of Islam yet there is little indication as to whether he actually converted to Islam in the theological sense by testifying to specific beliefs. Moreover, al-Husayn did not appear to ask him theological questions when he joined his camp. Even if there was a discussion about these, it seems unlikely in the heat of the battle that al-Husayn would examine the specific doctrines which al-Hurr adhered to. What was crucial, however, was that al-Hurr's moral conscience was ignited by the truth which al-Husayn stood for. Something within the deep recesses of al-Hurr's soul made him repent and transcend his own existence; this was the start of his journey towards God. Al-Husayn's immediate forgiveness not only shows him reflecting God's mercy in his own character but also shows that he saw al-Hurr's sincerity as more important. Al-Hurr chose a path of morality and ultimately, Godliness, even if this was not expressed in explicit terms. The same conscience was ignited in other martyrs who were not Muslim and joined al-Husayn's camp, such as the young Christian couple Wahb and Haniyyah and Wahb's mother, Qamar.

One can draw several implications for Muslim theology from this incident. It is generally thought that theology (*ilm al-kalaam*) began in the seventh and eighth centuries due to debates by philosophers and theologians on the nature of God's existence, free will and pre-destination. Doctrines that were formulated by both Shi'i and Sunni schools of thought from this point onwards were not necessarily derived from the Qur'an and the examples of Prophet Muhammad (*sunnah*) in isolation to create a static belief system; rather they emerged also in response to differing views on free will and predestination. So in Shi'i theology, the doctrine of justice (*adalah*) emerged as a response to the speculative theology of the Asharite school of thought which argued that God did not have prior rational justice. The Asharites believed that God's Will was paramount and, without intending to sound simplistic, He could put a murderer in heaven and a pious man in hell. The Shi'a and the schools of rationalist philosophy, the Mu'tazilah, responded by arguing that this went against God's justice and God must first and foremost be a rational Being. Sunni scholars did not always take this line and we find that schools of thought such as the Hanbalis and Malikis did not believe in discursive theology. Today, we need to reinvestigate the origins of Muslim theology to see how beliefs develop in response to personal circumstances, particularly in a pluralised and globalised world where we are all interconnected and are forced to learn about each other.

Al-Hurr's case shows a different type of conversion to Islam taking place. The question is, is it possible for faith to grow and that the process of this growth is actually the submission to God? The issue is how this submission arises in one's soul, which only God can know. Such a personal journey which at times cannot be codified but can be seen or nurtured in a person's character is currently outside the bounds of Muslim theology (though paradoxically, becoming a Muslim is a personal decision and one cannot perform *taqlid* – imitation of a jurist, here). The point is that theology neatly defines people in faith categories and recognises them in terms of whether they attest to theological doctrines. Key doctrines are important and it is not about forgetting these doctrines but rather how to recognise the process of faith (*iman*) in Muslim theology. This is crucial to encourage people to reflect on the nature of their existence and to welcome those who wish to find God from a more organic source, rather than one who only identifies with the outward manifestation of one's faith. Arguably, a case can be made that this 'nurturing' method was used by the Prophets of God in order to instil true and sincere faith in the people of their society, just as al-Husayn did towards al-Hurr.

The massacre of Karbala also has the potential to positively affect our social values and culture, particularly, to use the word of Charles Taylor, in an age of 'secularity'. This is an age which is disenchanted with the cosmos – a view that little is sacred and human beings are allowed to follow their own whims. Coupled with this is the decline in personal religious practice and withdrawal from one's community. Finally, there is a gradual fragmentation of our social order, where faith is one option among many. This is society living in a universe with no central point around which it revolves.

Taylor's concept of secularity is crucial. The lack of importance placed on a religious worldview and the disintegration of the community has resulted in a suspicion of any higher morality and transcendence than one's own. Notwithstanding the innate nature of morality in all human beings, religion, at the very least, afforded the idea that human beings could submit to a Being, force or system greater than themselves. For monotheistic religions such as Islam, Allah plays a central role in redirecting human beings to His beautiful names which include the Merciful, the Just, the Knower and the Light. These are meant to be reflected in a human being's character, thus cementing the personal bond between the Creator and created. However, when there is a disenchanted view of the cosmos, the values of our social order become fragmented, and morality descends into personal freedoms. If the massacre of Karbala was taught in schools, seminaries and universities as a universal event – just like World War I, II and the Holocaust – it could change the psychology of people and help them appreciate the nature of justice, suffering and patience. Yet the event needs to be seen as more than a commemoration; it must be written and spoken about in relation to social and cultural challenges. Even the practice of torture by certain governments, the plight of orphans and the maltreatment of women all have a link to the massacre of Karbala because that is what al-Husayn and his family endured. The event has huge symbolic power and many dimensions which can be tapped into and become a timely reminder for the re-evaluation of humanity's morals.

The massacre of Karbala can also be a source of unity for Shi'i and Sunni Muslims. Both sects accord respect to Prophet Muhammad and his family and acknowledge the wrong doings of Yazid. The Umayyad regime, it is widely recognised, was far removed from the caliphate and al-Husayn provides the moral and spiritual link to Prophet Muhammad. However, it is still the responsibility of Shi'i Muslims to focus more on the moral reasons behind al-Husayn's martyrdom not just for themselves but for fellow human beings to understand why so much emphasis is placed on commemorating the Day of 'Ashura. Beyond the tears and manifestations of grief, there needs to be a greater balance in the way people understand and remember al-Husayn.

A VERONICA ON THE EVE OF WAR

Martin Rose

> Cities also believe that they are work of mind, or of chance, but neither the one
> nor the other suffices to hold up their walls. You take delight not in a city's seven or
> seventy wonders, but in the answer it gives to a question of yours.
>
> Italo Calvino, *Invisible Cities*

Almost a quarter of a century ago, I was a young British Council officer
posted to Baghdad in the hopeful period after the end of what was then
called 'the Gulf War,' the pointless eight-year slugfest that devoured innumerable young Iraqis and Iranians between 1980 and 1988. I was still there
with my family in August 1990, when the Iraqi army invaded Kuwait, setting
off a chain reaction of hatred, calculation and violence that is still playing out
today, two 'Gulf Wars' later.

So much has been written about Iraq in the last two decades that it isn't
easy to remember the time when Saddam Hussein ruled unchallenged, supported by Western governments viscerally alarmed at Khomeini's Iran – and
when very little was really known in England about Ba'athist Iraq. I arrived
at the end of 1988, with my wife Georgina and our eight-month-old daughter in a country bled dry by its war with Iran, mourning countless sons,
deprived of every faintly luxurious import, from academic journals to pineapples, and from cancer drugs to carburettors. The Council nursed academic
and artistic contacts, donated books, ran English classes and medical exams,
and brought in theatre companies. It seemed that, with the war behind it,
Iraq would move slowly back into the community of nations.

This of course was to reckon without Saddam, a geopolitical autistic who
understood no language, at home or abroad, but that of violence, coercion
and bribery. As Baghdad cautiously expanded into peace, like a paper flower
dropped into water, he and his Ba'athist myrmidons were struggling with a

wartime legacy of massive debt, and unwillingness by his Arab paymasters to write it off; while oil, his one asset, was selling cheap, its value unsupported by those same Arab states. His 'answer' to this knot of problems came with a gesture at once highly symbolic, and highly coercive. The invasion of Kuwait salved a wound that went back to the emirate's creation by the British, as well as giving Iraq control of its vast oil reserves. It also punished a state that demanded debt repayment, but wouldn't reduce oil output to support the price; and it sent a clear message to the Arab oil ministers meeting in Taif as the Iraqi army crossed the border.

The measure of Saddam's unpredictability is that the invasion took the world by surprise. He may have believed that the Americans had given him a green light, or he may not have given a damn. But as an Englishman in the Middle East, I came to see clearly a deeper past in which my country had shaped his, seldom malignantly, often carelessly and always self-interestedly. I saw a history, insouciantly forgotten by Englishmen but remembered in painful detail by Iraqis. I quickly lost count of the number of times that the Balfour Declaration was raised as a polite reproach over dinner. And I slowly made out the shape of a different story of Iraq and its relations with Britain and the world, an account which made sense not just in its most warped and overblown form to Saddam; but in more thoughtful versions to most intelligent Iraqis; and to me.

In this unimaginably ancient and astonishingly anglophile country we found friends, surprises, challenges and an affection that has lasted twenty-five years. Most importantly, I learned that the world looks quite different according to where you stand; and that it is important to stand in as many different places as possible if we want to understand anything at all.

2 August 1990 was a day of high drama. Iraqi armoured units crossed the border into Kuwait in the early morning, annexing what was referred to bathetically as 'the nineteenth province.' We awoke to the World Service news, and lay listening for several minutes to the seizure of strategic locations across the emirate, and the detention of passengers on a British Airways 747 refuelling at Kuwait airport. I drove quickly into the office, where television sets were droning martial music behind grainy film of soldiers hoisting Iraqi flags on hot, flat rooftops. The mood of our Iraqi staff ranged from elation to the deepest gloom.

The previous evening we had had a small supper for Robin and Annabel Kealy, the *chargé d'affaires* and his wife, who were preparing to leave Baghdad at the end of their posting. We talked a lot about the breaking crisis in the south. Saddam had moved troops to the Kuwaiti border and was threatening to invade, but no one believed he would actually do so. 'No,' said Robin over coffee, 'it's sabre-rattling. He's trying to frighten the Kuwaitis into raising the oil price. He believes that they're plotting to bleed Iraq dry.'

A little after midnight we said goodbye in the dry heat of a Baghdad summer night, under a glittering sky, and they drove home to Mansour. Within minutes Robin was summoned urgently to the Embassy: the sabre was out of its scabbard, and the Iraqi army had invaded Kuwait. For several weeks he scarcely got home, sleeping on a canvas camp-bed in his office.

In the morning, our world had changed. We were living, suddenly, in a country at war, and there was an ignoble *frisson* of excitement as well as a quiet anxiety for our children and our Iraqi friends. Most Iraqis seemed exuberant, and there was a sense of real joy at Iraq's having retaken Kuwait, treacherously severed from Iraq by the British.

Later that day Robin called a meeting at the Embassy. I have a vivid memory of sitting in a conference room on the river side of the building, and looking out across the brown August lawn on a baking afternoon. The window frames were bright white gloss, and there were red and white flowers in tubs outside on the terrace. The cushions in the window embrasures were covered in flower-patterned chintz. Outside, the Tigris slid past, an oily brown stream. Robin had nothing for us but general reassurance, a brief account of events in Kuwait and instructions to stay closely in touch with the Embassy. It all felt quite unreal, in the shimmering heat of that almost absurdly English room; scarcely credible that we were tumbling into the whirlpool of an international crisis.

Robin told us that the airport was closed and would remain so for a few days, but that non-essential staff should prepare to leave when it re-opened. We did the rounds of the airline offices, trying to buy tickets, but it quickly became clear that there were no tickets for foreigners. Day after day we were assured by the Iraqi government that the closure of the airport was a technical matter, that the inconvenience was regrettable and that we would soon be able to leave. It was almost a fortnight before the word 'hostage' was spoken, and then only tentatively. We all colluded in this coy reticence, feeling that the longer we could postpone hearing and saying the word, the further off was the reality.

Real hostages came up from Kuwait, where British and other foreign nationals had been seized from their homes and from airliners in transit. They were kept in very difficult conditions in Kuwait and after a fortnight or so, shipped up to Baghdad in convoys of buses, many of them bedraggled families with babies suffering from the blistering heat of the long slow drive up from the Gulf. They were held at the Mansour Melia hotel, where they were denied consular access and contact with the outside world. The Embassy needed to know who, and how, they were. James Tansley, a young diplomat, and the Defence Attaché, John Cochrane, penetrated the hotel in one of the war's less-sung special operations. While the brigadier raged and swore histrionically at the front desk, mesmerising everyone in the lobby with a bravura performance, James dived into a laundry paternoster and managed to reach the top floor, exchanging hurried words with a member of the military mission before the *mukhabarat* (secret service) tumbled out of the paternoster behind him like Keystone Cops and bundled him away.

Before long the civilians were moved out of Baghdad and onto military and industrial sites around the country, as 'human shields' against the bombing Saddam began to expect. We knew, because the BBC kept telling us so, that we were likely to follow the same route with our two daughters, Fanny, aged two and a half, and Jossie, just five months old. Temperatures not infrequently pass fifty degrees in Baghdad in August, and any quarters without air-conditioning were likely to be quite difficult. We tried to work out what we should have ready to take with us when a lorry pulled up outside our house. It was dispiriting work, and we had no idea whether we would really be taken away, but it distracted us in those first few days. Georgina, stuck alone at home packing and repacking for all eventualities, was reluctant to leave the house while the BBC was our only way of receiving instructions from the Iraqi government. But at the height of her anxieties and preparations, there was a strident shout across the garden wall. Our amiably crazed neighbour, a war-widow called Hajjia Wasfia, wanted Georgina to go and mend her air-cooler. This somehow broke the spell, and doing something useful, however trivial, for our Iraqi neighbour made our own plight seem less all-enveloping.

Meanwhile, there was a distracting drama unfolding at the Embassy, which we watched with amusement. Soon after the invasion, a number of British employees of Bechtel, the US engineering giant, burst into the compound and demanded the protection of HM Government. Bechtel announced that it regarded their contracts as terminated, and their visas were cancelled by the Iraqis. The engineers could not leave the Embassy, but they were not entirely welcome inside it: the stage was set for a long-running culture war. The settlers were brisk and efficient and started establishing an orderly camp in the grounds. Rows of tents went up on the cricket pitch. Latrines were dug. Fireplaces and mess-tents followed. In due course they built concrete emplacements for washing-machines, and neat washing-lines appeared between the trees. Electrical engineers ran cables out of the Embassy power-supply and connected them to fridges, ghetto-blasters and arc-lights. Evening entertainments were organised, with singing and noisy jollity. Sunburned engineers lay about in little but khaki shorts, resenting being told when they might use the Embassy swimming-pool and when they might not. The engineers suspected that the diplomats were snobs, reluctant to share the pleasant walled enclave which, as British citizens (but mostly not, testy dips would sometimes observe dryly, as British tax-payers) the engineers felt they owned. Some believed that the engineers were cynical, freeloading parasites who had foisted themselves on the Embassy in a moment of well-judged panic. Disagreements escalated, coming to a head when gigantic sacks of rice and whole sides of meat arrived unannounced at the Embassy's wrought-iron gates for the campers. A shudder of horror rippled across the stiff upper lip. But gradually the sparring subsided and Chancery and Tent City learned to co-exist cheerfully enough. The snatches of ribald song and the whirring of washing-machines from the Embassy lawn were one of the more memorable accompaniments of the crisis months.

Iraq had put its head into a noose, but didn't understand what it had done. There was jubilation at Saddam's reuniting the motherland, but little real understanding of the likely consequences. A few days after the invasion, our neighbours asked us to a party to celebrate the 'Return of the Nineteenth Province.' I didn't at all feel like joining them, but we were uncomfortable showing outright disapproval in our wholly Iraqi neighbourhood of Adhami-yya, so Georgina and Fanny went briefly to toast Iraqi arms and the new *wilaya*, while I stayed at home with the baby. Some more thoughtful Iraqis were anxious about what would follow. Across the road our friends from Hit were sombre, and shook hands warmly, but very uncomfortably, when we called. They guessed more presciently what might come of their president's hubris, and what it might mean for us, and them. But in general, knowledge of the world was so thin, and filtered through such poverty of information and language, that few understood the enormity of the line that had been crossed.

Euphoria was maintained by two carefully manipulated dramas. The first was the return of prisoners from Iran. This had been in progress for some months, but after August it was orchestrated so as to provide a daily focus of attention. No family which had sons and uncles unaccounted for could resist clustering round the television screen for the daily drip of returns, the agonising procession of thin, bearded and often wild-eyed men coming down aircraft steps. This perverted circus was quintessentially Ba'athist. There was no concern of any kind for the prisoners as individuals (indeed they were regarded with deep suspicion as having been tainted by exposure to Iranian propaganda); nor for their families. Many of the conscript soldiers, and thus many of the POWs, were Shi'ites from the south, particularly liable, it was assumed, to the poison of their fellow Shi'ites in Iran; and only the officer corps was predominantly Sunni. There was little acknowledgement of what seemed an obvious truth to Western observers, that the Gulf War had solidified an Iraqi sense of nationhood, failing to rewrite loyalties along sectarian lines in Iraq, or along ethno-linguistic lines in Iran. In failing to acknowledge this obvious truth the Ba'ath was wiser, as it turned out, than Western observers.

After the circuses, the bread. Baghdad filled rapidly with the loot of Kuwait. The story of Iraqi troops tipping Kuwaiti babies from their incubators in order to steal them turned out to be Allied propaganda of the Germans-boil-nuns-to-make-soap school; but virtually everything else appeared in Baghdad's markets. Hotels were stripped of crockery, linen, alcohol, bathtowels, wardrobes and bedside lights. Cars with Kuwaiti licence-plates were openly driven in Baghdad's streets. Fruit that hadn't been seen in a decade, like bananas and pineapples, appeared in crates on the stalls of Baghdad's *suqs* as Kuwait's supermarkets were emptied. Palm trees were uprooted and carried north. Typewriters and PCs even appeared briefly for sale off the backs of lorries, an unthinkable breach of the *mukhabarat's* monopoly on type. Baghdad police were soon driving about in flashy Kuwaiti police-cars, firemen in Kuwaiti fire-engines and ambulance-men in Kuwaiti ambulances. Prices fell dramatically, so that televisions and stereos, cars and video-players all sold for a fraction of their July prices, often still in their cardboard boxes.

Iraqis reacted in different ways. Many became, quite understandably, acquisitive after a decade of rationing and war, sensing that this abundance wouldn't last long. Many traded in and out of these new commodities, making fortunes, sometimes despicably. But the one reaction I shall not forget was from Arshad Asad, the Council's effervescent, ingenious fixer, who had long ago asked to buy our television and other electrical goods when we left. I said to him that I wouldn't hold him to our bargain, now that the bottom had dropped out of the market. 'Don't be silly,' said Arshad, gently. 'This stuff from Kuwait is *haram*. And anyway, a Muslim doesn't profit from other people's misfortunes. The price is what we agreed'.

But soon after the first flush of loot, a cooler reality set in. Basic commodities began to run short. Ration cards were extended to a much wider range of goods than they had ever covered, and were issued to foreigners. Smudged pasteboard tickets covered the daily ration of basic commodities like rice, bread, oil and sugar. The rations were surprisingly large – the weekly packet of sugar testified to a national sweet tooth that no government dared defy. Beer continued to be available, though as time went by it became nastier, half-brewed and yeasty. By the late autumn it had virtually disappeared. Iraqis being the astonishing drinkers that they were, this may not have been clever.

At the British Council we kept as much of a sense of normality as possible in these strange circumstances. Peter Elborn, the Director, insisted that teaching continue. We all felt that if our claims to be an institution apart from politics meant anything – and if Mrs Thatcher's claims to be in dispute with Saddam and not with the Iraqi people were anything other than hot air – then we should stick doggedly to our work with ordinary Iraqis, who made it very clear that they valued us. The Centre teachers were all out of the country for the summer, but we still had a couple of young men running summer-courses at the Saddam Medical School, and they roughly retrained Peter and me. A small teaching programme was re-established. But somehow the British press got wind of it and started making enquiries, and finally the order came out from Downing Street that the British Council was to close its teaching centre. Four hundred students turned up at the gates when we closed finally, to protest and to support us.

This was an early sign of the malign jingoism into which Britain descended as war loomed. The papers delighted in suggesting that we were giving aid and comfort to the enemy, and closing the teaching centre was a craven concession to this press-driven 'patriotism.' Small-mindedness, as so often in that ugly era, prevailed over (while masquerading as) principle.

There was much coming and going of people: diplomats could cross the Jordanian border, and each week the diplomatic bag was picked up by the lucky dip whose turn it was for a weekend in Amman. Back he or she came with our letters, books and papers – the Guardian Weekly, the TLS, the Saffron Walden Weekly News and so on. The BBC brought us news, unblocked, and even the telephones worked well enough, so that we were never out of touch with England – just unable to get there.

This was the period when CNN and other global channels were coming into their own. For the first time, communication crossed the battle lines insouciantly and effectively. There was a constant stream of journalists coming into the country. John Simpson of the BBC was in and out, and once arranged to interview us at home. He sent a researcher to do the leg-work and voiced over so carelessly that he called our six-month-old baby girl 'Jonathan' throughout the piece. More interesting was Patrick Cockburn of the Independent, fast becoming a leading Iraq expert. And once I found myself taking Carl Bernstein of the Washington Post to lunch at the Rashid Hotel. I must have been rather star-struck, because I remember nothing at all, alas, of our conversation, or even why I had ended up looking after him.

All this gave a very odd quality to our detention in Iraq. You could half shut your eyes and often forget, particularly at first, that you were being held hostage. Sometimes, though, the comings and goings of journalists, politicians and diplomats left a bitter taste. Many were crisis tourists, and all of them could leave Iraq when they had got their story or their adrenalin rush.

Others came to demonstrate solidarity with the regime in the face of Western aggression, and Saddam organised a welter of protest marches and festivals of outrage to accommodate them. Such demonstrations were got-up affairs, carefully staged and filmed so as to exaggerate the paltry numbers of dragooned participants. Different groups were scheduled for particular days, and would arrive by bus. That the participants weren't entirely willing was illustrated for me by an academic friend who was ordered, with all his colleagues at Baghdad University, to pullulate noisily about the gates of the British Embassy before handing in a copy of his latest book, with a ferocious note of protest on the flyleaf. 'And did you?' I asked him, ingenuously. 'Are you mad?' he replied, 'I'd never have got another British visa in my life. I stuffed it up my jumper.' Other demonstrations were made up of doctors, engineers, children and nursing mothers. All were window-dressing, but the nursing mothers, protesting the evil Western plot to deprive Iraqi children of powdered milk, finally proved the last straw for an already much-tested James Tansley, who marched red-faced down the Embassy drive with an album of photographs of dead Kurdish children, to show the puzzled matrons real cruelty. A couple of days later he was declared *persona non grata* by the Iraqi government, and had to leave for home. Naturally, I envied him.

Our detention seemed quite surreal in the light of these comings and goings. Relatively few of the 'human shields,' as we were euphemistically called by the Iraqi government, were able to move freely around Baghdad. Those of us who were (who had been living in Baghdad itself before the invasion), felt sometimes like the living dead. We'd sit at dinner with people who brought news of friends, or plays in the West End, or politics: we felt increasingly hollow, and had growing sympathy with Sami and Girgis, the restless and much-taunted tigers at the Baghdad Zoo.

For six weeks it was unclear how the situation would develop. Even at this stage it was obvious that governments were doing deals with Saddam to get their nationals out of Iraq. The Thais left in exchange, it was said, for a planeload of rice, and suddenly Phayom, our children's nanny, was gone. Though it was made explicitly and pugnaciously clear by our own prime minister that there would be no deals over British hostages, Saddam started dimly to realise that holding women and children hostage was not doing him any good, either with wavering Arab governments or with those in the West pressing for peaceful solutions. There was a memorable charade when he tried to show that we were all honoured guests by asking a young British hostage called Stuart Lockwood to sit on his knee. The five-year old refused heroically, live on Iraqi television, and a British woman muttered audibly, 'I think it's disgraceful, hiding behind women and children'. Not long afterwards, in mid-September, it became clear that women and children were to be released. We got exit visas for Georgina, Fanny and Jossie.

We had a few days to pack and prepare ourselves for their departure. Of course my main feeling was relief that they were going to be out of danger – but there was also a good measure of fear about being alone in Baghdad, and forced to confront the increasing nastiness of the situation, and its possible outcomes, without the comfort and distraction of my family. I saw them off at the airport where we had arrived eighteen months before, and stood with very hollow stomach watching them disappear through passport control, wondering if I would see them again. Georgina arrived at Amman a couple of hours later, and was interviewed for ITN by Brent Sadler, who asked her slightly inanely how she felt about leaving her husband in Iraq. She fixed him with a steely look, and said just 'Bloody awful'. Georgina continued to talk to the press, though the *Cambridge Evening News* and the *Ham & High* were more usual vehicles than the national papers. But mostly she settled down in Hampstead to looking after the children, and to doing whatever she could to support me in Baghdad.

Suddenly, there was little distraction left for me in Baghdad. What was more, the remaining hostages and I were members of a diminishing group. Starting as a fairly large collection of the male citizens of 'belligerent' Western countries, it shrank steadily. I was reminded of Monty Python's *Exploding Blue Danube Waltz*: one by one whole sections of the orchestra disappeared. I noticed this particularly at the Italian classes I attended. 'Where are the French?' we'd say one week: 'Where are the Germans?' the next. Then the older men went, and so on. By the end, in December, the remaining hostages were almost all Britons, Italians and Spaniards of military age. Almost every other government seemed prepared to do deals, and often for more metallic commodities, I think, than rice.

In our echoing house in Hayy al-Shammasiyya I lived alone. Some days I managed to be cheerful, others not. What I knew of Iraqi politics was not reassuring, and I was uncomfortably aware that Saddam had a well-tried technique for ensuring the loyalty of his Revolutionary Command Council colleagues, by making them shoot traitors, with a video camera running to record their complicity. It occurred to me often that if he realised what lay ahead, he might well consider British hostages, in particular, excellent coercive film material for the war, and the last stand, to come.

There was more time for morose thoughts after the family had left, and I had my share of them, sitting as I was, trapped, in the capital city of a country against which my own was preparing to invade; a country ruled by a family with a peculiarly developed reputation for elaborate and careless savagery. And there was not a great deal to do. At first we had picnics in the country, but as petrol-rationing began to bite, and as we grew anxious at being too far from where capricious decisions about our futures were being made, we left Baghdad less and less. That we could do so at all was bizarre. All around us were Europeans held prisoner in military aerodromes and factories, the human shields who were supposed to discourage Allied bombing. To our constant surprise, we were free to roam Iraq, but tied psychologically to Baghdad where we apparently fulfilled our own role as human shields by living amongst Iraqis across the city.

I went into the office every working day, but we had little real work. Friends at the Embassy were preoccupied with crisis-management; and Council colleagues had mostly been on holiday already when the crisis broke in August. Our Iraqi friends were very precious, but they had their own lives, and their own anxieties and fears to manage, and so I tried to ration my demands on them. I found it increasingly difficult to concentrate. I had little stamina when it came to reading, my mind wandering constantly to the unanswerable question of my own and my family's future; and to the juggernaut of war that was rolling slowly towards Baghdad. The high point of each day was a morning telephone call with Georgina in Hampstead, but as I put the phone down, I often felt a dark blanket wrapping itself round me.

There were long deserts of time that had to be filled. The Italian Cultural Centre set up and ran excellent Italian classes for hostages, and prompted by this I read many novels about Italy. It was a fantasy of escape – what the Romanian writer Sorin Antohi calls, exquisitely, 'geocultural Bovaryism,' or 'a disposition to leap into some better place'. But increasingly I brooded and became quite seriously depressed. It didn't occur to me that there was a problem beyond simply feeling miserable, nor that there might be a solution. But when Peter rather diffidently gave me a slip of paper with the name and address of an Iraqi psychiatrist written on it, and suggested that he might be helpful, I was pleased as well as surprised.

And so, one day in October 1990, I found myself in the dingy waiting-room of a well-known Iraqi psychiatrist. The weather was warm, and I sat gloomily on a torn leatherette couch by an open window, looking across a noisy street in Mansour. The other patients were stubbly, and to my mind rather wild-eyed, Baghdadis, and I felt no urge to talk. After a quarter of an hour or so I was ushered in to see the doctor. Tall, black-haired and courtly, he extended his manicured hand gracefully to me. I explained that I was looking for help in dealing with persistent depression. 'And what do you think is the cause of your depression?' he asked me in the perfect English of an Iraqi doctor. Abashed to a degree that I had not quite expected, I said something about the war, about being held hostage in Iraq and being separated from my family; and I said that I was finding the whole situation claustrophobic and difficult to deal with. 'Ah,' he said, with only a tiny flicker of self-parody, 'it sounds to me like what we doctors call exogenous depression'. 'And what does that mean, exactly?' I asked, uncomfortably. 'It means,' he said, in the same unruffled, gentle voice, 'that as soon as you leave my fucking country, it will go away.'

He prescribed anti-depressants, which worked astonishingly. I quickly found myself much more able to cope with the situation – much more able to see patches of light as well as dark, and to snatch the small crumbs of comfort that were, when I looked dispassionately, many. What I think the medication did was to allow me the mental and emotional space to see that, however grim I might find my predicament, I was simply living the life that all Iraqis lived; that fear for oneself, and one's family, uncertainty and a constant sense of helplessness before a capricious tyrant were the normal state of things for most Iraqis. I told myself, and found the telling useful, that I was fortunate: that however grim I might think my situation, it could be resolved by a single signature on a single piece of paper, and a flight out of Baghdad. Our Iraqi friends were not so lucky. Even were escape to become possible, it would be a long, messy and traumatic business of families split and endangered, of relatives punished; of professional lives cast aside; of language lost, of childhood left behind; of the void of exile. And being able to leave, for them, required much more than a single signature on a scrap of paper.

Friends in England sometimes sent music with their letters (what else was as welcome and as neutral?), and I listened to it, loud, in the car. The Pogues' album *Peace and Love* arrived one day and I have a vivid memory of driving through many nights along Baghdad's ugly freeways with *Blue Heaven* filling the car. In the way that music has of retaining emotion, that song still evokes for me the brassy emptiness of dark days in Baghdad, and I listen to it, very occasionally, with cautious pleasure and sadness. *In my blue heaven, there's a bottle of Pontchartrain . . . Chalmette by moonlight, to take away the pain . . .*

But there were other things to occupy my mind too, and amongst these was the little group of my fellow hostages at the British Council. Peter remained completely unchanged by being held hostage, a condition which, anyway, he entirely declined to recognise, maintaining that he wanted to stay and that therefore his not being allowed to leave was an irrelevance. Self-contained and controlled, he sailed through the crisis like a pond-skater walking across water. He was practical, funny, supportive and imaginative, but allowed none of us a glimpse of what he was feeling. Others displayed their anxieties openly. There were the two sensible but occasionally panic-stricken teachers from the Saddam Medical School, who shared meals and tensely amusing evenings with me over beer and pizzas. Together we went from time to time to the home of the Italian Cultural Attaché, whose house reputedly had fourteen bedrooms, for his fourteen absent children, and floated on a cellar of Italian wine: he gave fine parties.

And then there was Jack, the squash-coach who we had brought out to give the national squash team some intensive training. Sport in Iraq was deadly serious, if not always very competent, with substantial rewards and punishments meted out to national players. The Iraqi Olympic Association (IOA) was unusual – possibly unique - amongst Olympic Associations in having an elaborately equipped prison and torture-chamber in the base-ment of its Baghdad headquarters, used to punish and encourage under-performers. The IOA was the private fiefdom of 'Uday, the more brutal (if such comparisons are meaningful) of Saddam's two sons; and the building was a centre, among its many criminal uses, for the distribution of looted Kuwaiti property. To support 'Uday's Olympic pretensions, the British Council had been encouraged to bring a coach to Iraq to work miracles with the demoralised squash team: Jack, a young man in his early twenties who had never travelled abroad. He came from Essex, and he brought his girlfriend with him.

He was a cheerful fellow, genially ignorant of the world, incurious and innocent. Even before 2 August he was causing us problems. His girlfriend, who was a tall young woman with a remarkable figure and long blond hair, would walk from their hotel to the IOA dressed in a very short tennis skirt and very tight shirt. Not surprisingly, this turned a few heads on Saadoun

Street. In fact, she attracted crowds, and the Information Ministry asked us to have a quiet word with her boyfriend about the lenient standards of modesty expected in pre-war Baghdad. He was astonished. 'Well,' he said, 'I noticed that she attracts a bit of attention. I reckon it's because these people haven't seen blue eyes before.'

His moment of glory came when he was training the team in the squash court at the IOA. He was working them quite hard one afternoon, when a sudden hush fell, and his players dropped their rackets, sidling awkwardly towards the door, eyes lowered and in silence. 'What's up?' he asked, and then noticed a swarthy man in squash kit who had just come onto the court with a partner. 'Oi!' he said to the man whom his players recognised as 'Uday Hussain, though he did not, 'Oi! Off the court – I'm booked till 4.00.' The players began to run for the exit, pale as death. 'Uday scowled horribly. Jack, alone with 'Uday and his squash partner, looked at him quizzically, still quite unaware of who he was speaking to, and intoned gaily, 'SMI-LE!' He then walked off the court leaving 'Uday dumbstruck. There was no retribution: he walked away and reached his hotel unscathed. Even he, insouciant as he was, was chastened to discover that he had been chaffing Baghdad's most voracious junior butcher.

But he too was a hostage. He became in a perverse way rather good for the rest of us, a source of constant amusement as well as worry. He simply wouldn't accept it, and spent hours on the telephone to the British and international Olympic authorities trying to get released. When he wasn't harassing the Foreign Office or the BOC he was dictating hilariously naïve (but alarming) despatches to his local paper. We waited each week in trepidation for the latest column of mixed-up politics and intercultural incomprehension to be faxed through from London, praying all the while that Olympus might smile on him and whisk him away. At last it did, and he disappeared, back to Essex, leaving us in Baghdad with one more weight off our shoulders.

Over the four-and-a-half months of the crisis, Iraq came into a very different focus. I was certainly aware of victims of the Iraqi state, but never was it clearer to me how sharp was the distinction between Iraq and its rulers. As I walked in the streets of Baghdad, complete strangers would sidle up to me and take my hand, and say quietly in English 'I am so sorry,' or 'I am ashamed for my country,' and move quickly on. Officials whom I didn't know well made appointments to see me, and talked about nothing: the point of the meeting was the moment at the end when they squeezed my hand and, looking me in the eye, said a few short words of shame and support. Not once in those months did I hear a single hard word, or curse, or even see a hostile look. It was as though the worm had turned. Very soon after the invasion Mahmud and Hamid, two young reserve officers, one an academic, the other a chemical engineer, screeched to a halt outside our gate in Mahmud's car. They marched up the drive. I was surprised, because although they were frequent visitors they always parked several streets away to avoid attention. 'Why are you parked *here?*' I asked. 'Allow us our little braveries,' said Mahmud. 'Now is the time when we must make statements, however small'. Another friend, Jafar, arrived unannounced one evening soon after Georgina left, carrying a tray of kebabs and a bottle of the ubiquitous Johnnie Walker Black Label. Our neighbours shyly offered tea and sympathy. Very, very few friends vanished. It was a deeply touching time, and I remain to this day immensely grateful to have seen Iraq in its moment of cautious, frightened hope and generosity. As Jafar said to me, halfway down the bottle of Black Label, 'You see, Martin, we know war is coming, and we accept responsibility for our weakness, for the moral failures and the cowardice in letting this ...', he waved his hand helplessly, 'this *man* rule us. We know that we will lose sons and brothers and cousins in this coming war, and we know that it is necessary, made necessary by our own wrong decisions. I just pray that if you start this war, you finish it properly, right to the end'. He told me too, on this and another occasion, that he and his wife had made a hiding place at their house, and that 'if it gets very bad,' I was to go there and weather the storm. I hugged him, and told him that I deeply appreciated his courage and generosity, but that I couldn't put his family to that risk. Fortunately we never had to argue it out as Baghdad burned.

Even more important to me were Farouk and Jane and their five children who became my family, making me endlessly welcome in their little flat and giving me moments of normality and friendship that helped restore my sagging spirits. We were already very fond of them, and had seen a lot of them in what I might – without too much irony – call the good times. Georgina and Jane had been pregnant together, and the family was often at our house. Now I found a different kind of friendship, which did more than anything else to keep me afloat in these dreary, frightening times. Of all the many things I remember from that time, most vivid, because like Jafar's offer it represented a serious risk, was a conversation that Farouk had with me one evening, taking me gruffly aside. 'If things get really difficult,' he said, 'we will take you to Rawa, and from there you will be taken by my cousins across the desert to Syria.'

We made other attempts to shift the log-jam. A few years before this I had lived in Jordan, travelling the Middle East as a representative of Macmillan, the publisher. Our local agent was a genial, clever fixer who earned his commission on selling English language text books. We had travelled together a good deal in the early 1980s, and I had become fond of him. His brother was close to King Hussein, a senior officer in state security, and I knew him a little, too. When Georgina flew back to England in September 1990, I asked her to telephone my old colleague. He was sympathetic, a sentimental and generous man. The brothers got to work and pulled strings, over a period of several weeks, and my hopes were cautiously raised, until he phoned Georgina again in London and told her that nothing he or Jorda-nian intelligence could do was going to help: Saddam Hussein was treating the hostages as a personal dossier, and taking all decisions himself: such decisions weren't going to include me.

I wasn't sure what to think of all this. It was a very passive position to be in, waiting for something to happen and wondering whether I would be shepherded across the desert to Syria, or left to make what I could of Bagh-dad during an allied assault on the city. From time to time a European was rumoured to have made it to Syria, but there were unpleasant stories too of would-be escapers recaptured near the frontiers. That sort of attempt seemed at this point still unnecessarily melodramatic and unlikely to suc-ceed. There was little for us to do but wait upon events.

At the Embassy the crisis continued, in one sense, very satisfactorily. For young diplomats, and particularly the young and single, to find themselves in the thick of a major global crisis was seventh heaven. It was what they had been trained for, the apogee of a diplomatic career. Adrenalin and other hormones flowed fast. Days were long and unpredictable, our host govern-ment capricious and dangerous. They certainly earned their keep, but there were also moments of more than mild hilarity.

One winter evening – it must have been 13 November – I found myself sitting by the swimming pool at the Embassy, holding a large drink, while Chancery staff put on a choral performance of *Joseph and the Amazing Technicolour Dreamcoat*. Surreal enough in itself, the evening became more so when, at the interval, James wandered across and said quietly, 'Tonight may well be the night, Martin. Sleep in the safe area of your house.' My stomach tightened, and I went home with my mind buzzing at the prospect of an allied bombing run on Baghdad. I took a sleeping-bag to the 'safe area' of our house – the archway between the kitchen and the living-room which somebody had suggested might provide slightly more shelter than elsewhere. I doubted this, but dutifully laid out my bed, torch and bag of food. Then I phoned Georgina at Hampstead and began, rather unhappily, to say goodbye – that there might be a period in which we couldn't communicate. She was mystified and rather impatient. 'Martin, none of this matters. There are much more important things happening here. Geoffrey Howe has resigned with a blistering speech in the Commons tonight. Thatcher's in trouble. Listen to the BBC'. I did, for much of a sleepless night on the kitchen floor, until the dawn crept palely in through the window onto an un-bombed sleeping-bag. It seemed rather anti-climactic, glad though I was to be alive on that cold Baghdad morning. I drove into work and began my day, which included a morning meeting at the Embassy where Howe's resignation was much discussed.

'What was last night all about then?' I asked James afterwards in the hall. 'Well, we got this,' he said, shiftily pulling a large sheet of paper from the bundle in his hands and unfolding it, 'and it seemed wise to take precautions.' He handed me a faxed front page from the London *Evening Standard*, carrying a photograph of RAF bombers, and an enormous scare-headline about imminent bombing of Baghdad. James looked a little rueful, and I have never taken official information quite so seriously since that morning.

Margaret Thatcher was on the skids. I watched her approaching nemesis with principled delight and unprincipled relief. Her uncomprehending despatch was swift and ruthless, and the pictures of her walking tearful down the steps of the Paris Embassy have for me no overtones of tragedy, simply grim satisfaction. That image and her final loss of power signalled the beginning of the end, the possibility of a solution for us in Iraq which her intransigence had made unattainable until that moment. Not only did I know very well that her stubborn stand on hostage negotiations had made it impossible for Saddam to concede anything while she remained in power; but I also detested the jingoistic, chauvinist populism she evoked.

Her appeal was to those of whom Hugh Trevor-Roper had written to Bernard Berenson during the Suez Crisis: 'The world of lower middle-class conservatives who have no intelligence but a deep belief in violence as a sign of self-importance; who hate foreigners, especially if they come from 'inferior' races; and who [are] gratified with the spectacle of violence against such people, even if it fails in its object'.

Quite what broke Saddam's resolve over the hostages is hard to know, and there are many competing claimants, from Richard Branson to the Coptic patriarch of Egypt. I suspect that it was a more gradual and cumulative realisation on the part of the Iraqi dictator, fed by streams of visitors who spent many hours in excruciating conversation. One after another international luminaries like Jesse Jackson, Edward Heath, Willy Brandt and Helmut Schmidt appeared, processing down the steps of their aeroplanes, being convoyed off to Karradat Meriam, or some other Las Vegas-inspired palace, to run through the arguments for letting Saddam's hostages go free.

My own favourite, to my surprise, was the earnest, grey figure of Tony Benn. He spent a morning with Saddam explaining, probably at tiresome length, why the continued holding of hostages was undermining the peace movement in the West, and meant that Iraq could never effectively claim the moral high ground. The meeting ended in the late morning, and Benn was taken back to his hotel. He had evidently impressed the Iraqi dictator by talking almost as interminably and relentlessly as Saddam did himself. After lunch he was summoned back, and asked to run through the arguments all over again, which, wearily, he did. And shortly afterwards we began to see movement.

Each of the international visitors left with a small number of hostages in their private jets. The number and the identity of each 'bag' were carefully calibrated comments on their importance and their national policy. It made great theatre, but of course never included the young, male and healthy, adding to our sense of being within a constantly contracting perimeter, like castaways watching the tide coming in around the edges of a small desert island.

But something else was beginning to happen alongside these high-profile political mercy-missions. One by one at first, and then in groups, individual mothers and wives were allowed into Iraq to intercede for their men. This was essentially theatrical, and Saddam milked it for all it was worth, with television interviews and bizarre ceremonies where the benign despot graciously handed men over to their wives and mothers. He was trying, with typically clumsy misunderstanding of PR, to establish a counter-narrative, one in which he figured as the proud victim who, despite all, was prepared to offer clemency to the individual agents of Western aggression. Naturally it didn't work – rather the opposite, as Western publics watched women being humiliated, forced to beg a tyrant for mercy in front of the cameras. But it provided a barometer of the approaching weather, and soon the mercury began to rise. From lone individuals trying their luck, the clemency business gradually became a production-line: it dawned on us all that any woman who could make it to Iraq would be given her man back.

As this became clear, my family in London started to discuss how to handle it. War was approaching fast, and time might well be short. They decided that rather than Georgina going back, and leaving two small, orphan-able, children in London, my mother would fly to Iraq. She was 62, and not well-travelled; scared, certainly, but determined to fetch me back from Baghdad. She set about the long process of visas and AIDS certificates, and made contact with other determined women on the same mission. By early December, she was ready to travel. In Baghdad I was apprehensive, grateful, but above all humbled by the way my mother was prepared to put her head in the lion's mouth.

It was at this point, with Iraqi reservists recalled to their units and my mother packing in Hampstead, that I received one of the stranger invitations that came my way in Iraq. Mahmud came into my office and announced that he would be defending his thesis the next day at Al-Mustansiriyya University. *Christology and Inscape in the Poetry of Gerard Manley Hopkins*, his research project, had reached its final fence just days before the outbreak of war, and he insisted that I be at his *viva*. It was 2 December. 'But Mahmud, is that sense? You'll be going back into the army in Kuwait the next day – do you really want a foreigner at your viva? A foreigner, what's more, who's an official of a country that's about to attack Iraq, whose army you're going to face across the desert in a few days' time?' 'Well, I shan't

defend the thesis at all unless you come.' He was not to be dissuaded and so
the next day, my 36th birthday, touched and puzzled, I went to Al-Mustansiriyya and was ushered to a seat of honour in the middle of the front row
in a lecture hall of banked, semi-circular benches. With a cold bottle of
Sprite and a plate of sticky buns by my elbow, I felt like an aficionado at the
bull ring, waiting for the first bull.

In came Mahmud, in dark suit, scarlet BA hood and long black gown. He
stood on the podium, extraordinarily handsome, eyes glittering, and faced
the picadors. They were three Iraqi professors from different universities,
leaders in their field of English Literature. I waited for the lances to be
lowered at the bull. One by one the professors asked questions designed to
show off their expertise. Mahmud parried impeccably. It became clear that
the professors were not entirely comfortable with Hopkins's sprung rhythm,
or his vocabulary – or indeed his Christology.

Gradually it dawned on me that I had mistaken the bull for the picadors
and the matador for the bull. Slowly, and with exquisite courtesy, Mahmud
led them on. A flash of his cape would tempt one of them into a risible
misunderstanding of a phrase or allusion. Another flash of red silk would
offer them a word to pronounce which fell horribly outside their ken. In
another delicate *veronica*, red silk draped across the bull's eyes, he would
respectfully ask them to read aloud a line about which they were asking him,
and one of them would butcher it in a wild misreading of metre. There was
not a trace of triumph, just courtesy and diffidence, but he made complete
fools of all of them, without any one of them noticing.

I looked round to see how others were reacting to this curious verbal
corrida: they weren't. It seemed as though they were entirely unaware of the
drama being played out. So too were the examiners, who nodded gratefully
at Mahmud's clear and courteous answers, making occasional notes and
looking at the candidate with what seemed to be admiration, before they
blundered unawares into the next trap. And the next, and the next.

Slowly it dawned on me why I was there, what my role was in this odd
play, beyond being Mahmud's friend and a representative of Britain. I was a
witness to a cryptic, scarcely perceptible statement by a clever man, about
his own country. It was a silent engagement with a regime that he despised,
not just politically, but intellectually and in almost every other. The professors led the applause at the end of the viva, and I joined in.

Mahmud never hinted at my real role, but I realised that what he had wanted was someone there who understood, so that his exquisite demonstration of intellectual superiority and of the inadequacy of his seniors should really have *happened*. And all that was required was that I sit there and testify to his subversion with a slight nod of comprehension. Without me, his bravura performance would have been like the roaring of the waves in a sea-shell not held to an ear – not just unperceived, but non-existent.

At some point in late November the centre of gravity shifted and after months of wondering *whether* we would escape, we somehow knew we would, and wondered only *when*. Each day, news of more releases came to us through Iraqi television and through the Embassy, and by the first week of December, with my mother finishing her travel arrangements, and Mahmud pressing his hood and gown, I was beginning to hope that her trip might not be necessary. On 7 December the word went round that the foreign ministry was issuing exit visas. By refusing to take no for an answer, I was one of the first to get my passport in – and my visa back.

The next morning in London, my mother was at the Iraqi consulate, submitting her AIDS certificate, when the clerk told her quietly that there was good news. It had just been announced in Baghdad that all the hostages were to be freed.

For us in Baghdad the question that morning was how to leave, and it was an aesthetic as well as a practical question. Richard Branson had been keeping a Virgin 747 at Amman airport ready to collect the hostages from Baghdad. Not only did I think that it would take some time to sort out its departure for London; but I also had an appalling vision of an aerial gin-palace full of loud Britons, patriotic, jingoistic and anti-Iraqi. I did not think I could bear it, wanting to experience this revolution in my life quietly and alone. I drove into the office early and talked it quickly through with Peter, who had decided to stay a few more days. 'Why not try the Iraq Air flight to Amman?' There was a daily flight to Jordan, the only scheduled flight out, sanctions having closed every other route. Someone phoned Iraq Air for me, and came back with the news that there was one seat left on the day's flight; and that if I could get to the airport in 50 minutes, I could have it. Leaping into an office Land Rover, our driver raced to the airport at appalling speed. We made it, and I checked in.

I remember very clearly the sense of utter exhaustion and anticlimax that drained through my whole body as the plane climbed over the dun landscape of the Iraqi desert and headed north-west along the Euphrates. Suddenly, my entire life was transformed, and long before we left Iraqi airspace I had my life in front of me again, full of infinite possibilities. But I knew that I was leaving behind people who couldn't make the same journey – who were still living with the fear that I was quickly sloughing off, and facing the looming prospect of a war which could only be weeks away.

The flight to Amman is short, and we were soon descending. I hoped to find someone there from the British Council to meet me. What I hadn't realised was that I was the first hostage to leave Iraq after the announcement of our release, and I emerged from the baggage carousels through the sliding glass doors to find an arrival hall packed with journalists expecting an entire plane full of hostages. I felt like the little *Man Who* in a Bateman cartoon, and had to speak to a stream of journalists, with a strong sense that until all the hostages were out it would be best to say as little as possible.

My family had been more concerned for me than they let on, worried among other things that I had become dependent on anti-depressants, and would need gentle looking-after. In the event, I threw the medicine box into a bin at Amman airport and forgot it. The psychiatrist had been quite right about exogenous depression and its all-too-exogenous cure.

The aerial bombing of Baghdad began just over a month later, on 17 January 1991.

PRESCRIBING DEATH

Jalees Rehman

I stood in front of the black Sphinx statue in the midst of a bustling crowd of fellow medical students who were rushing up the stairs to the next lecture. In Greek mythology, the Sphinx is thought to have guarded the entrance to Thebes. It used to pose a riddle to anyone wanting to pass through the gates. But standing in front of our Sphinx in the anatomy institute of Ludwig-Maximilians-Universität in Munich, I was the one who had a question. My silent question directed at the mute Sphinx was evoked by my recent visit to the Dachau concentration camp memorial site: Why did you fail to guard the entrance of our medical school in the years leading up to the Third Reich?

Dachau is a Bavarian town located roughly twenty kilometres northwest of Munich. Prior to 1933, Dachau was a well-known refuge, serving as a summer residence for the Bavarian royal family and as a sanctuary for German artists who were inspired by the melancholic beauty of the surrounding wetlands and forests. However, soon after Adolf Hitler and the Nazi party came to power in January 1933, Dachau became an infamous symbol of the Nazi terror and atrocities. In March of 1933, the Nazi government announced the opening of the Dachau concentration camp on the site of a former ammunition factory. The Dachau camp was one of the first concentration camps in the Third Reich and its initial purpose was to detain political enemies of the Nazis such as social democrats, socialists, trade union leaders and communists. The Nazis and the paramilitary SS (*Schutzstaffel*) organisation used the cynical expression 'protective custody', suggesting that they were merely detaining their political opponents in order to protect them from the righteous anger of the public. The official purpose of the Dachau concentration camp was to 'educate' the political dissidents to think in a manner that would conform to the Nazi government's ideology.

The initial prisoners of the Dachau camp were primarily left-wing political opponents of the Nazis. The prisoner population massively expanded during the subsequent years and soon included members of many other groups persecuted by the Nazis, such as Jews, Gypsies, homosexuals, members of the clergy, and later on Poles, Russians and other prisoners of war captured during the Second World War. The Dachau camp was never a death camp or extermination camp of the likes of Auschwitz, but thousands of prisoners died in Dachau and many Jewish prisoners held at Dachau were also sent to their death to the extermination camps. Exact numbers of prisoners held and murdered at Dachau are difficult to obtain, but current estimates suggest that during the years of 1933-1945 at least 200,000 prisoners were held at the Dachau camp and at least 41,000 prisoners died. The common causes of death were executions, starvation and the spread of epidemics such as typhoid. After the war, the Dachau concentration camp was converted into a memorial site and museum which would allow visitors from all over the world to help remember the atrocities and convey a realistic portrayal of the Nazi terrors.

The burden of the Nazi legacy has been one of the cornerstones of German post-war education and culture. The atrocities committed by the Nazis in the Third Reich and the horrors of the Holocaust are the most widely covered aspects of the German secondary school curriculum. We extensively studied the Third Reich not only in our history classes, but also in classes about literature, ethics, philosophy, art and even music, because the impact that the Nazis and the trauma of the Second World War had on German culture and society was so pervasive. The Nazi atrocities and the role of the general German public as passive or not so passive accomplices of the Nazi criminals were the topics of numerous discussions that we had in our classes and in essays that we had to write. Many German school classes also supplement the theoretical learning about the Nazi atrocities with visits to museums or concentration camp memorial sites. However, even though I had also visited the Dachau concentration camp memorial site on multiple occasions when I was still in school, my most recent visit just prior to starting medical school was haunting me in a manner that I had not previously experienced.

In school, we had learned about the six million Jews that had been murdered by the Nazis and their SS-commanders, and we also learned about the millions of non-Jewish victims, such as the Sinti and Roma (Gypsies), Poles, Russians, disabled citizens, clergy members, socialists and communists who had perished during the Nazi reign. Unlike many of my German classmates, I had the luxury of an immigrant background. The term 'luxury' may seem odd, because in the 1970s and 1980s (and to a certain extent even today), being an immigrant in Germany was often associated with a lower socio-economic status – quite the opposite of a 'luxury'. However, there was one key area of German culture, where we immigrants were granted an unspoken privilege: *The Past*. Like many fellow immigrants, I enjoyed the comfort of knowing that my ancestors had no part in the Nazi crimes, because during the years when the Nazis were perpetrating the genocide, my ancestors had been subjects of the British Empire in India.

Throughout my childhood, I was convinced that even if my family had lived in Nazi Germany, we would have probably also ended up as prisoners in a concentration camp. Growing up as a Muslim, I was aware of the many similarities between how Muslims and Jews practise their religion and I had always felt a deep kinship with Judaism. I assumed that with my dark-skinned appearance, I would not have met the Nazi standards of a respectable human being. I only had a few unfortunate encounters with German neo-Nazis or skinheads in the 1980s, and in one of the exchanges that I still remember, the Neo-Nazi yelled that I and my ilk deserved to have been 'gassed' in a Nazi concentration camp. All of these experiences made it easy for me to think of myself as someone who would have been a potential victim of the Nazis, if I had lived during the Third Reich. This enabled me to avoid the torturous introspection that many other Germans had to undertake when trying to understand their families' or communities' guilt and complicity in the Nazi crimes. Some of my class-mates had grandparents who had been members of the Nazi party or the SS. I remember how they described the painful conversations they had with their grandparents, interrogating them about their motives for joining the Nazi party and whether they felt shame for their actions.

During all my previous visits to the Dachau concentration camp, I had been horrified by the crimes committed by Germans who had lived in or near my home city of Munich. I could sense the palpable evil exuding from the walls of the buildings of the Dachau camp, and I was able to feel the pain and suffering of thousands of human beings that had been murdered there. During these visits, all my relativistic musings about the nature of evil that are so common during adolescence would usually disappear. Moral relativism is an intriguing approach for class-room debates, but at the concentration camp site, I knew that true evil did exist and had taken place at this very site only half a century ago. The magnitude of the Nazi evil was so enormous that it always remained beyond my comprehension. In order to understand and describe evil, we often use categories and numbers to enumerate the victims or types of atrocities committed. On a subconscious level, I think that these abstractions are just our way of processing evil without having to directly confront it. Most of us have difficulties to emotionally and cognitively process news about a tragedy in which a single family is killed. The murder of a few hundred or a few thousand humans lies so far outside of our experience that it transcends our ability to comprehend the extent of the tragedy. In the case of the Holocaust, we may cognitively know that millions of human beings perished, but it is unlikely that any of us are able to even remotely grasp the extent of the tragedy and suffering of these millions of innocent human beings.

This recent visit to Dachau in the autumn of 1990 forced me to confront one aspect of the Nazi atrocities that had previously eluded me: medical experiments on human beings. Learning about the details of the horrific and deadly experiments carried out by German physicians on the Dachau concentration camp prisoners had shaken me to my very core. I had previously known that medical experiments on human prisoners were performed in the concentration camps, but I had just seen it as yet another proof of the monstrous nature of 'those Nazis'. During this recent visit, I not only saw the specific sites where the medical experiments had been conducted, but I also read details about the suffering and torture that the prisoners had to endure. The fact that I was about to start medical school is probably why I took a much deeper interest in these crimes than I had in the past. My reason for going to medical school was that I wanted to become a scientist, a physician who would not only treat individual patients but someone who would also study the mechanisms of disease and help develop novel therapies. Up until that Dachau visit in 1990, I had always assumed that combining the profession of a healer with that of a scientist was the pinnacle of nobility and morality. My naïve idealism in regards to my future career as a physician was shredded when I realised that many of the horrific human experiments were carried out and supervised by German physicians who had studied medicine at some of Germany's leading universities and then gone on to murder the Dachau prisoners in the name of medical research.

Standing in front of the Sphinx, I knew that some of these murderous physicians had probably walked past this same statue. I tried to tell myself that the vast majority of German physicians did not partake in the Nazi crimes and did not conduct experiments on prisoners at the concentration camps, but somehow this did not provide me the comfort that I sought. A strange memory of an analogy surfaced, which my elementary school teacher in third grade had taught us. She was telling us about the pollution of water by oil and that a single drop of oil could pollute a thousand litres of drinking water. I knew that only a fraction of German physicians had committed the crimes in the concentration camps, but somehow these physicians had tainted the whole profession. I was now struggling with my own aspiration to become a physician before my career had even begun. As I walked away from the Sphinx to finally attend the anatomy lecture, I knew that I needed to learn more about how and why physicians had actively participated in the Nazi crimes. I also realised that my exuberant passion for medicine and science would be replaced with a cautious enthusiasm, always keeping in mind that there is a dark side to medicine and research that should not be forgotten.

In the weeks, months and years that followed, I read a number of books about the atrocities committed at Dachau. I think that deep down, I had initially wanted to prove to myself that these murderers had not been scientists or physicians. I wanted to believe that they constituted a special breed of monstrous individuals, a cruel and unique aberrancy in the history of mankind that had occurred during the Third Reich, products of their time which had now gone extinct. I hoped to find signs of severe mental illnesses, not to excuse their crimes but to in part to help restore the mystique of nobility to the professions of medicine and science. If the Nazi physicians were indeed mentally deranged murderers, one could hardly blame the medical and scientific establishment for the crimes committed by these individuals. In retrospect, I attribute my silly aspirations to my youthful immaturity and naïveté. During the subsequent years, I learned that many of the Nazi physicians were not mentally ill, they did not constitute some genetic aberrancy and they did see themselves as physicians and scientists. They weren't even rabid anti-Semites or passionate followers of the Nazi ideology. Instead, they were middle-class physician-scientists, who saw human experimentation and murder at the concentration camps as an opportunity to advance their medical research and careers, fulfill their ambitions for fame and prestige and pursue their quest for scientific truth. More recently, I have also come across literature about the careers of the physician scientists who actively or passively supported the torture and suffering inflicted on human beings in the name of science. It was shocking to find out that a number of such individuals were able to avoid the postwar prosecution for their crimes and instead, they went on to become faculty members at German universities. I know that most of my professors in medical school were in their forties, fifties or sixties and were either born after the Third Reich or were only children during the Third Reich. Knowing that none of my teachers participated in the Nazi crimes provided me some solace, but I also know that their mentors and professors likely included people who participated in the Nazi crimes.

There were numerous physicians who conducted human experiments in the concentration camps, but I just want to highlight the atrocities committed by one such individual. Sigmund Rascher was born in 1909 into a middle class family in Munich. His father was a physician who encouraged his family to actively play classical music and was a big supporter of the anthroposophic philosopher Rudolf Steiner. This probably explains why Sigmund Rascher's father enrolled his children in a Waldorf school. Waldorf schools were founded on Rudolf Steiner's philosophy which strives to achieve a balanced and holistic education by targeting the mind, body and soul of the student and by fostering the student's creativity. Sigmund Rascher appears to have been an average student and completed his A-Levels at the age of 21, after which he entered medical school at the University of Freiburg. In 1933, Rascher joined the NSDAP (Nazi party) and in 1934 he decided to move to Munich, where he completed medical school in 1936. Instead of starting a clinical practice, Rascher focused on medical research and worked in a cancer research laboratory in Munich. It appears that he impressed his peers and mentors by developing innovative tests to diagnose cancer. He then decided to voluntarily join the SS and was also conscripted into the

Luftwaffe (air-force) as a physician. Most biographical sketches of Rascher explicitly describe him as being ambitious, talkative and attention-seeking. It may therefore come as a surprise that he would have joined the SS instead of pursuing his burgeoning career in cancer research. However, by joining the SS and by using some personal connections of his wife, Rascher had gained access to the head of the SS, Reichsführer Heinrich Himmler, who was one of the most powerful men in the Third Reich. Thus joining the SS may have been a strategic career move for Rascher.

After Rascher was conscripted into the *Luftwaffe*, he contacted Himmler to see if he could get his medical research career back on track. The SS had full control over the concentration camps, so Rascher proposed performing experiments on the camp prisoners to study the effects of high altitude on air-force pilots. He explained that the experiments could not be performed on the pilots themselves, because they were too dangerous and potentially fatal. However, if prisoners from the Dachau concentration camp were used, one could mimic high altitude conditions with a low pressure chamber and monitor the responses of the prisoners to these potentially fatal conditions. Himmler and the *Luftwaffe* agreed to these proposed studies and Rascher began his first series of experiments. He documented the experiments with photographs of the prisoners as they suffered in the low pressure chambers. Of the 200 Dachau prisoners that were forced to participate in these studies, at least seventy or eighty died a painful death during the experiments while some of the survivors may have been executed after the experiments. Rascher reported his results directly to Himmler, who took a personal interest in these studies. In one series of experiments, Rascher reported the death of ten out of ten Jewish prisoners due to fatal air embolisms to the brain and there are reports of Rascher dissecting the bodies of prisoners after the experiments while they were still alive.

These horrific high altitude experiments represent only some of the unimaginable pain inflicted by Rascher on the Dachau prisoners. After reporting his results, Rascher suggested a different set of studies to Himmler. He wanted to study the effect of severe cold on human physiology to mimic the conditions that an air-force pilot might encounter if his plane had been hit while flying over the sea. Rascher received approval to complete these studies in which naked prisoners were placed in near-freezing water. A horrific table of numbers that Rascher generated from one of these sets of experiments is forever etched into my memory. In this specific table with the title '*Exitus*' (medical terminology for death), Rascher lists the data for seven prisoners who were placed in near freezing water and logs the time it took for them to die and the body temperature at which they died. One prisoner was kept in the near-freezing water for ninety-five minutes and then died five minutes after he was pulled out of the water. I have stared at this table so many times, but the thought of the prisoner's painful and prolonged death in the freezing water still brings tears to my eyes. It is estimated that at least 90-100 prisoners were murdered in these hypothermia experiments.

In an odd twist of events, Rascher and his wife were arrested in 1944 on grounds of suspected kidnapping of children. The exact circumstances of these accusations remain somewhat mysterious, but even Himmler's intervention could not save Rascher. He was imprisoned in a concentration camp, transferred to Dachau and executed by the SS, just days before the Dachau camp was liberated by the Allied Forces in April of 1945.

When we find out about a genocide, our first natural reaction is to empathise with the suffering of the victims and view the perpetrators as non-human monsters. If we dig deeper, however, we are bound to find that in most cases, the perpetrators were, sadly, very human. In my readings about the Holocaust, especially in regards to the role of physicians and scientists, I have been terrified by the realisation that the perpetrators bore characteristics that are all too common among most human beings, including myself. Many of us carry within ourselves the potential to be ambitious and opportunistic, to seek prestige and power and to believe that the 'ends justify the means'. In the case of the Nazi physicians, it seems that these characteristics were the primary drivers for their actions; the Third Reich just represented a fertile ground that allowed these characteristics to give rise to horrific crimes. This realisation has had a profound effect on how I relate to the Holocaust and on how I approach the practice of science and medicine. I have lost the immigrant immunity that I had issued to myself when it came to dealing with the crimes of the Third Reich. I forced myself to undergo the same kind of introspection that non-immigrant Germans had routinely undergone during the post-war decades. Even though my genetic ancestors had not been part of the Third Reich, the German physicians who committed the atrocities shared many of my German cultural roots. They had probably also read the poetry of Goethe and Rilke in school, they would have listened to Beethoven's symphonies and probably studied the philosophy of Immanuel Kant. They wanted to leave their mark on science and break new ground in scientific discovery. I found similar ambitions within myself, my colleagues and my students. Importantly, I realised that these desires and ambitions needed to be kept in check by necessary ethical safeguards, so that we physicians and scientists will never again sacrifice the well-being of our patients and fellow human beings for our goals.

In the quest for novel medical cures, it is all too easy to fall into the trap of neglecting the well-being of individual research subjects for the purpose of the 'greater good'. Claus Schilling, a physician who specialised in tropical medicine and infectious disease, conducted numerous experiments at Dachau in which he infected prisoners with malaria and watched scores of them die as he tried out novel cures that ultimately failed. When he was placed on trial for his crimes against humanity after the fall of the Third Reich, he did not deny that he had been in charge of the medical experiments that resulted in the death of so many prisoners. He merely believed that the experiments were necessary to find a cure for malaria and apparently viewed the victims of his experiments as collateral damage. He was found guilty and executed as a war criminal in 1946. Other German physicians who had participated in the atrocities of the Third Reich were tried before a US military tribunal in Nuremberg, in what became known as the *Nürnberger Ärzteprozess* (Doctor's Trial in the city of Nuremberg) and many of the defendants either received the death penalty or life imprisonment for the crimes that they had committed.

In addition to these punishments, the tribunal also released an important document, 'The Nuremberg Code', which would help enshrine the ethical principles of how medical research should be conducted. The first of the ten principles of the Nuremberg Code is that for medical research to be ethical, one requires voluntary and informed consent of every research subject participating in the experiments. They cannot be directly or indirectly coerced into participating in research studies. Furthermore, all the risks and benefits of the experiment have to be fully explained to the potential research subjects, so that they can reach an informed decision as to whether or not they want to be a part of the research. This principle of the Nuremberg Code is a direct response to the medical experiments at Dachau and other concentration camps, where prisoners were coerced into participating and often did not know that the experiments would likely result in their death.

The Nuremberg Code itself is not a legally binding document, but many of its principles have found their ways into modern day laws and regulations of how medical research can be conducted. In the United States, all research involving human subjects has to be approved by an Institutional Review Board (IRB). The IRB committee at each research institution consists of practicing physicians, scientists and non-specialists who carefully assess the risks and benefits to an individual participant in a proposed research project. They try to ensure that potential research subjects are not coerced into participating in a study. Contemporary IRBs do not only look into obvious coercions such as forcing prisoners to participate in a research study, but they also try to ensure that less obvious forms of coercion are avoided. Refusing to treat a patient with standard medical therapies because he or she decided against participating in a study of a new experimental therapy, for example, would be a form of indirect coercion that the IRB would identify. The IRBs also curtail other subtle forms of pressure exerted on research subjects. For example, excessive monetary reimbursement for participation in high-risk studies is carefully scrutinised, because such a study could attract poverty-stricken research subjects whose decision to participate may be driven by financial pressures that confound their decision-making in regards to the risks and benefits of participation in the study.

In my work as physician scientist in the field of regenerative medicine and stem cell biology, I often come across colleagues in the US who complain of the over-reaching authority of the IRBs. Many proposed research studies in the US are rejected by the IRBs because of legal and ethical concerns about the risks that these novel therapies pose to human subjects. While I can sympathise with the concerns of my colleagues that medical progress is delayed due to these restrictions, my knowledge of the crimes committed by physicians and scientists at the concentrations camps allows me to under-stand and support our contemporary restrictions on medical research. When deciding about the safety of a medical experiment or the autonomy of the research subject, it is safer to err on the side of protecting the rights and well-being of the individual subject than invoking the 'greater good' argument. I have noticed that my colleagues who complain the most about IRBs have limited knowledge about the history of how regulations on the ethics or medical research evolved. Many of them know little about the crimes committed by physicians at the concentration camps and do not understand why we nowadays place such a high value on the individual's rights and autonomy. I have a simple prescription for these colleagues: visit the Dachau concentration camp!

INSIDE EVIN

Ramin Jahanbegloo

A few days before my eventual release, I put pen to paper for the last time within the walls of Evin Prison, and on a little torn-off piece of a Kleenex box, wrote an aphorism: 'A philosopher puts himself in danger because of his thoughts; for his philosophy is like a tightrope on which he walks, with the world threatening deep below.' My ideas had landed me in this prison. To get out I would have to convince my captors that I regretted having these thoughts. No other lifeline remained.

In the early morning of 27 April, 2006, I was on my way to Brussels to attend a conference. Inside Mehrabad airport in Tehran, after I had checked in my luggage and gone through the security check, I was approached by four men. One of them came up and called me by my first name. 'Ramin, could you follow us?' he said. I looked them over quickly: they wore ordinary suits without ties, and they all had beards, giving them an oddly generic quality. The one who had spoken stood impatiently waiting for me to comply. 'I'll miss my plane', I said.

'We just want to ask you a few questions'. People around us were watching, but nobody moved. Quickly I realised that I had no choice but to go with them.

I was led to a waiting car. Two of the men sat in the front as driver and passenger, and the other two got in the back with me, keeping me in the middle. Then they pushed my head down and the car took off toward another part of the airport, to a garage where another car was waiting. Here, with fewer people around, the men became more aggressive, pulling me out of the car and throwing me into the other one. Again they put my head down and this time one of them covered my head with his blazer. This blazer, which smelled of rotten onions, had a hole in it, so that I could see one of the rear windows. The car left the airport very quickly and soon we were on the highway, heading for northern Tehran. Then I heard one of them say into a walkie-talkie: 'We have the package. The package is arriving.'

I was terrified, and feared for my life. I knew there had been cases in Iran where people had been taken away like this and executed without notice or trial. Their mutilated bodies were found in suburban areas of Tehran. Abductors similar to these men, who by now I knew had to be intelligence officers, had been picking up intellectuals and activists and killing them on the spot. An agitated voice kept escaping from me, though I felt I was not speaking. It kept echoing, bouncing around inside the car, falling back into my throat and escaping again—'Where are you taking me? Where are you taking me?' And the simple, hollow reply: 'Shut up,' over and over again.

Never in my life had I thought I would be relieved to be approaching the grim walls of Evin prison. But relief is exactly what I felt when I recognised, through the hole in the blazer, a nearby square in the area of Saadat Abad which signalled its proximity. I knew then that I would not be murdered. We passed the first gate and when we stopped at the second gate I heard the driver presenting his identification card to the guard: 'We have a package for 209.' I later learned that 209 was a section of Evin prison that was administered by the Ministry of Information. It was an interrogation centre where no one, not even members of the government, could enter or leave without a permit. It is the autonomous kingdom of Iranian security officers and interrogators who formulate and carry out whatever policy they like toward the prisoners. In their view, prisoners of section 209 are spies, traitors, enemies of Islam or the Revolution who deserve humiliation and sometimes the harshest treatment. Those who are less known to the public are dumped into solitary cells without any medical attention and ignored by prison staff.

Blindfolded, I was led by the arm from one room to another, and listening to their voices, I heard them say that we were going to the administrative room. In this room I heard someone say, 'Where are his belongings? Go and bring a prison uniform for him.' They asked me to sit down. This was when I felt a hand on my shoulder and a voice that said, with an unforgettable ominousness, 'This is the last stop.'

I recall the sound of a heavy steel door closing behind me. I took off my blindfold and found myself trapped between four cold walls. I looked around, my eyes adjusting to the blinding light as if emerging from a dream

– or, strangely, as if waking up into a nightmare. It was a very small cell, maybe three by three metres. A high ceiling and old cement. All in green. An intense yellow light was coming from a single bulb high above. There were two blankets on the floor, next to a small vent by the wall. I could hear the horror of the walls somehow, the voices of past prisoners whispering a painful welcome in my ears. I could even see traces of these past guests on the wall despite the green paint that was supposed to cover years of torture in this cell. I had no way of knowing whether they had survived the time they had spent here. What about me? Would I be able to survive solitary confinement without going insane? The truth is, when you are in solitary, you never know when you will break. So many questions were storming my mind. I was isolated and bewildered. I heard my own breathing and then, as if from an impossible distance, the sound of someone moaning. It was coming through the vent. Later on I would find out that he was another prisoner who was in such a bad condition that he could barely move. He had to be helped by the prison guards to go to the bathroom. I came to the conclusion that he must have been tortured. Should I expect the same fate? Disoriented, I eventually fall asleep.

'Wake up, wake up.' It was the raspy voice of a burly prison officer standing in the doorway. 'Get ready for the interrogation,' he said. I was led into an interrogation room, concrete like all the other ones, covered with soundproof corks. Though blindfolded, I could smell the disagreeable odour and flat taste of rotten cork. I was ordered to sit on a single chair facing the wall at the far end. After what seemed like hours I heard footsteps behind me. It sounded as if two men had entered. But they said nothing, and seemed to be waiting for something else to happen. I could hear the sound of their breathing. And then I heard the low mumble of voices. I held my breath and waited. Eventually a third man came in, and he was the first one who talked to me.

'Oh, very interesting, Mr. Jahanbegloo, the great intellectual is here. What are you doing here in prison?' he asked ironically.

'I think there has been a mistake in bringing me here,' I said immediately.

'No, no there is no mistake,' he said drily. 'You have been brought here because you are accused of a conspiracy against the Iranian state. You are implicated in a *barandazi narm*.'

I had never heard these words before. The direct translation from Farsi would be a 'soft overthrow;' later on I supposed that what he meant by that was a Velvet Revolution. But I asked him then, in my confusion, to clarify what he meant.

'You know better than I what a soft overthrow is,' he responded.

I could already see that the thread of a normal conversation was quickly slipping away. There would be no rational basis in our discussions to come.

The principal interrogator, the man who had spoken, had on old brown dress shoes, flattened at the back in the customary Persian way, and with no laces. The others referred to him as *Hajj Agha*, which literally means someone who has been to Mecca for pilgrimage, but it is actually the way interrogators called each other as a sign of fidelity to Islam. Hajj Agha pretended to be a 'university professor,' and though he tried all the time to use the word 'methodology', he did not seem like someone with a humanist education. The other two were much more reticent and merely served as echoes of this chief officer. Their false names were Hajj Ali and Hajj Saeed, and judging by their shoes I could tell why they were mere background characters. The first had on a pair of raggedy tennis shoes, and the second always walked around in household sandals.

After I told him that I still could not understand what I was being implicated in and what he wanted from me, Hajj Agha proceeded to lay out a conspiracy theory which they must have spent a lot of time constructing, though in the end it was nothing but a web of nonsense.

'You see, Mr. Jahanbegloo, we know for a fact who you're working for. We've been through your emails. We have two rooms full of documents – video clips and writings, newspaper clippings and voice recordings – on you and all that you have done with your life. It all testifies to your guilt. So you're better off telling us from the beginning what your role is in this soft overthrow, and the details of how your employers have instructed you to carry it out.'

'What employers? What are you talking about?'

Hajj Agha exhaled his cigarette smoke slowly, patiently, and I felt it enveloping me from behind like a fog of uncertainty.

'The United States and Israel, of course. Do you think we're stupid? We know you've been meeting with American and Israeli scholars, with politicians, with activists. You've done it all out in the open. There are video recordings of your meetings with them, countless articles and books that you've collaborated on with them. Shall I go on? You know best what role you've played in working with them, and your intention has been to change the government of the Islamic Republic to better suit their interests.'

What could I say in this situation? How could I convince these men that I was innocent? How could one talk sense to men who had swallowed the revolutionary ideology of the Islamic Republic? It was like confronting absurdity in human form. I was already guilty in their eyes, and they supposedly already knew what I was guilty of. In a way my innocence was working against me, because what in a normal society is supposed to make you a decent man actually becomes an anomaly in the Islamic Republic. There was nothing to say. I could only respond to their questions with shorter questions that clarified nothing. Our language game, with the rules all in disarray, had turned into a life or death struggle which constantly drew near to madness.

The interrogations continued. Hajj Ali used to come to Evin prison at one o'clock and ask the prison guards to take me out of my prison cell. He had made it his vocation to turn me into a good Muslim. Each time when we were alone, he would ask me to remove my blindfolds and to sit next to him on a machine-made carpet on the floor. And each time the conversation would revolve around religion and the fact that I had lost my faith. Once he looked me in the eyes and asked:

'Do you consider yourself as a true Muslim?'

'What exactly do you mean by this?' I replied.

'Do you know the names of the 12 Shiite Imams?' he backfired angrily.

'Yes, I do,' I reacted with confidence and did some name dropping: 'Ali ibn Abu Talib, Hasan ibn Ali, Husayn ibn Ali, Zayn al-Abidin....'

'Enough. I am sure you don't know how to pray?' he said.

'My grandmother taught me how to pray when I was 12, but....' I was trying to find an answer to get out of his trap. He cut my phrase and added:

'No wonder you became a spy. You come from a family of non-believers. Is it true that your father was a communist?'

'My father was an idealist and his great ideal was to change himself and to enrich the world.'

'But he failed and went to prison. In the same way that you failed because you made the wrong choices in life.'

I was listening to my inner voice murmuring in my mind: did I make the wrong choice? Maybe, because I was born in a period of history in which people have no respect for anything. But I did not choose to be born in the twentieth century. I chose neither my parents nor my country. They chose me. I got back to him with a little more confidence: 'We usually make a living by what we get but we can make a life out of what we wish.'

He stood up and responded furiously: 'Stop philosophising. We are not in a classroom and I am not your student. I am not here to listen to you. You have to listen to me. If I have to I will make sure that I can keep you in this cell for several years or even more. Then you would not get to see your daughter. I want to try and save you in spite of yourself, so I'm making an attempt to save you; but you need to collaborate with us.'

Now, I was no longer looking at him. I had my eyes fixed on the machine-made carpet which largely set the tone of our conversation. The designs were neither warm nor relaxing; the busy carpet patterns served to hide stains. I was fearful, shocked and terribly angry and asked him: 'What do you mean by collaboration? I have never collaborated with any government. I am not interested in power.'

'But power is beautiful when it is on the side of God. We are servants of Islam and Iran,' he responded.

'I always thought that you cannot serve God and politics at the same time. You can't serve two masters,' I said.

'Well, I serve the Guide of the Revolution and his will is that of God.'

I nodded without adding a word.

'You have to collaborate. You have to confess,' he continued. And then he dialled a number on his mobile and started talking to another person about a business plan. I wasn't listening to his phone conversation. I was still thinking of his words 'collaborate' and 'confess,' which hit me like a rock. This was the first time in my life that someone was asking me to confess something. What was I supposed to confess? I hadn't committed any crimes and didn't recognise myself as guilty. I was shivering with rage.

Hajj Ali ended his conversation on the phone. He looked towards me again and realised that I was deeply tortured by my thoughts. 'Think of what I told you. Put your blindfolds back on and return to your cell.' He called one of the prison guards by his number. 'Number 430, come here and take the prisoner back to his cell.'

Fifty days passed. I kept track of the days by making scratches on the wall. In ordinary life, fifty days often carry little weight. They can pass by fleetingly as we go about our daily tasks, caught in the transient flow of life. When one is in solitary confinement, sleepless, and under constant pressure, days become heavy and oppressive. Each hour becomes another stone on one's back. It is a different kind of suffering from physical torture; it spares the body and goes directly for the soul. And yet, despite the difficulties I was facing, I was always aware that others inside Evin were undergoing even worse tribulations. On that fiftieth day my wife, Azin, and daughter, Afarin, came. She came on a sweltering day in June to bring a hint of salvation.

While I was locked up in solitary confinement trying to keep my sanity, not knowing how my wife and child were doing, she had been outside fighting to see me and to get me out. The day after my arrest, the participants in the conference I was supposed to attend in Brussels had become concerned; and one of them, Ron Asmus, whom I had met in 2002 at an Aspen Institute conference in Istanbul, had contacted Azin to tell her I had not arrived. My wife and my mother had been left without any news from me for 48 hours, but two days after my arrest, on a Friday morning at 10:00 am, I was handcuffed and taken to my apartment for a search. I was taken blindfolded in a car with two heavy weight security officers while another car full of three men followed us. They asked me to open the door of my apartment with my key and to make sure that my wife would not make any noise. It happened that my mother and my in-laws were also present at our apartment and were all very worried about my fate. They were all happy to find out that I was in good health, though they could tell from my unshaven and tired face that I had had two rough nights at the prison. As soon as the security officers entered our apartment they started searching for any document or paper which could prove their conspiracy theory. One of the security officers was filming the whole scene and he looked in the cupboards for pirate DVDs and alcohol. My mother was trying her best to argue with my jailers, hoping to persuade them to have mercy. I was asked to sit on a chair and remain silent. I could not say a word about my situation in prison. The security officers confiscated most of my writings and photos, finishing their four hour search with five big boxes of documents that they took to prison. I never forgot the last word my mother told me before I returned to prison. 'My son', she said, 'stand firm for your convictions. Your father also went to prison.' These words gave me confidence and courage. The jailers put back the handcuffs, blindfolded me and took me back to section 209. My mother's words rang in my ears, and they reminded me of Rumi's: 'Ignore those who make you fearful and sad, who degrade you back towards disease and death.'

It did not take Azin long to take up the Herculean task of contacting every person she could and pull every string to have me released. She secretly met the Italian ambassador, Roberto Toscano, throwing on a chador and going through the back door of his residence in the Farmanieh area of Tehran to tell him what had happened to me. We had been friends for many years and Roberto was ready to do everything he could to help me. With the help of Roberto talks soon began with members of the Council of the European Union. Javier Solana, the Secretary General of this council, was contacted, and a petition was started which was passed at first throughout Europe and later in Canada, the United States, India, and many other places. At the time, I had no clue that any of this was happening. I knew I had friends and sympathisers out there, but never imagined the scale of their response, the generosity and the compassion they showed during my time of crisis.

But I knew nothing of this when Azin came with our one-year-old baby in her arms and stood outside the gates in the unbearable heat until she could see me. The massive series of arrests that had been made that day following a demonstration for women's rights had brought dozens of pro-testors straight to Evin, and while they were being processed, the visitors simply had to wait. Finally, when the interrogators came to my cell in the afternoon and announced that I had a visitor, I became confused, and then, when my thoughts cleared up and I knew who it was, I grew very excited. Preparing me for the visit was a ridiculous process. Hajj Ali retrieved some of my clothes from my suitcase, which I had been planning to wear to the conference, and told me to put them on. They shaved me so that I would no longer look like the Count of Monte Cristo, and Hajj Ali even insisted on spraying me with cologne. All this was meant to make me look presentable and in good shape. There was good reason for this as I was to learn later, but at the time my captors told me nothing and, to be honest, as thrilled as I was, it barely mattered to me. I was blindfolded and escorted out of section 209, then put into a car and driven past the inner gates, down from the secluded hilly area to the main gate where the visiting rooms and the guards' dormitories stood.

We had ten minutes. Before I entered the room where she was sitting and waiting for me, Hajj Ali told me this with special emphasis. Ten minutes. And, he whispered, I was not to forget what he had told me: if I said anything about what had gone on in there I would not be able to see her again. He sat me down on the sofa next to her and removed my blindfold. She seemed very excited and I could tell her heart was beating fast as her large searching eyes looked me over. Afarin was clinging to her very tightly. It was obvious she was scared in this filthy, gloomy environment. The place where we found ourselves was not a regular visiting room. The sofa we sat on was dirty and full of holes; the walls were covered with stains and chipped paint. In the corner there were some pillows and blankets which I assumed were for guards to sleep under. This was a special meeting room that had been arranged so that other prisoners and visitors could not see me. I was nervous and didn't know what to say. We wanted to have contact with each other, to embrace, but Hajj Ali was sitting right there, behind a desk in front of us. So we sat on the sofa staring at each other, and she would ask, 'How are you doing? Is everything OK?' and I would reply, 'Yes, I'm fine. Are you OK?'

There was so much that I wanted to say, but the words kept fading as soon as they reached my lips. 'Don't bring Afarin here anymore. I don't want her to have memories of this,' I finally said. Azin gave me a knowing look, then reached into her bag and took out two books: the autobiographies of Gandhi and Nehru. 'These will help,' she said.

Hajj Ali took the books away from me immediately and informed me that they would have to be checked. Most books were fine, he said, but any notations or sections not written by the author were forbidden; they could contain secret communications. And finishing this explanation, he quickly informed us that our time was up.

The departure was hurried – there was barely any time for the pain to set in. As we said goodbye, Azin leaned over and whispered in my ear, 'Everything is OK outside. Be strong.' I found strength in her words; even as I headed back to the bleakness of my cell, even as I was forced to change back into prisoners' clothes, I was filled with new hope and determination. Soon, I told myself, I will leave this place, and I'll be together again with my wife and child.

A few days later, sometime in the early hours of the morning, just as I finished my daily exercises and started my reading, I heard a banging against the iron door. The slot opened and a voice announced that I was to prepare myself for a visit. A minute later, two guards came in and led me straight outside, away from section 209 and into the Evin gardens. These gardens seemed extremely out of place in such a hostile and grim setting, but they immediately offered a little comfort – a reminder of other things out there in the world, a reassurance that such things still existed. A few trees, some patches of grass, scattered wildflowers and a bench. Hajj Ali and Hajj Saeed stood next to me, saying nothing and gazing about impatiently. A few soldiers in military clothing passed by. I looked around and, noticing a nearby hospital, realised this must be a resting area for doctors and patients, offering a brief respite from all the bleak activities of each passing day. Later I learned that many of those tortured or on hunger strike would be taken to this hospital. Ordinary people rarely know that the so-called Evin prison doctors are anything but doctors. They are not there to save lives, but to keep the prisoner alive so that the interrogations continue.

Despite the uncertainty, I tried to enjoy the moment, breathing deeply to take in the fresh air, listening to the singing birds, hoping the expected visitor would be Azin. And to my surprise, a minute later, I saw her figure emerging in the distance. She was accompanied by her father and they were both walking toward us from the main gate. Seeing her approach was like the gradual manifestation of a dream figure, a person alive every hour in my thoughts now made real, in the flesh. My interrogators had told me so many times that I may never see her again that I had started to believe them. I kept myself composed as she finally reached us, but the image I projected was one of exhaustion and desolation. I could see that in her eyes, too, there was a real sadness. She held her hands out to me and looked me over with concern.

'How are you, my dear? How is Afarin?'

'We're both fine,' she responded softly. 'You look terribly thin.'

'Do I? How is my mother? And the rest of the family?'

'Everyone is well. We're worried about you. Do you know when you'll be freed?'

It was a painful question for both of us, and she asked it with such feeling that the words broke something in her and tears finally fell down her eyes. She had been so strong, but it was impossible to hold it back anymore. Hajj Ali and Hajj Saeed, who had been overseeing our conversation, turned away and walked off a few steps. I reached out and put a hand on her shoulder, looked her in the eyes. 'I will get out of here eventually. Have hope,' I said, trying to inspire in her the same feelings that her visit had brought me.

Little did I know that she had recently met with Judge Saeed Mortazavi, the city's Prosecutor General, who had told her that it was very unlikely I would be freed. So her tears kept falling even as she handed me the copy of Hegel's *Phenomenology of Spirit* that I'd asked for. She hugged and kissed me, and as we walked away we constantly looked back at each other.

As soon as we reached section 209 again, I was unexpectedly taken to a new room where a taciturn barber gave me a quick shave and a haircut. What were they preparing me for now, I thought. When the barber finished, Hajj Ali came in with some of my clothes and told me to change.

'Put these on. You have to look good for the camera.'

'The camera?' I asked. 'Are you planning to film me for something? I don't want to be filmed.'

'Shut up and do as you're told,' he suddenly yelled. He rarely let his anger flare up like this with me. But then it became evident why he was so upset. 'That wife of yours is creating a lot of problems for us. And now you will do something for us to cancel out those problems. Anyhow, this is part of your interrogation, and you have no say in the matter.'

I knew what he meant, even though he wasn't willing to say it openly and Azin had had to conceal it in front of them: the campaign to secure my release had gained a lot of momentum and pressure was mounting on the prosecutors to charge me formally. And to charge me, they would require more evidence: a confession.

It was comical how they had arranged everything in such a makeshift way, considering their status as agents of the state. I walked the distance from my cell to the interrogation room blindfolded. Once in the room, they took off the blindfolds, but asked me not to move my head in any direction. One of the interrogators who never showed me his face was sitting on my far right so that I could not see him and he would not be on camera. The room they took me to was similar to all the other interrogation rooms, except that here they had replaced the usual metal chair with a brown leather chair; behind it stood a blue screen and in front of it a table with a microphone; a single plant next to it was supposed to give the place a more pleasant look. Two camera-men waiting at the other end of the table looked me over as we came in and said they were ready to begin filming. Hajj Ali sat me down on the leather chair and barked out his instructions: 'You are to repeat everything we tell you in front of the camera. You may not change any of the words, and you have to say it all as naturally as possible. Listen closely and memorise the words well, because we don't have all day. Most importantly, we will be standing to the side and you are not to look at us at any point in time. Keep your eyes averted, or else we will have to stop the tape and start again, and it will not turn out well for you if you keep wasting our time. On the other hand, if you comply and do exactly as you're told, there may be some hope for you after all,' he finished in a more reassuring tone.

It soon occurred to me how cleverly they had actually orchestrated everything. They had taken me to see my wife, and immediately afterward, knowing I would be filled with excitement and anxiety to be released, had brought me here to force a false confession out of me. More than anything they had used the element of surprise against me, so that it all happened as if in a whirlwind, leaving me no time to contemplate my next move. It was very effective. Images of Azin lingered, freshly burnt into my consciousness – her cheerless eyes, the tears streaming down her cheeks, her trembling lips. I had to do whatever I could to get out of there, to be with her and my daughter again. I was not going to be like Socrates, ready to drink the hemlock; unlike him, I had too much to lose. 'Tell me what I have to say,' I told Hajj Ali.

I had nothing to confess. I merely repeated their words. Keeping my eyes down the entire time and reciting it all as bluntly as I could, I explained how my work on nonviolence was directly tied to United States interests and designs, how American agents had approached me and put me in contact with people at the NED (National Endowment for Democracy), and how this gave shape to my plans and aims. I continued with the words they had asked me to repeat: I prepared a final report comparing Iranian civil society with that of Eastern Europe at the time of the Velvet Revolution. I was also supposed to have been in contact with people at the Woodrow Wilson International Center for Scholars in Washington D.C., namely Haleh Esfandiari – who, they had told me to mention, is married to a Jew. The aim of this organisation, I explained, was to continue the work of the NED, to foment unrest and eventual revolution in Iran.

'Now that I am looking back at my activities over the past few years from America to Iran,' I finished with suppressed bitterness and pain, 'I see that my activities have placed me in the camp of Iran's enemies rather than on the side of its national interests. And I am disappointed in myself for these things and I think that I have to rectify this in the best way possible.'

To my relief, the camera was turned off here and I was congratulated on having done a good job. This, Hajj Ali told me, would really help my case. With a strange mixture of satisfaction and disgust, I returned to my cell and hoped for the best. As I lost myself in the pages of Hegel's *Phenomenology of Spirit*, the transcript of my 'confession' was distributed, so it was soon known publicly that I was a known traitor and spy who had willingly confessed. The tape itself would not be released until a year later, when it was combined with other forced confessions from Haleh Esfandiari and Kian Tajbaksh in a programme entitled 'In the Name of Democracy'. This short documentary, which aired on a state-run broadcast station, depicted the three of us as agents working in the interests of foreigners to undermine the Islamic Republic. It began by talking about nonviolence and revolution, and with interspersed interviews and discussions, made the usual claims about the United States' diabolical schemes and the mechanisms it used to achieve its aims. To this day, certain labels have stuck to me because of this kind of propaganda. It is true that my intellectual work revolves around nonviolence and resistance, yet I have never been a civil activist or – it goes without saying – an agent employed by any government. One of the reasons such accusations have been thrown at me, however, is my involvement with many different thinkers, some of them known radicals.

I passed the days spreading my feet on the floor and walking silently in my cell. Freedom is all I wanted. My desire for freedom mocked absurd justice. But absurd justice denied my freedom. Then the moment I was waiting for arrived one day at the doorstep of my cell.

'Get ready,' shouted one of the prison guards opening the iron door of my cell. 'Someone will take you to the Revolutionary Court.' I had a few seconds of silence, thinking this was the end, and then replied back, 'OK. I will be ready!'

The words 'Revolutionary Court' sent a shiver through my spine. I had not known such fear and I can hardly explain how I felt at the time. An hour later a man came, blindfolded me and took me to a car. He took off the blindfold. I was sitting in the back of an official car with the guard next to me. I was handcuffed and he had a pistol at his side. The driver was going fast towards downtown Tehran. He was taking the special road that is reserved for police officers and official cars. This was my first time out of Evin prison after three long months. I was in my prison uniform and unshaved and people who stopped at the red light next to our car looked at me like a circus animal. I suppose they considered me a criminal or a drug dealer. Maybe people were afraid of me because they did not understand me. For them I was just a prisoner because I was in prison uniform.

The car drove up near the bazaar and parked in front of the Revolutionary Court. I was taken to the first floor where I sat with my guard for an hour waiting for General Prosecutor Mortazavi to see me. I was surprised to see Hajj Saeed coming out of the room and asking me to follow him. Mortazavi was talking to his secretary and did not even notice my entrance. He looked shorter than he did in his photos with a three-day beard and moustache. His spectacles made him look even more atrocious than his nickname 'the butcher of the press' implied. I knew him for his role in the death of Zahra Kazemi, the Canadian-Iranian photographer who was tortured, beaten and raped during her detention in 2003.

Mortazavi gave me a harsh look and said: 'Mr. Jahanbegloo, you are accused of spying against the interests of the Islamic Republic of Iran.'

'But I have never been connected with any foreign intelligence.' I replied.

'Listen to me carefully. If you contradict me you will go on trial facing charges of communicating with a hostile government and I can easily ask for death penalty,' he responded ferociously.

'But I am not a spy; I am a philosopher,' I said shyly.

'That doesn't interest us. What interests us is with what foreign institution you are connected,' he fired back.

'None!'

'And who recognises you as a philosopher? Americans, Canadians, the French?'

'I... I have taught at many universities. But I haven't done anything except serve people.'

'Is that so? And why do you have Canadian citizenship? This is a proof that you are a spy.'

'But many Iranians have dual nationalities,' I said.

'You are not an Iranian; you are an ugly Canadian.'

'But I have lived and worked in this country. I have written books in Persian.'

'Forget the big words. Your writings are of no use to us. They do not serve Islam and they do not serve Iran.'

Angrily, Mortazavi turned to Hajj Saeed and said: 'Take him to the other room and read him all the accusations.'

I was taken to the next room and Saeed came with a paper on which there was a long list of accusations: spying, working with foreign intelligence, plotting against the security of the Iranian state, preparing a velvet revolution, collaboration with Jewish institutions, writing lies about the Holocaust, and so on.

'Sign this,' he said.

'But I haven't done any of these,' I replied with a disoriented tone.

'Look. If you don't sign, we have to start all the interrogations from scratch. This means that you will stay here for a year or two with no contact with the outside world.'

I felt that I was signing my death sentence and that it would be used against me as long as the Islamic regime remained in place in Iran. But so many prisoners had done the same thing before me, just to save their lives and be with their families again. I was thinking of my daughter Afarin. What would she think in twenty years from now? Would she say that her father was a hero, a coward, or simply a man who met his destiny on the road he took to avoid it?

I was taken back to Evin. My supper was already waiting for me in the room; colder than usual. The blindfold was taken off. The iron door was closed behind me. That night I ate and slept with shame.

GRAVEYARDS

Hamza Elahi

An old man, a first generation immigrant from Pakistan, is dying in his modest Wanstead semi. There are half a dozen relatives gathered around his bed; his breathing is laboured, his grip weak. He has worked hard, reared children, made his share of mistakes, but by and large has lived honourably. He has even had the foresight, in his will, to allot a sum of money for his burial. He might not have been rich, but there is enough here for a decent grave. Should he be buried in the nearest graveyard, for ease of accessibility? Should his tombstone have a hyperbolic epitaph, or be painted in the colours of the 'homeland'? Should his loving children pool their money and put up a mausoleum in his honour? What can or ought to be done? Does Islam have anything to say?

In the 'Gardens of Peace' cemetery in Ilford, the graves appear to have come off a production line. Rows of identical mounds of earth crowned with a simple stone slab stretch obediently as far as the eye can see. They resemble some kind of chant, or repeat binary code; they are like insistent questions to which you always get the same answer.

The day I visit the sky seems struck by some kind of illness. It is only midday but it is black and bulging, ready to be operated on. I kneel at one of the graves. The stone slabs have only the most basic information: a name, a date of death, an age. The only other information is a code denoting the plot the grave is in (the graveyard has about a dozen plots) and an exact location in that plot. I still can't be sure whether the code is deeply dehumanizing or refreshingly free of any sentimentality about death. There is nothing else that differentiates the graves; there is nothing else remarkable about them. Bouquets of flowers are daring and very occasional interlopers, for even they are not encouraged – it is made clear in the graveyard's guidelines that they are for the benefit of the living, not the dead. Those who visit the dead – they are everywhere, mumbling under hoods and umbrellas – must leave only prayers as a mark of their visit.

I approach a group of people in the cemetery's Hall of Remembrance, a low, light-filled building used largely for prayer, to ask what they think of the graveyard. One or two offer no opinion. Al Amin, who is of Sudanese descent, praises the fidelity to Islamic principles, and seems to be knowledgeable about what those principles are. 'Modesty in death as in life. There is community here'. Karim, who came from Pakistan eleven years ago, knows nothing about the principles, but intuitively grasps the reasons behind this treatment of the dead. 'Now they are in the hands of God'. He raises a hand at the sky, to which the first incision is being made. He is smiling broadly under his prayer hat. Rain begins to fall, with a clarity of sound and form I haven't seen or heard before.

In the graveyards of many other religious traditions perceptions of the deceased, and the material inequalities of life, are perpetuated in tombstone inscriptions and in hierarchies established by the time and expense lavished on the grave. In the 'Gardens of Peace', the headstones are not an aide memoire to the deceased's personality or achievements, and in the graveyard there is no aristocracy or proxy sink estate. Death has come. The time for revision or redemption is over. Partisan tombstone retrospectives amount to nothing more than the polite contortions of the mason's chisel. Ostentatious graves only invite deadly vines which strangle cherubs and clip the wings of angels. The living really should know better. The dead, by now, almost certainly do.

There does seem to be some consensus, based on various traditions of Prophet Muhammad (*hadiths*), that this is how things should be done. A Muslim's grave, the orthodoxy suggests, should be plain and humble, and the material used in its making should not be expensive. A Muslim graveyard should value simplicity and orderliness. Collectively, the graves should be akin to believers standing in line in the mosque, in God's presence; anything that violates this equality should be avoided. Walls surrounding a grave, provided they are not decorated or painted, are permissible, but only in order to mark out the grave. It is certainly not permitted to build a dome or any other construction over the grave in order to embellish or aggrandise it. Although some *hadiths* forbid tombstone inscriptions, following the Prophet's own practice after the death of his son Ibrahim, scholars have viewed it as permissible to write on the gravestones only the name and the date of death.

But this approach is not supported by other graveyards. This is something I quickly realised when I went to Brookwood, just outside Woking in Surrey, the resting place for some of Britain's earliest Muslims, and also some of its most distinguished. Incorporated by Act of Parliament in 1852, Brookwood was at the time the largest cemetery in the world. It remains the largest in the country and one of the largest in Western Europe. A private London terminus was used to carry coffins and mourners direct to Brookwood Station, and an exit from the station leading directly to the cemetery remains to this day. Privately owned at its founding by the London Necropolis Company, Brookwood is now in the hands of Erkin Guney, a Muslim of Turkish-Cypriot descent.

Between the leaves of Brookwood's many trees, the sun falls thick on my bare arms. Doom-laden clouds are gathering towards the west; later it will rain. Brookwood feels very lived in: the trees grow to impressive heights, lichen-covered tombstones slant and fade – this is a place of deep slumber. Those buried in Brookwood are an extremely eclectic bunch. The vast majority of the graves are those of Englishmen, but there are also sections for Latvians, Swedes, Serbs, Czechs, Poles, Turks, and military plots covering about half a dozen nations. Muslims rub shoulders with Zoroastrians, soldiers with scholars, the long dead with those merely wet behind the ears. Of the Muslims there is a bewildering array of nationalities and sects, including Ismailis, Ahmadis, and Dawoodi Bohras. To this extent Brookwood promises the possibility of comparisons across time, sect, class and culture.

Right by the station entrance are the Muslim graves. They are exclusively Turkish or Kurdish – and they couldn't be more different from those in the 'Gardens of Peace'. Nearly all have tombstones and a kerbset covering the body in its entirety. Epitaphs are commonplace and effusive, both on the part of the living ('a gentleman to his dying day') and the dead ('to live in hearts we leave behind is not to die'). There are photographs of the deceased. The material used in the grave-making is almost invariably marble. Flowers are unexceptional, as are windmills, wind chimes and other mementos. Although most of the graves seem to have had some significant thought devoted to them, there were several that had not, and even one where it was left to a series of peeling stickers to spell out the name of the deceased. (I am reminded of this grave a few days later, when I visit the Henley Road Cemetery in Reading. Here there is a whole section for those, all of Christian heritage, who cannot afford tombstones – and in that section, you will find, propped or draped against the cramped sunken graves, football scarves, model angels, model cars, wind chimes, even chilled cans of lager.)

The rest of Brookwood's Muslim graves are a mish-mash, from the splendour of the mausoleum of Sharif Al Hussein Ben Ali, and the strange, interconnected tombs of the Dawoodi Bohras, to the relative conformity of the Ahmadiyya and other Muslim graves. The graves of Marmaduke Pickthall and Abdullah Yusuf Ali, the translators of the Qur'an, within a few yards of each other, are all made of stone, have very short epitaphs and a verse from the Qur'an, but are otherwise simple and unadorned. Interestingly, the dead of Indian and Pakistani descent mostly follow the same blueprint. The graves of Sufi master Idries Shah, the Indian painter Maqbool Fida Husain and the last King of Yemen, Muhammad al-Badr are also to be found at Brookwood.

The most distinctive graves, and those that are closest in appearance and philosophy to those in the 'Gardens of Peace', are Brookwood's Ismailis. These are completely flat, and the headstones, equidistant from one another, are very small, pentagon-shaped objects that list only the most basic information about the deceased. From a distance the headstones appear to be stepping stones to some enchanted Elysium tucked away behind a set of hedgerows. Nearer, I am reminded not only of the 'Gardens of Peace' but of Brookwood's numerous military cemeteries. For there is the sense, whether real or imagined, of those in each resting place having lived and died for something bigger and more important than themselves: the soldier for his nation, the Muslim for his Lord. The fellowship in common cause and the enormity of sacrifice are moving; and there is an understanding that any proofs of that sacrifice, in epitaphs charged with mush and tales of derring-do, are unnecessary, even offensive. But even if all of this is imagined, what cannot be disavowed is the sense that, irrespective of rank or station in life, death is democratic. Private lies beside general, porter beside surgeon, father beside son. Equality is a truth common to all graveyards, but is best made in graveyards such as these. Seek all the power you want, and the wealth, but it's no good being the richest man amongst the dead. Even if you have a bone to pick with the iniquities of life, you cannot possibly have a bone to pick with graveyards.

As we rattle along in his 4x4, raindrops tinkling on its old steel roof, Erkin Guney explains that there is no hard and fast policy when it comes to Muslim graves at Brookwood. If the family wants an image of the deceased on the tombstone, that is permissible; if the family wants a mausoleum, and can afford one, that is permissible; the same goes for flowers, unbridled epitaphs, mementos. I ask whether such ostentation is desirable in Islam. Or if it might amplify the suffering of the deceased, or at least do nothing to ease it. Guney makes it clear that the family's wishes will always prevail. But if there is any doubt, an imam is always at hand to provide guidance.

After visits to some other cemeteries, I begin to come to some tentative conclusions about national and cultural preferences. Tottenham Park Cemetery in north London and the Muslim section of the Henley Road Cemetery lend weight to the theory that Muslims of Indian and Pakistani origin tend to have the simplest of graves. Those of Turkish and Kurdish descent are less rigid: photographs of the deceased on headstones are commonplace in their section of Tottenham Park Cemetery. The graves are often accompanied by pictures of things associated with the deceased: a sports car, a pair of running shoes, a comb and scissors. There is a smattering of mausoleums and an ease with left objects, and no bar to long and effusive epitaphs.

When I contacted the 'Gardens of Peace' they were very precise about how and why they maintained their graves as they did: the graves are in a mound shape because there is a hadith which states that the grave must be like the hump of a camel and about a span in height; the stone markers simply denote the fact that there is a grave underneath; and ostentatious graves and mausoleums are absolutely not permitted in Islam, a position which they state, quite categorically, is backed up any number of hadiths. This then brings them to their central point: that it is Allah who should be worshipped, not a grave.

There are undoubtedly those who will, like the trustees of the 'Gardens of Peace', put fidelity to Islamic principles (as they see them) front and centre. Others see things differently; and wish to accommodate the wishes of the living. But it is almost impossible to unravel motivation. Some might bury their dead in the 'Gardens of Peace' simply because it is the nearest Muslim cemetery (a fact the 'Gardens of Peace' acknowledge, though they also list many other reasons why people might end up choosing them, including the methods of burial that follow the example of the Prophet, the *sunnah*). Some, otherwise very pious, might erect a mausoleum, because they can afford it and because it is what their fathers and forefathers did. There is a complex matrix of motives, influenced by culture, sect, proximity to graveyards, or fidelity to orthodox principles, that determines how the living treat their dead.

The fear of death, and grief for the departed, can find expression in that reaching, parrying interface between the living and the dead, the grave. Through the grave we may channel and commune. We may cling to the dead, and the dead may cling to life. Perhaps the most important thing about graves is that they needn't be important – or at least they needn't be self-important. They can be meaningful memorials, certainly, but equally they can perpetuate, paralyse, indoctrinate. Perhaps without realising it, how we bury the dead in many ways reflects our attitude to life.

CAN MALAYS KISS?

Shanon Shah

Global Ikhwan is a multi-million dollar business network in Malaysia. Their headquarters is based in Rawang, an hour's drive from Kuala Lumpur, where they have established a community, with clinics and restaurants, a bakery and beauty salon. The name Ikhwan, meaning Muslim Brotherhood, suggests that they are a religiously devout community. A branch of Al Arqam, a religious movement banned in 1994 for 'deviant' beliefs, 'Global Ikhwan' has now become a recognisable brand in Malaysia. While their way of life may evoke mystery and even suspicion amongst certain quarters, it is their attitude to sex which is most fascinating.

In June 2011, Global Ikhwan established the Obedient Wives Club (OWC). The group promised sex lessons to help wives 'serve their husbands better than…first-class prostitute[s]' to protect marriages and curb social ills. Its vice-president, Dr Rohaya Mohamad, said a religious wife should also possess good sexual prowess and go beyond being a traditional 'good wife or good cook'. But why were these sex lessons needed? According to the group's secretary, Hajiera Hartley, they were merely responses to questions from members, for example on kissing. 'Honestly, the Malays do not know how to kiss,' she lamented.

It is important to clarify here that 'Malay' in Malaysia is usually synonymous with 'Muslim' – the Federal Constitution defines ethnic Malays as Muslims. Of course, Islam has been part of Malay culture for centuries, but this constitutional provision means that in contemporary Malaysia, it is illegal for someone of Malay ethnicity to profess any belief other than Islam. So it should be clear that the 'Malays' I refer to are all Muslims in Malaysia – if not by personal conviction, then by constitutional definition – whether they know how to kiss or not.

Later, in October, the OWC published its first book: *Seks Islam, perangi Yahudi untuk kembalikan seks Islam kepada dunia* (Islamic sex, fighting Jews to return Islamic sex to the world). The book launch was accompanied by a stage performance in which the performers declared that Islamic sex is 'many times more amazing than the forbidden sex of the Jews'. The book itself was filled with explicit tips on sexual relations, including encouraging Muslim spouses in polygamous marriages to have group sex.

Women's groups and Islamic officials condemned the book immediately for its tawdry take on gender and marital relations, and the government eventually banned it. These condemnations, however, do not explain why OWC's advocacy on ideal Muslim marriages should entail such blatant anti-Semitism and yet make virtually no mention of love. Not that a marital guide could automatically be less exploitative just by admonishing spouses to be more 'loving' instead of asking wives to be 'first-class whores'. 'Love' rhetoric can be and certainly has been used to keep many a good woman down, especially those stuck in abusive relationships.

My point is that it is curious how the OWC's media rhetoric of sexual intimacy played up eroticism so explicitly and yet remained so silent on love and romance in the context of marriage. More curiously, the groups that criticised OWC defended equality and respect for women, and condemned sexual exploitation and even OWC's 'backwardness', but similarly steered clear of love-speak.

Where, then, do we locate love in expressions of Malay culture? There is curious linkage, or rather the lack of one, between love and these sorts of sex-positive Malay-Muslim approaches to marital relations. After all, this is not the first time that the burden of an ideal marriage has been placed on a Malay woman's shoulders, and specifically called for her to be simultaneously wife and whore. To examine an earlier instance of this linkage as an artefact of Malay culture, we need look no further than Malaysian film-maker U-Wei Haji Saari's 1993 cinematic foray, *Perempuan, Isteri dan Jalang* (Woman, Wife and Whore). Film censors eventually removed '*jalang*' or 'whore' from the title after public outcry, but I will continue to quote the title in its uncensored entirety.

Let us begin our comparison with the film's opening: a naturalistic, seven-minute long scene of a group of villagers engaged in last-minute preparations for a wedding feast. Womenfolk huddle indoors, chattering and arranging flowers, and more men and women prepare food outdoors and yell at scampering children, warning them to stay out of trouble. Under the hot sun, the wedding band plays Malay pop classics with gusto. Then the groom and his procession arrive and the *kompangs* (traditional Malay hand drums) start up.

But something is not quite right. The bride will not emerge from her chambers. The women chatter worriedly and the groom is now scowling and stomping his feet. Then someone cries, 'Zaleha is missing!'

That the film is set so firmly in the Malay 'heartland' speaks of its historical context – this was a time when the Malaysian government was firmly in Prime Minister Mahathir Mohamad's grip. Much has been written of Mahathir's modernity, authoritarianism, defensive ethnic and religious politics, and even his anti-Semitism. What I want to point out here, however, is that under Mahathir's twenty-two-year premiership beginning in 1981, Malaysia experienced dramatic, state-directed urbanisation and industrialisation. In 1970, 33.5% of Malaysia's population lived in urban areas while in 2010, the figure was 71.0%. This rapid development was always part of Mahathir's grand project for Malaysia. What we need to understand, though, is that these changes also affected social arrangements, especially how rural Malay families fragmented and got reconfigured. These dynamics were far from smooth or untroubled. Thus, *Perempuan, Isteri dan Jalang's* village setting needs to be read in this historical context when many young Malays were experiencing rapid modernisation in their *kampungs*, or were moving from *kampungs* to cities themselves. The closing of the film's introductory scene is thus profoundly unsettling – where has Zaleha gone?

The next scene shows a typical Malay wedding ceremony in progress – the *akad nikah* (sealing of the marriage covenant) with everyone sitting cross-legged in front of the *imam* and key witnesses. Only this time, the ceremony takes place in Golok, in largely-Muslim southern Thailand – and it turns out Zaleha is not only a runaway bride, she has eloped with another man. Southern Thailand is often where Malay Malaysian couples run to get married when to do so in Malaysia might be difficult or impossible. For instance, Malay men often sneak to places like Golok to marry second, third, or fourth wives. This is because while it is wrong under Malaysian *sharia* laws for husbands to contract polygamous marriages without their current wife's permission, once the marriage is contracted it is nevertheless valid. The perpetrators merely need to pay a small fine for their infraction.

In *Perempuan, Isteri dan Jalang*, it is not clear if Zaleha is contracting a polygamous marriage. We assume that she and her new husband are getting married across the border to avoid controversy back home. But then they return to their motel room only to be accosted by the jilted groom, Amir. After a violent and slightly long-winded confrontation, Amir pulls out a gun and kills Zaleha's husband and kidnaps her. Amir rapes Zaleha and then loans (yes, loans) her to a pimp, still in southern Thailand, promising to return after six months.

Thus, one major difference between *Perempuan, Isteri dan Jalang* and the OWC is that Zaleha only wanted to elope and marry another man, but vengeful Amir forces her to become a whore as punishment. The OWC on the other hand is asking wives to willingly behave like prostitutes. The implication is that Amir unwittingly unleashes Zaleha's sexuality and we do not know how controllable it is or will be. The OWC wants to train women to unleash and have power over their own sexuality. On the other hand the similarity between the two cases is that this female sexuality, potent as it is and regardless who unleashes it, needs to be deployed for male pleasure.

In Amir and Zaleha's case all hell breaks loose (naturally). Amir might have intended to teach Zaleha a lesson by turning her into a whore, but ends up becoming a kind of Dr Frankenstein to Zaleha's sex monster. This is foreshadowed onscreen mostly through fashion and coded bodily practices. Zaleha now wears figure-enhancing outfits and chain-smokes (which when done by a female character in Malay-language cinema is code for 'will have sex with anyone').

In addition, Zaleha is now crafty, too. When Amir makes it clear he has no intention of marrying her after her six-month sex-work stint – thus allowing her to regain her honour – she orchestrates a visit by Islamic morality enforcers to their motel room. She thus 'tricks' Amir into marriage because of the ensuing humiliation and threat of punishment toward him.

This is another Malaysian peculiarity. The country's rapid modernisation also entailed an increasingly bureaucratic administration of Islamic laws. By the 1990s, Islamic departments had special divisions in charge of enforcing all kinds of *sharia* legislation on personal beliefs and moral conduct. A Malay man not attending Friday prayers at the mosque could be fined or even jailed. Malays caught skiving off the Ramadan fast could similarly be fined or jailed. There were also the *khalwat* or 'close proximity' laws – an unmarried man and woman were forbidden from sharing the same private space. Thus, Zaleha-the-whore's appropriation of *khalwat* rulings to re-legitimise her social status is interesting and subversive.

When she and Amir return to the village as a married couple, Amir continues beating her (somewhat frequently) and verbally abusing her (somewhat more frequently). Apart from whimpering and crying during these acts of violence, Zaleha proceeds to turn the entire kampung topsy-turvy. She flirts with the itinerant Indian-Muslim textile merchant, Si Majeet, thus ensuring his business becomes brisker amongst the local women. At the local seamstress Asiah's house, she encourages the other womenfolk to try out more figure-hugging, albeit traditional, clothing designs. She then takes one of them, Kak Maria, to town, and they end up watching a movie with a strange man with whom Zaleha plays in the darkened, half-empty cinema. On another occasion, not content with bathing at home, she sashays to the river with arms and shoulders exposed and splashes around, inviting the other women to leave their washing and frolic with her. Later, she even encourages one of the nubile kampung virgins, Mina, to flirt with her admirer-cum-stalker, Bakri.

But just what are the consequences of Zaleha's instigations? The menfolk claim that when girls want to have fun, men starve. After all, when wives and daughters pursue leisure instead of housework, who prepares dinner? One night, Zaleha does not have enough salt to season her curry and Amir rips the sleeve off her new dress. On another night, Kak Mariah does not cook in time because she is late returning from town with Zaleha – her husband slaps her in front of the rest of the village. Yes, the women in *Perempuan, Isteri dan Jalang* are not able to juggle their sexual awakening with their cooking duties and have to be physically disciplined by their husbands. How unlike the good wife-whore utopia promoted by the OWC.

I can hear the protests that these are untypical, unrepresentative stereotypes of Malay culture. While this is true, it misses the point I am making. I am interested in how Malay culture is represented or spoken for especially in the arena of intimate relationships. Let us note that Amir and Zaleha are fictional characters created by a Malay man, a film director keen to critique Malay society through film. Similarly, whatever criticisms and ridicule the

OWC has courted for promoting lewd, anti-Jewish, 'Islamic' sex, let us not forget that it consists of Malay women speaking on their own behalf.

Granted, they all have a stake in society and draw on specific cultural resources to fortify their own identity boundaries and push their own agendas. The question is, are they drawing on a culture that is filled with stable and eternal meaning? Has the idea of marital intimacy in Malay culture, as Islamised as it has been for centuries, traditionally been divorced from the idea of love, at least in art and literature?

Yes and no. On one hand, the scholar of Malay literature Muhammad Haji Salleh says there seems to be a dearth of literary examples that privilege romantic love. He speculates that this might be because marriage in Malay culture was usually pre-arranged. He goes on to say that there is hardly a Malay equivalent of *Romeo and Juliet* or *Laila and Majnun*.

On the other hand, this might be a chicken-and-egg question. Muhammad also notes that there is a paucity of studies on love in Malay oral or literary traditions, making it hard to comment decisively. Besides, even if there are no love-centric stories *per se*, classical Malay literature contains several instances of pivotal love episodes, for example the romantic exploits of the warrior hero Hang Tuah. In short, there is no proven absence of love in literary representations of Malay culture – it could just be hiding in places we have not thought to seek with contemporary eyes.

Nevertheless, Muhammad says the *Hikayat Raja Kulawandu* (The Story of King Kulawandu), a Malay literary text copied in the early nineteenth century, could be classified as a 'proper' love story. There are plenty of references to giddy, passionate love in its pages, expressed in the hybrid sensibilities of Malay culture and Islamic piety. There might even be a reference to pre-marital physical lovemaking, justified on the grounds that the two lovers are already married 'in their hearts'. This cannot be entirely verified, though, as Malay texts tend to avoid graphic depictions of sexual acts. They usually opt for coy allegories. If need be, behaviour that is tabooed among humans is sometimes transferred onto non-human characters.

The lovers in *Hikayat Raja Kulawandu* eventually do get married officially and the tale ends happily ever after. The point is that from first sight to marital union, their relationship is not only depicted as passionate and sensuous, but they also declare and demonstrate mutual love constantly, albeit poetically.

Talking about love in 'Malay' texts is difficult, though. The boundaries around Malay 'identity' in archipelagic Southeast Asia have always been fluid, even after the coming of Islam. It is arguably only in recent decades that a more defensive and politicised policing of the boundary of Malay-ness has emerged. Not only that, this ethnic boundary is now seen as coextensive with the equally rigidly drawn boundary of Islam.

But can we blame it all on nationalism? Again, the picture is not black-and-white. For instance, in the early twentieth century Malay novel, *Faridah Hanom*, we find similar threads of eroticism and loving intimacy between the two protagonists, Faridah and Shafik. Nevertheless, we can see in *Faridah Hanom* how Malay literature developed nationalist and Islamic reformist ideals at the turn of the twentieth century. For example, even though there is ferocious marital rape later in the story, the novel is, on the whole, opposed to the idea of forced marriages. It is an eclectic tale, one in which the 'emancipation' of Muslim women is portrayed as part of the greater nationalist project.

'Nationalist' seems like a strange word, though, chiefly because *Faridah Hanom* is not set in 1920s Malaya (as contemporary West Malaysia was known then), but in the world of the Arab elite in Cairo, Egypt. In fact, it remains a mystery whether the writer of *Faridah Hanom*, Syed Sheik Al-Hadi, adapted his tale from an existing Egyptian story or if he was merely influenced by the eclecticism of the era's transnational Islamic reformism. What is even more curious is how big a hit the novel was amongst Malay readers in Malaya. This is by no means exceptional – Malay culture has historically borrowed and adapted heavily from Chinese, Persian, Indian and even European cultures. From the start of the eighteenth century, increased contact with the Arab World, specifically Islamic centres of learning in the Arabian Peninsula and Egypt, resulted in increasing influence from those regions, too.

The paradox, then, is that contemporary Malay advocates and artists such as OWC and U-Wei are drawing upon a cultural resource that, in turn, has drawn from a variety of other transnational influences over the centuries. What, then, does it mean to speak of a 'Malay' notion of love, or sex, or indeed of anything at all?

Perhaps it is better to rephrase the question and ask what exactly contemporary Malays, Malaysians in particular, are doing when they define and redefine intimate relationships using cultural and religious imagery. Rather than theorize in the abstract, I would like to try something literary of my own. I would like to create a character, a composite of the many Malay women I am friends with – let us call her Aishah.

Aishah was born in 1978, into a family of the emerging Malay middle-class of the 1970s and 1980s. Her father comes from a family of fruit sellers and craft makers in the *kampung*. He was one of the children who finished secondary school during British rule and went on to become a civil servant in the newly-formed federation of Malaysia in 1963. Her mother is also from a *kampung* not far from her father's. Thus, while Aishah's immediate family is urban middle-class, she is equally at home in her grandparents' *kampungs* because the extended family congregates there every Eid (or Raya, as it is known in Malaysia).

Aishah grows up in a pretty relaxed but traditional Malay family. They listen to Malay pop songs and watch Malay films on television. Her father is a gentle but authoritarian patriarch. The family is very happy when Aishah's eldest sister manages to enrol in university in the early 1980s. Soon after this, the sister starts wearing the *hijab* (or *tudung*, as it is known in Malaysia). Another sister starts wearing the *tudung* some years later, after graduating from university and getting engaged. This is not such a big deal, as Aishah has several cousins and aunts who have started donning the tudung as well. What shocks the family is when Aishah's older brother, the eldest child, becomes an Islamic preacher after university, joins the opposition Islamic party PAS, and starts having political ambitions – something Aishah's civil servant father finds rebellious and misguided.

Meanwhile, Aishah does not wear the *tudung*. She used to, in boarding school, but then after getting a scholarship to go to university in Australia she stops. This creates a great rift with her PAS-supporting brother, but surprisingly not with her sisters or parents.

Already we see in this biography the implications of the Malaysian state's modernisation-cum-Malay-nationalist agenda – numerous Malay students were given scholarships to study medicine, engineering, accounting and finance in local and overseas universities. They were then expected to serve the government or government-linked corporations that sponsored their studies – this was often specified in the scholarship agreements. It was typically Mahathirist nation-building. Thus, after graduating, Aishah starts working at the government-linked corporation that sponsored her studies. She starts as a junior executive and is now manager of the finance department of one of the company's newer subsidiaries.

This is where Aishah meets her first proper 'boyfriend' – a Malay man working at the same company. He started work at the company a couple of years before her and, although his family is privileged 'old money', he managed to obtain the same scholarship as Aishah, albeit two years before her, to study in the US. He has returned to Malaysia with an American accent and a desire to ascend the corporate-political ladder as swiftly as possible, even if it means exploiting some 'old money' connections along the way. It is with him that Aishah becomes sexually active, although she regrets it. They eventually break up when Aishah discovers his womanizing ways. Besides, she is furious that he requires a certain kind of deference from her to aid his corporate-political ambitions.

For a couple of years afterwards, Aishah is very depressed. Her mother and sisters try looking for suitable men for her, but she is disheartened with all the Malay men she is introduced to. 'Maybe it's true,' she thinks. 'Malay men are useless.' This is when she meets Dave, an American expatriate in Kuala Lumpur. She is smitten from the start, because although Aishah grew up on Malay love songs, she also came of age watching *Sex and the City*, *Ally McBeal* and Hollywood 'chick flicks' like *Clueless* and *Legally Blonde*. Dave is her American knight in shining sedan.

But while they have much in common, Aishah wants to continue living her life in Malaysia. So, if she and Dave are to get married, they need to settle down here. Dave is all up for it, but there is a catch – under Malaysian law, a Muslim can only marry another Muslim. Dave has to convert to Islam. Dave is actually game for this, even in a post-September 11 environment. He and Aishah pick up books on Islam from the shelves of Malaysian bookshops and collect information for new Muslim converts from the Muslim Welfare Organization. All this is, of course, information strictly controlled by the Malaysian authorities – most of the books on Islam they find seem to have been written by Saudi-approved authors. While Aishah takes this for granted, for Dave, the more he learns about 'Islam' the less certain he becomes about converting.

He starts asking Aishah about things like polygamy, domestic violence, rape, homosexuality, jihad, and anti-Semitism. Although uncomfortable,

Aishah tries to engage with Dave's questions. She does her own research but is overwhelmed by the sheer amount of contradictory information on Islam she encounters. Finally Dave says, 'I can't do this. I can't embrace a religion that wants to take away so much from me and the people I love.' That is the end of Aishah and Dave.

To make matters worse, earlier, one of Aishah's cousins spies on her and Dave on a romantic date in a classy Kuala Lumpur restaurant that serves alcohol. Aishah's family is appalled. The cousin fails to report that Aishah drank apple juice and ordered a seafood dish, while Dave's dish was vegetarian. Aishah is shunned by her family for a while. After her breakup with Dave and the onset of even deeper depression, Aishah's PAS-supporting brother says to her, 'You need to repent.'

At this juncture, what options are available to Aishah, exactly? To forge on with her 'modern' job and lifestyle would erode her already-eroded Malay identity. To be a 'true' Malay would require a rejection of some of the things she holds dear, like her freedom in choosing a life partner. This is a woman who, although steeped in Malay culture, is more familiar with films such as *Perempuan, Isteri dan Jalang* than literary works such as *Faridah Hanom* and *Hikayat Raja Kulawandu*. Add to this the fact that life in a largely xenophobic Australia was traumatic and made Aishah yearn for her *kampung* childhood. Lastly, for nearly a quarter of a century, she has known only one prime minister, Mahathir Mohamad, who has goaded her generation to pursue modern ambitions while adhering to authoritarian versions of 'Asian' and 'Islamic' values.

So yes, while Aishah might yearn for love, the forces of nationalism, capitalism and religious chauvinism have constrained her options, in particular her expressions of gender and sexuality. She is conflicted – she is not even a wife yet and already she is convinced she is a whore. And just where has it landed her? A failed relationship with a Malay jerk and another failed relationship with an American coward.

At this point, Aishah might 'repent' in her own way. She may or may not wear the *tudung* again full-time, but she might start going for religious classes and memorising longer Quranic verses. She might attend lectures for women at her local mosque. Although all of this might make her uncomfortable, she sets these discomforts aside, momentarily, in her quest to get closer to God. After all, what else is an educated Malay woman to do in Malaysia?

The Aishah I know could be lucky. She could, in a few months, find a nice Malay-Muslim man who has been through parallel experiences and knows what it is like to have found and lost love in an uncertain world. They could fall in love, get married and try to remake themselves as reflective, albeit normative, Malays and Muslims. Or she could go on searching and, in the process, drift further away from Islam and Malay culture, finding them both oppressive and 'backward'. She might even move to Sydney or Brisbane, preferring to remake herself as a full-fledged Aussie.

Or she could find a good enough Malay-Muslim man with severe conflicts and insecurities, who wants to treat her well but also be more assertive in his Malay and Muslim convictions. They too might get engaged and eventually married. This Aishah and her husband might both submit to a continual cycle of 'repentance'. This Aishah might wonder how on Earth she is going to juggle her responsibilities as corporate manager, citizen, wife, daughter, sister, Muslim, Malay, and eventually mother. Whatever it is, this Aishah must be relieved to have a chance at married life which also fulfils the expectations of her family and society.

Furthermore, this Aishah might be relieved that something like the OWC now exists. For this Aishah, love might be the ultimate quest, but there are other hurdles to jump through first. Some of these will undoubtedly pertain to her sexuality. How will she learn to harness a force that she regrets unleashing all those years ago? Maybe the OWC can help teach her how to kiss properly as a good Malay wife.

But do not mistake Aishah for someone who is perpetually sad or weak. Aishah has always been, like many Malay women, funny and confident. She jokes about sex because her mother and sisters joke about sex, albeit not in front of men. Even then, there might be some leeway – jokes can be told through allegory. This is, after all, Malay culture we are talking about. Furthermore, Aishah is not about to give up her day job. She might consider modifying parts of her professional life to ensure that she does not usurp her husband's authority, but these changes will probably not be too dramatic.

I have not told the story of this Aishah's husband, but it is easy to imagine what kinds of pressures he might be subjected to as well. Again, he is not an 'evil oppressor' and we do not need to cast him in the role of a villain. He, too, is most likely funny, confident, gentle, and genuinely loves Aishah and their children. But we must remember that he, too, is of the generation that grew up during the Mahathir administration, and he, too, has been shaped by films such as *Perempuan, Isteri dan Jalang*. Let us also not freeze Aishah and her husband in Malay 'culture', as though it is static and saturated with politics. But let us also not underestimate how their worldviews and experiences have been shaped by the contradictory forces of modernity, Malay nationalism, and Islamisation. Most importantly, let us not deny Aishah and her husband their agency as social actors. They do not passively consume Malay 'culture' and get influenced by it unthinkingly. Yes, they might consume Malay entertainment, literature and art, but they also contribute to the constant redefinition of Malay culture through their consumption patterns and tastes.

So has 'love' in Malay art or literature been redefined, by cultural producers and consumers? Here's a clue. The biggest 2011 box office hit was *Ombak Rindu,* a film which contains a pivotal sequence where the Malay heroine is violently raped by the Malay hero. Yet, through the power of the heroine's prayers, the hero changes his behaviour, marries her and becomes a terrific husband. She becomes his second wife in a polygamous marriage, by the way. Many Malaysian feminists, including Malay women, were disgusted at what they saw as a justification and even glorification of rape and polygamy. They were flabbergasted at how so many Malay women loved this film so unreservedly.

Over informal conversation, some friends of mine – makers of Malay films and television programmes – offered a different perspective. They said perhaps the women who watched the film focused more on the heroine's piety. After all, even though she had to endure rape and abuse, her closeness to God is what saw her through. Even though she had to endure attacks on her sexuality, her patience and prayers were ultimately rewarded. Some people might see it as her marrying her rapist, but to her, she married the man of her dreams. As macabre as this might sound, perhaps this is how modernisation, authoritarianism, and transnational Muslim trends have transformed Malay culture. These processes have all affected how different Malays want to fall in love, think they should fall in love, and actually fall in (and out of) love. I suspect there were quite a few Aishahs who felt *Ombak Rindu* articulated their desires and fears.

This argument is of course not meant to trivialise or justify the very real violence against women that occurs even within Muslim marriages in

Malaysia. These remain inadequately addressed and, as we have seen with *Perempuan, Isteri dan Jalang* and *Ombak Rindu*, have become normalised in Malay culture. That these aspects of marriage are so casually ignored by groups like OWC who, instead, juxtapose marital sexuality against anti-Semitism indicates that analysing 'love' might help us understand how Malaysian society is changing. With apologies to Cher and her *Shoop Shoop Song*, perhaps this is an important part of how some Malay Malaysians want to 'do' culture – in how they kiss.

What I am getting at is that perhaps with *Perempuan, Isteri dan Jalang* and the OWC, it is not that 'love' has been divorced from ideas about marital intimacy in Malay culture. It is still there. It is just that other concerns and anxieties are now stronger determinants of how intimacy is forged among Malays in Malaysia. Among contemporary Malays, kissing is totally political.

NETWORKS OF LOVE

Samia Rahman

It was blurry. She could make out only shapes and figures. The tension in the air was palpable and she had the distinct feeling that all eyes were upon her. An entire life had been building up to this occasion, and now it was time. 'Here, take this,' said a voice she recognised and yet didn't know. A tray was placed in her hands. It was heavy, too heavy, and teetering with cups and a teapot. 'Whatever you do, don't make any mistakes'. She walked into the room and it felt cold and strange. He was there, sitting at the far end. She mustn't stare. But how can she not? Her fate could be sealed in this moment.

This is how I remember one particular *rishta* encounter. The word *rishta* literally means relation; but it is most often used when a marriage suitor comes calling, family in tow, to ask for your hand in marriage. I was in my early twenties and the last thing on my mind was a *rishta*. Thankfully, I had suffered little pressure from my parents to consider marriage, although there is no doubt it was constantly on their mind. I should have suspected something was in the air when my mother started talking to a particular *Aunty-ji* who was renowned for arranging introductions. She asked for my 'bio-data'. My mother hastily filled out a form with my essential details with the trepidation and hope of someone applying for a job. The *Aunty-ji* gently informed her to keep her expectations fairly low. 'Doctors are out of your daughter's league', she warned. I had studied a subject entirely lacking in status (English literature) and was pursuing a career in journalism so could not possibly hope to reach such echelons. There was no need to entirely despair though. I did have some attributes to speak of, such as a 'fair complexion'. Though the fact that I can't make *roti* was a seriously negative point. Before long the Aunty found a match. I was lucky, she told my mum, because eligible men were thin on the ground.

She had identified a nice boy in his late twenties who worked in IT. A date was scheduled for him to come to my house with his family. It was a prospect that made me cringe. My parents were even more nervous than me. My mother was adamant that I should not wear my glasses; it could reduce my appeal. This meant I could only make out the features of my suitor by staring at him intently. I thought I was being discreet, but according to my family my attempts to glimpse at my possible intended meant I looked wide-eyed and crazed. Needless to say, the *rishta* was a disaster.

My experience is hardly unique but we ought to spare a thought for our parent's generation. They did not always have the luxury of veto that we (mostly) now enjoy. My mum was a university student in Karachi when her family was gripped with wedding fever at the news that a relative now settled in the UK would soon be arriving to marry. Preparations were afoot, outfits were made and excitement mounting as the day approached. It was only when mum found herself embroidering a wedding dress that had been made to her exact measurements that it dawned on her that she was to be the bride. In her time consent was understood in a very specific way: if a girl said 'yes', it was fine; if she said 'no' it was because she was too shy to say 'yes' and it was fine. Thankfully, my parents enjoyed a happy and loving marriage. Others have been less fortunate.

The emergence of assertive young men and women who are not easily emotionally blackmailed by their parents, and who politely direct the *rishta* procession out of the house, has played havoc with the networks of *Aunty-jis*. 'These days boys and girls they want this click thing', sighs Aunty Sadia. She has found her match-making activities severely tested by the 'choosiness' of those placed on her books by their parents. 'They turn down perfectly good *rishtay* because they didn't get this click and then they complain they are getting older and still unmarried. Things are very different now compared to my day'. Alas poor Aunties. Little do they realise that there is no better way to quash any potential chemistry between a couple than to place both sets of families in the room at a first meeting. It's a bit like spectators watching a blood sport. No wonder, the *Aunty-jis* are now being by-passed by less daunting options available to young Muslims seeking a life partner.

Take the Emerald Network. It was established, some eight years ago, by Rooful Ali, an accountant and freelance photographer. Emerald is a hugely popular Muslim social networking forum that hosts regular meetings and activities. These meticulously organised and professionally executed gatherings have included comedy nights and charity fundraising dinners with tickets priced at £25 or more depending on the nature of the event. It became popular though word of mouth and attracts a professional crowd. Ali points out that it is not a profit-making enterprise; he only charges to cover costs. Emerald is marketed as a meeting place for Muslims, somewhere to expand their social circle and make useful contacts. It has enabled young Muslims to meet marriage partners in a relaxed, informal and thoroughly halal environment. Ali can count almost thirty Emerald wedding success stories within his group of friends alone. There are likely to be many others who, through friendships and introductions initiated at an Emerald event, have eventually met the person they will marry.

Emerald is successful, Ali argues, because the traditional routes to finding a spouse are simply not working for his generation. 'It is an urban myth that you will meet someone at a family gathering, wedding or function. They are completely over-rated'. He identifies other routes to marriage that have had a modicum of success, such as meeting someone at university. Young Muslims could possibly meet someone at the meetings of their University's Islamic societies. But the quality of Islamic societies, Ali points out, is inconsistent, ranging from apathetic to riven with in-fighting. A large numbers of Islamic societies are unhealthily obsessed with gender segregation. Such rigidity inevitably leaves youngsters with no social skills whatsoever when it comes to dealings with the opposite sex.

What about criticism of 'free-mixing'? Emerald has received a fair share of censure, Ali admits. He has become expert at dealing with the sniping. 'It comes down to a person's intentions. Nobody is forcing you to attend, never mind make you speak with a brother or sister. People need to get out of the bubble of being something at home or in the mosque but completely different everywhere else. After all, you mix with members of the opposite sex at work don't you? How did you get to this event? I'm guessing on the bus or the tube? That's a lot of free-mixing and suddenly when you're at a Muslim social event you become totally inept and unable to lower your gaze!'

Other routes to finding a partner have also sprung up during the last few years. One could attend a Muslim-style speed-dating soiree one evening and saunter off to a formal marriage event with or without a chaperone the next. These undoubtedly provide a path to romance for some but the stigma of attending a marriage event is likely to put off others. There is also the disheartening regularity with which Muslim women outnumber Muslim men at these events. Ali suggests this is indicative of the higher ratio of women to men in society in general. There is also the 'marrying back home' factor prevalent among British Muslim men who passively allow marriages to be arranged. It's the option requiring least effort. Women on the other hand are much more proactive. As such, they are more likely to attend a speed dating event or a matrimonial function with their female friends.

Those who do not feel comfortable attending marriage events could always visit one of the many talks and gatherings that regularly take place or involve themselves in charity or volunteering projects. City Circle is a popular and thriving Friday evening public discussion event set up by a group of young Muslim professionals. Certainly at its inception in the early 2000s, the City Circle volunteers were of a certain demographic and a number of successful marriages resulted. But that demographic has now grown up, got married, had children and the social aspect of attending a City Circle talk does not offer the same opportunities. Ali observes that City Circle is perfectly placed to assist young Muslim singletons looking to get married but the infrastructure just isn't there. 'It's a wasted opportunity and I think that's a shame because City Circle is extremely successful. The talks are packed out but at the end that's it. People melt away in their cliques and there isn't anyone making it their business to draw newcomers in and ensuring people get to know one another and perhaps continue the discussion by moving on as a group to a restaurant'.

This is where Emerald has been so effective. Ali is a social butterfly. He takes great delight in bringing people together, networking and socialising. But not everyone can be as enthusiastic. He gets a lot of pleasure when he sees his friends hooking up and marrying. The friends and friends-of-friends network is another route by which young Muslims come together; and marriages can be made. There is, as Ali notes, a problem. Friends sometimes are not pleased to see others settle down before them.

This hasn't stopped him from organising a specific marriage forum called MeetMyMuslimMate.com, which he hopes will take the stigma out of the Muslim dating game. The concept is simple: a single Muslim can attend with another single friend, preferably of the opposite sex in order to maintain the male to female ratio. The website states the philosophy behind the initiative:

We have no particular target towards any ethnic group, as this is being promoted via friends of friends, it simply depends on the diversity or otherwise of one another's circle of friends, which we anticipate in the majority of instances to be of South Asian or Arab descent. With regards to whether they're previously married, their profession, location and age – it will be up to you to find out through conversation with them. MeetMyMuslimMate endeavours to break down the notion of pre-judging and dismissing people on paper labels, therefore we encourage everyone to make their own decision having at least spoken to someone first hand.

This approach seeks to transcend many prejudices that exist in the Muslim community. Ali describes these prejudices as 'flag over faith'. Many young Muslims, perhaps due to pressure from the family, want to marry someone from their own ethnic or national background; or worse, from their own clan. 'Those who clung on to the belief that they must marry someone from the same country of origin as them or the exact same background - they're still searching. The successful marriages are between those people who have moved the goalposts and weren't held back by ethnicity or nationality'.

Ali also expresses disappointment that married couples do not do more to pair up their still solitary friends. Newlyweds are often introduced to a whole new social circle via the friends and relatives of their spouse and could be considerably more creative in instigating connections. Match making can be a fun and rewarding hobby for married couples!

That's exactly what Farah Kausar discovered. A GP and a mother, Kausar has not forgotten those among her friends who have yet to find Mr or Ms Right. She decided to help her single friends with a distinctly twentieth century approach to matrimonial orchestrations.

It all began when Kausar was on the phone to a friend who was moaning about his lacklustre love life. Frustrated with his woes, she appealed for a suitable girl by detailing his desired wifely credentials on Facebook. The response was overwhelming. 'My inbox was full – so many people messaged me. People I knew ages ago or vaguely were contacting me with suggestions. It struck me that there was a real need for this. I had put it on Facebook in a jokey way so was shocked by the number of people who got in touch'. Of those who responded, not all were coming up with suggestions for her friend. Some asked if Kausar could do a similar 'shout-out' for them or a single person they knew. The strength of social networking as a matchmaking tool lies in the fact that it is less of a shot in the dark than dating websites such as Shaadi.com or singlemuslim.com. 'Although it's online, it feels safe because it's through friends or friends of friends', Kausar explains. 'You are linking together people who someone you know can vouch for and that feels more reliable'. Kausar has been so inundated by the details of single Muslims looking for a marriage partner that she has had to create a database to keep track of everyone and who had been introduced to whom. Unlike 'real-life' marriage events where women over the age of thirty outnumber the men, who are likely to be younger anyway, social networks have an extended, mixed-gender reach. 'Because it is done in a tongue-in-cheek way, nobody is made to feel desperate,' Kausar says. 'Everyone assumes that there are too many girls who can't find a husband but there are actually a lot of great guys out there. It's just that the girls are proactive and many guys would never dream of going to a marriage-related event yet feel much more comfortable doing this'. She never discloses a person's identity via Facebook, simply informally states their vital statistics and that of their required match.

Kausar describes her social networking matchmaking endeavours as the perfect balance between public and private. The message is relayed out to all her (considerable) Facebook friends and those who are interested and wish to find out more can message her privately. Everyone's dignity remains intact. Once she has facilitated an introduction the rest is up to the couple. Crucially it is a highly targeted method. Someone who specifically wishes to marry a Pakistani male aged between thirty-four and thirty-nine who has not previously been married can be assured that only someone who fits their criteria will respond. At a marriage or social event they may have spent time acquainting themselves with a male who turns out to be too young or, divorced or, shock, horror, isn't Pakistani.

I wonder whether this targeted approach may take the romance out of meeting a potential spouse and compound the 'flag over faith' specificity that Ali bemoans. Some rather more conservative Muslims may consider this is a good thing. The irony has not escaped the notice of Kausar who wrote on her Facebook:

I am looking to get married but I'd only consider a doctor/dentist who lives within a 5 mile radius of my house

OR

I know I'm only 4ft nothing but I wouldn't consider marrying anyone less than 6ft 2

OR

I'd like to marry a hindu-punjabi, must be vegetarian and of east African descent. Ideally Kenyan, I could 'cope' with a Tanzanian but definitely not Ugandan

Seriously people! And you wonder why you're in your 30s and single?? Good luck!

Marrying according to clan or ethnic background is essentially a generational phenomenon. Second and third generation Muslims in Britain tend to be much more open minded then their parents. Indeed, there has been an increase in mixed-ethnicity marriage among second-generation Muslims (with parents sometimes just relieved that their over-thirties children are marrying at all!). However, for many young Muslims the pursuit of love is at the risk of death. Highly publicised honour crimes provide a glimpse into this obnoxious reality. The murder in 2003 of seventeen-year-old British-Pakistani Shafilea Ahmed and the conviction of her parents in June 2012, provides a good illustration of the pathology of a minority. Of course, one should point out that honour killings have nothing to do with Islam, nor are they exclusive to Muslim communities. But it would be dishonest to deny that this horrific crime has snuffed out the lives of far too many young Muslims. What is also indisputable is that such atrocities are almost always carried out against young women deemed to be cavorting with the wrong sort of suitor and therefore bringing shame upon their family. A culture that thinks it is shameful for one to marry outside one's ethnicity and not shameful to murder a young and innocent person has lost all its ethical bearings.

Big cities, such as London, Manchester and Birmingham, provide some anonymity for young Muslims in their quest for a marriage partner. Perhaps this is why organisations such as the Emerald Network thrive in the metropolis. But in smaller towns, where individual freedom is sometimes stifled, the story can be rather different. 'Everyone knows everyone here', says Waqas Ahmad. He is looking for love in Bradford. 'If your parents have no problem with you going to a social event to look for a wife fair enough. But if your brother-in-law's cousin happens to also be there or if your uncle who's a taxi driver clocks you, then it's gonna get around and people start chatting all kind of things. It's worse for girls because if you get a reputation you're done for and then who's gonna want to marry you?' It is not possible for many young Muslims in small towns to go against their parent's wishes. 'How can I not involve my parents in the most important decision of my life?' he asks. He has a university education, is street-wise, and a steady job. He is no mummy's boy. And he will happily date a woman he likes – of any religion or race. But when it comes to marriage he must meet the expectations of his parents. 'If I fell in love with some girl they didn't introduce me to or they didn't approve of, it would kill them, seriously'.

So *rishta* processions are not going to disappear any time soon. *Aunty Jis* may be needed for the foreseeable future. And family friends will forever be dropping hints. An old friend of my mother suggested her archaeologist-turned-primary-school-teacher son now living in London meet with her daughter. After much nagging from his mother, he dutifully came round to my house some months later. Dressed in a crumpled shirt with long hair and no assets to his name he was so laid back he spent most of the visit watching the Wimbledon final on TV. As he was leaving he wrote my email address on a scrap of paper, which I was sure he would lose; and announced he would be away travelling for a month. We emailed every day.

MY BRITISH HIJAB

Khola Hasan

I am a very unfashionable woman.

I grew up in the only Wahhabi household in North London in the late 1970s. My father had studied in the strict Salafi universities of Saudi Arabia, and our understanding and idea of Islam was therefore very different to the cultural Islam practised by the vast majority of Asian Muslims. Our entire family stood out of the crowd within the small Asian community of Wood Green. My father lectured at universities for his day job, but also helped establish mosques and Islamic Centres with Saudi money wherever possible. My mother had turned our three-bedroom house into an evening school for local kids. She taught the Qur'an and Islamic studies to a community that had no mosque and was unused to such a disciplined and religious family. My siblings and I grew up in a home that had plenty of laughter and silliness, but was also very puritanical and religion-centred. For many years, I was one of those odd-looking women you see walking down the streets of Mile End and Small Heath, wearing a long and flowing black robe, large black scarf and, for a short while, even a veil to cover my face. As I wear glasses, the veil would force my breath up my face and steam up my glasses, which was incredibly uncomfortable. To be perfectly honest, I found the veil oppressive, but loved the scarf and gown. It looked elegant, like the dress of a medieval lady.

Some years ago I attended a medieval re-creation in an Essex castle, complete with a jousting tournament, court jesters juggling, princesses in brocade finery, and the servant classes tending to their needs. Music was played, the knights rode and duelled impressively, and the princess waved her handkerchief perfectly. During the event one of the organisers came up to me and my sister, both of us wearing long flowing gowns and pretty scarves, and thanked us for coming in costume - dressed as medieval English ladies. His comment made me wonder why my outfit was considered so out-of-place in modern Britain if it fitted fine with medieval British fashion. After all, fashions do come and go. Nevertheless it was considered out of place in North London, and it certainly made my childhood rather difficult.

I rarely wear the long, black robe now, preferring jackets in pretty colours with long skirts or trousers and matching scarves. Issues of integration and citizenship, as well as theological debates on the reform of classical understandings of Islamic law now dominate my thinking. But why have I changed my appearance so drastically? Having worn the veil to cover my face for so many years, why do I frown on women who continue to wear it?

I can date the change in my outlook very precisely: 7 July 2005. I was in a gym (women only) on that bleak Thursday morning, burning away the calories on an electric treadmill. The music programme blaring out from the radio was suddenly interrupted by a newsflash, with news of a series of bomb blasts in central London. Bombs had exploded on underground trains and a bus, all within an hour of each other. The death toll was as yet unknown, but it would certainly be high. This was the height of the morning rush hour, and commuters would be filling the trains and buses in London in their hurry to get to work. The sweat drained from my face as one by one all the women stopped their exercises to listen to the news. The first blast was thought to be an accident, but as more bombs exploded, this explanation was shunned. The attacks seemed too co-ordinated to be an accident. The dreaded word 'terrorist' was now being used.

Please God, I whispered to myself. Please, please let it not be Muslims. Please let it be a mechanical problem that caused the explosions. Please let it be Tamils, the IRA, anyone. Please let it be anyone but Muslims.

Tears streamed down my face as I ran into the cubicles to change. I was desperate to get home to watch the television news. And I was very frightened. Terrorist attacks happened in other countries, not here in London. Not at home. My mobile phone rang. It was my mother, frantic with worry as I had not been answering my phone at home. 'Where are you?' she asked in Urdu in a hushed whisper. 'There has been a bomb in central London. I am not letting your brother go to uni today, and you need to stay at home as well. *Allah rahem karay*.' (May God have mercy on all of us.)

As I waited at the bus stop, I could hear other passengers whispering among themselves about the rumours of a terrorist attack on London. They whispered heads down, refusing to make eye contact with me, refusing to allow me into the conversation. Would they be whispering if I was not here, with my head scarf and long gown, I wondered. Am I the eternal stranger among people I consider to be my own?

The rest of the day was spent glued to news channels, hoping constantly that some remote group would accept responsibility for the horrific attacks, and so absolve us, the British Muslim community, from the crime. But that did not happen. Images of the dead and injured emerging from the bus wreckage and out of underground stations were shown, innocent people, on their way to work. My neighbour Jennifer used to travel to work in central London early every morning at the same time as the bombs went off. On that terrible morning her husband David was in New Zealand to watch England play international rugby. He heard the news but could not contact her as the sheer volume of calls had put an immense strain on London's telecommunications system. It was a full 24 hours before he could speak to her and know that she was safe. I could not imagine the pain he went through and the sense of sheer helplessness he endured. More than fifty people were killed that day, hundreds were injured, and all four suicide bombers died. It was the worst terrorist incident on Britain's transport network. The four men, all Muslims and all from West Yorkshire, had left video films about the reasons for the attack. These were mainly the war on Iraq and Afghanistan, and the continued suffering of Palestinians. I fully agreed that the invasions of Iraq and Afghanistan were unjust, and that the suffering of the Palestinians remained a terrible tragedy. But how was the death of fifty civilians in Britain justifiable in this context? The dead were not combatants in the field, they were not supplying arms, and they had not killed anyone in Iraq or Palestine. How was their killing justified? The twisted logic of the bombers seemed to be that because non Muslims were killing Muslims in various countries, it was perfectly acceptable to kill any non Muslims anywhere in the world. And because the Prime Minister, Tony Blair, sent British troops to invade Iraq, it was acceptable to kill anyone in Tony Blair's country.

I had been aware for many years of the hatred some British Muslims felt for their government, which had colluded in the suffering of Muslims in various countries. But this was the first time I realised the intensity of the anger. Worse still, it was the first time I became aware that ordinary English people were also targets of this anger.

It was upsetting to hear the media using the opportunity to vilify Islam, to condemn it as barbaric and unjust. That was painful. But it was even more painful to hear some Muslims trying to justify the bombing, and to make the bombers look like heroes. They were not heroes but murderers. My faith was adamant that such people were murderers, pure and simple. The Qur'an says, 'Whoever killed a life unjustly, it is as if he killed the whole of mankind. And whoever saved a life, it is as if he saved all of mankind.' So how could these men be heroes?

The statement that stuck in my mind was from Mohammad Siddique Khan, one of the bombers who left a video film explaining his actions. 'Your democratically elected governments continuously perpetuate atrocities against my people all over the world,' he said. Given that Britain was his home, Khan should have seen Britain as his own country. But he saw it as the country of his enemy, while all Muslims were his own people. There was no sense of belonging or loyalty to Britain. I began to realise how distant many Muslims in Britain were from their own countrymen. They saw loyalty only in terms of religion, not in terms of the country in which they lived, laughed and prospered. And the Islam they purported to serve was a twisted and warped version of the truth, filled with hate for all non Muslims simply because of their faith. The ghetto mentality of large Muslim communities in Bradford and Leeds had helped breed this isolationist doctrine, and needed to be combated. For the first time I began to analyse my own sense of identity and belonging.

'Where is home for you?' My elderly friend Pauline had once asked me. Surprised at the question, I had instinctively answered, 'London!' Years later I now began to wonder what had prompted Pauline to ask me the question in the first place. How was I coming across in my daily interactions with ordinary Englishmen? Did I not behave as if London was my home, rather than a stop in my journey to an Islamic state? I realised I needed to make more of an effort to interact with my local community, to make friends with my neighbours, to smile at strangers I passed on the road. And I needed to change the way I dressed. My hijab was important, but did it have to look so foreign? So Middle Eastern? Could it not be adapted to the climate, fashion and lifestyle of Britain? For the first time in my life, I toyed with the idea of wearing long skirts, or baggy trouser suits with my scarf.

For the first time in almost twenty years, I decided to leave my house without my long, flowing, black gown.

My decision did not go down very well with many Muslim friends. During a lecture I was giving at Whitechapel's London Muslim Centre, I asked the audience why Muslim women felt compelled to dress in the austere fashions of the Middle East, given that neither our climate nor our lifestyle were conducive to such fashions. Instead of an intelligent debate, I was faced with the sight of many of the women walking out of the hall in protest. I was preaching heresy and they did not wish to know. Sadly, this is sometimes the standard of debate in Muslim communities.

So here I am today, still unfashionable because of the headscarf, but generally in bright colours and in skirts or trouser suits. And I have completely gone off wearing black. I was born in Saudi Arabia, in the holy city of Madina, but my parents were not Saudis. Their families were originally from India but during Partition in 1947, they were forced to flee to Pakistan. My father (who I call Abbu) was only five at the time but still remembers vividly the dreadful journey in a crowded train, with people clinging to the external ladders and doors, and crowding dangerously on the roof. It was a time of blood-letting, war and hatred. Mobs of Sikhs and Hindus rushed to the trains, armed with swords and knives, decapitating and mutilating any Muslims they could force off the trains. Even though the Muslims were leaving, the wave of hatred that Indian politicians had induced through their racist and hysterical propaganda made all Muslims the enemy, regardless of age or gender. Those refugees who finally arrived in Pakistan, exhausted, dishevelled and traumatised, were faced with grinding poverty. Their properties in India had forcefully been confiscated and they had fled with only the minimum of cash. One aunty described how her mother had made preparations for Partition by sewing small bags and filling them with dried fruit and nuts. She knew that when the order to run came, it would not be in a calm atmosphere but in one of panic, fear and chaos. There would be no opportunity to pack bags or even carry them, as looters would take everything away from the fleeing Muslims. A little cash sewed into the lining of their clothes and the bags of nuts would be light enough to run with. When the family were finally forced to flee by angry Hindu mobs, armed with torches with which to burn their homes, it was this collection of nuts and dried fruit that kept the family alive for many days.

Abbu's family had to struggle in Pakistan, having lost their homes and wealth. My grandfather, Sheikh Abdulghaffar Hasan, was an emerging Islamic scholar at the time. He became politically active with the founder of the Jamaat-e-Islami political party, the late Maulana Mawdudi. The two men, the scholar and the politician, joined forces in their new country. When both spoke out against the Qadianis, a minority sect they believed to be heretical because of their views on the finality of the Prophet Muhammad (which is a basic component of the Muslim creed), they were both imprisoned. Abbu was the third child in a family of eight children. With his father in prison, the financial situation became dire. But Abbu wanted an academic career, and nothing was going to stop him. By day he studied in college; by evening he tutored local children to help pay his fees. At the age of 18 he received a scholarship to study Islamic theology in the prestigious Islamic University of Medina in Saudi Arabia. He made his first journey by ship, which took two weeks. A few months later, my grandfather was offered the post of lecturer at the same university and so the entire family moved to Saudi Arabia. After her marriage my mother too moved from Karachi to join her husband. Hence Saudi Arabia became the country of my birth.

When Abbu graduated, he was offered a post by the Saudi government department responsible for religious affairs, called Dar al Iftaa (Ministry for Religious Propagation). By now Saudi Arabia was basking in the oil boom. The Saudis follow what is often called the Wahhabi school of Islam, a rather austere and dry interpretation of the faith. Their great wealth led to an equally great desire to spread their brand of faith. Abbu was employed as a representative and his first post was in Kenya.

His job in Nairobi was to introduce Salafi Islam to the rather laid-back Asian community. Salafism is a movement that aims to return Islam to its alleged roots, which means the earliest generations of the Muslims (*salaf salih*). It is a desire to cleanse Islam of what Salafis see as heresy and distortions that have accumulated over the centuries. One of the key characteristics of Salafis is their dislike of saint-worship. The practice of venerating saints and sages is common in many Muslim communities. The plethora of saints and pious men are highly revered and are sometimes believed to possess semi-divine powers. Mausoleums and shrines are built to these dead saints and attract thousands of devotees, pilgrims and funds. Salafis regard this practice as heresy and condemn it in no uncertain terms. Another example of what Salafis call heresy is the annual Mawlid, the celebration of the birthday of the Prophet Muhammad. Religious songs are sung, hot food is eaten and inspirational talks are given in an atmosphere of great gaiety and enjoyment. The Mawlid celebrations of Nairobi were always great fun. The ladies wore beautiful clothes and jewellery, they ate dishes such as biryani and *zarda* (sweet rice), and the evening ended with everyone standing to sing the melodious notes of the *salaam* (greetings) on the Prophet. Bowls of rose-water were often passed around, with the guests dipping balls of cotton wool in this and using them to fragrance their ears and wrists. There was an expectation that there would be a visit from the soul of the Prophet, so the participants had to be well-dressed and fragrant. All of which makes the Salafis rather angry.

Kenya was home to a large, settled and well-off Muslim community, originally from India. They were scandalised at the presence of this very young and very unusual Imam who spoke so passionately of cleansing Islam of heresy. The shock of Wahhabis in their midst was clearly too much for some of them to bear. This district was home to a large, poor and generally illiterate community of Somali Muslims. A small mosque had been built in the area with Saudi money. But Abu also wanted a school for the community. His dream was to begin with a small primary school, complete with boarding quarters for fifty local children, both girls and boys. The hope was that by the time these children had completed their primary and intermediate schooling, there would be funds to expand the school. Education, food, uniform and boarding would be free for the students, and so would help take the children away from the life of drudgery and child labour many of them would otherwise have to endure. The local community became wild with excitement as the project began to take shape in their midst. Here was a concrete opportunity to improve the lives of their children. They pooled together to help build the school and boarding rooms. Young men whistled as they dug the ground to lay the foundations and raise the walls. The building was completed within a year in an atmosphere of great joy and expectation for the future. It had five classrooms and eight dormitories; each room boasted three bunk beds to sleep six children.

While Abbu devoted himself to his school, writing the curriculum, teaching and employing other staff members, Kenya was experiencing radical change. In the 1970s, Africanisation policies began to be introduced in

Kenya, Uganda and Tanzania, with work permits often refused to non-Africans. The prosperous and well-established Asian communities were forced to leave the country. The first community to leave was from Uganda when, in 1972, President Idi Amin expelled more than 80,000 Asians. My parents watched events unfolding in neighbouring Uganda with foreboding while many of their friends packed tearfully and attempted to liquefy their assets. As the situation in East Africa became more dangerous, with increased reports of violence, murders, confiscation of property and refusal of work permits, many of our friends made the difficult decision to emigrate to Britain. In 1976 Dar al Iftaa decided that life in Kenya was becoming too dangerous for us, so my father was advised to migrate to England too. I was nine years old and very excited with the prospect of moving to London.

One of my first memories of life in London is the Silver Jubilee of Queen Elizabeth, celebrated soon after we moved. Our street celebrated in style, with a week spent hanging banners, balloons and bunting from the lamp posts and walls. On the morning of the celebration, a series of long tables were laid out in the middle of the street and covered with paper in festive red, white and blue. Our neighbours filled these tables with plates of sandwiches, sausage rolls, cakes, crisps and biscuits. A gramophone player was brought out and played the national anthem and Vera Lynn records. I watched the proceedings shyly from the lounge window, wanting to participate but too shy to go out. Aunty Vera saw my face pressed against the window and beckoned me to come out, so I did. We wore paper hats, ate and drank, danced in the street and partied until late at night. It was a wonderful welcome to life in England.

We lived on a typical, north London street in Wood Green. The houses were terraced, with small front gardens that boasted rose borders and chrysanthemums. The garden at the back of the house had a swing on which I used to sit with my head as far back as possible to see if I could get my long hair to touch the ground. The lawn was covered in daisies which I regularly picked to make daisy chains for my wrists. My brothers and I joined Lordship Lane Primary School and quickly settled in. Classes were streamed according to ability and I was immediately placed in the bottom stream with children who generally had learning difficulties. After three days the teacher finally consented to ask me my name. She had assumed I could not speak English and made no effort to draw me into the lesson.

When I responded in fluent, if accented English, she looked shocked. She handed me a short book on the exploits of Sue and Tim, with which the class had been struggling all week. I raced through the pages at top speed, bored at such an easy task. I had studied in a private school in Nairobi and was more than an academic match for other children my age. I was moved to the top stream the next day. In class I sat next to Claire, who had long blond hair that fell to her waist. I had never seen real blond hair before but had read in my collection of *Grimm's Fairy Tales* of princesses with golden hair. I remember coming home very excited, telling Ammi that a girl with real golden hair was in my class. Perhaps she too was a princess.

Ramadan, the month of fasting, began soon after we arrived in London. I was too young to fast but the day of Eid at the end of the month was celebrated lavishly. I wore new clothes, matching pink sandals, and had a pink ribbon plaited into my hair. But the most important embellishment was the red henna that covered my hands and nails. Ammi filled a tray with samosas, pakoras and halwa for Aunty Vera. I ran next door with the tray and knocked loudly. Her smile turned to horror as she saw my patterned hands. 'I have some bleach in the kitchen', she exclaimed. 'Come in and I'll see if we can get these horrible stains off'. She shook her head in disbelief as I explained that the red patterns on my hands were considered pretty in Asian culture. But worse was to come a few years later when a friend in school confided quietly in me. 'I know why your nails are an orange colour', she said in a whisper. I assumed she had discovered that as henna wears off, the colour fades from a pretty red to a faint orange. But my face turned red with embarrassment as she explained further. 'It's because you smoke. My mum told me.'

The Asian community in our area was very small at the time and consisted mainly of first generation immigrants from the Indian subcontinent with their young families. Racism against 'coloureds' and 'pakis' was openly practised and widely accepted. The new immigrants generally felt at best tolerated and at worst very unwelcome. It would be at least fifteen years before Indian culture, fashion, music and cuisine would become trendy, fashionable and even desirable. And it would be twenty years before school fetes in London would add henna painting to their stalls, and Hollywood brides would dress in Asian wedding outfits. This was a long way in the future. All I knew at the time was that being Asian and Muslim was something to be ashamed of, and to keep very quiet. For many years after my friend's confidence, I refused to wear henna on my hands, except during school holidays. And I still never wear it on my nails.

The time came to begin secondary school. For Asians generally and Muslims in particular, preference was given to single-sex schools. Our parents lived in fear that we may come home one day with that most dreaded of beings....a boyfriend. Arranged marriage was the norm and for anyone to marry for 'love' would have been enough for them to be stigmatised by the community for life. Worse still was the thought that this boyfriend might be a gora (white) boy. With a union like that in the family, the best option for the poor parents would be to sell up and move home. The Asian community was very tight-knit, judgemental and, to be perfectly honest, incredibly nosy. Parents kept a tight leash on their children, especially their daughters, for their own salvation but also to be able to survive in the community. Scandal was not considered desirable as its repercussions would be felt for decades. Mixed education obviously put temptation in the way of young people, so single-sex schools were preferred. We did not realise that we were incredibly fortunate that such schools still existed, and that soon most of them would be phased out in favour of completely mixed education.

At High Cross School I met for the first time a sizeable number of Asian girls, from Hindu, Sikh and Muslim families. Despite our different religious backgrounds, we all shared a lack of confidence and pride in our cultures and religions. We loved sitting in Asian-only groups, talking about Indian films, music or wedding outfits, all in whispers. Ours were not religions or cultures to be proud of; we were coloured immigrants, unwanted and strange. Many of us pretended we spoke in English at home with our parents, ashamed to admit that we had our own language. It was a secret we had to guard if we were to be accepted by our black and white friends. This was the time of rising skinhead and racist violence in many parts of England. News reports often carried stories of stabbings and gang attacks by skinheads against Asians and blacks. The skinheads were gangs of young men who shaved their heads completely, wore army-style clothing and big black boots. They looked and sounded incredibly intimidating. Not surprisingly, I was terrified of skinheads, and would walk with my head and eyes down whenever I saw any shaven heads walking in my direction. I could not understand my mother, who seemed to fear no-one. Her neck would visibly grow taller and her lips would purse in a determined manner whenever she saw gangs of young men walking toward her. While I shivered and kept my eyes glued to the ground, she looked them straight in the eye. What made it worse was that she wore the hijab: a headscarf and a long gown long before it became fashionable and long before it became a political symbol among the Muslim masses. None of her friends wore the hijab. Many had worn it in Pakistan before migrating, but spoke of it now as a symbol of backwardness. Their own daughters wore jeans and T shirts in public; they were desperate not only to sound English but to become English. My mother's refusal to join their ranks was considered to be a sign of inferiority and backwardness.

An important issue for me in secondary school was that of the daily prayers. My father asked my head teacher if I could use a classroom during the lunch break to offer my midday and afternoon prayers together, and she agreed readily. I was instructed to report to her office each lunch time to collect the key, pray in the room, lock it and return the key to her. She was most impressed and often asked me why other Muslim girls were not doing the same. For many years I was the only girl in the school praying so diligently.

I was a lanky twelve-year-old with long pigtails when my parents suggested I should think about wearing the headscarf. I always knew that I would have to wear it one day. The problem was that it was not a common sight in the streets of Wood Green in the late 1970s. In fact I would be the only girl at High Cross School for many years to wear it. Although I accepted the scarf as my duty to God, I was not too happy at having to wear it. It was bad enough being Asian, being brown, being different. But that scarf was like a neon beacon, telling everyone within a mile's radius that I was even more different from them than they had previously thought. My religion made me very different. It was not a quiet, unassuming religion, but one that required me to look odd. The first day I wore my headscarf to school is a day etched into my memory.

I was late for school as I had an appointment with the dentist that morning. I walked into my English lesson with the shameful piece of cloth burning into my head. As I opened the door, the class slowly shushed as everyone turned to stare. No one spoke. The journey to my desk seemed like a mile long as I dragged my heavy feet toward it, my ears hot, aware of everyone's looks and smirks. My teacher broke the silence with a loud guffaw. 'Why are you dressed like an old woman?' she asked. 'My religion says I have to,'

I mumbled, wishing the ground would swallow me up, wishing I would die now, wishing I had never been born. I hated the scarf. I hated getting up in the mornings for school as I knew I had to wear the dreaded thing. I hated standing at the bus stop where everyone stared, where the boys smirked at my strange outfit, where the girls looked me up and down in amusement. I grew accustomed to walking with my eyes glued to the ground, ashamed of my appearance, ashamed of being Asian and Muslim, and never daring to look at other people in the eye.

So why did I continue to wear the scarf if I hated it so much? I did not wish to disappoint my parents. They were celebrities within the Muslim community; people watched every move we made, often hoping to see signs of religious weakness or conflict within our incredibly tightly-knit family. I did not want to be the centre of any gossip. And I was really afraid of God. I was convinced that were I to remove the scarf, His wrath would descend upon me. It took me many years to realise that the scarf was probably not as important in the general scheme of things as I had imagined it to be.

My close friends were aghast while the not-so-close friends found a subject for ridicule. Not for me the latest trends in fashion, jewelry, make-up and parties, they assumed. The truth is that women in hijab do have a lot of fun, but it was difficult to explain. It was a very hard decision for me at that time, when there were no other girls in hijab in my community or in my school. I spent many a night dreading the taunts and smirks the next day would inevitably bring. My close friends were supportive but confused, especially when I wore my long raincoat in the middle of a hot and dry summer.

'Why is a woman's hair such an obsession with Islam, and why don't you just make it easy by wearing a hat?' they asked. I was too inexperienced to reply that it is a woman's beauty and body that are covered, not just her hair. 'After marriage will you dress like this at home, and in bed?' was a common question. The situation became worse when Abbu's friend, Uncle Idris, saw me going to school one day and decided his daughter too should wear the headscarf. Ruby disliked the scarf just as much as I did, but unlike me she was happy to rebel. She would leave home in the morning with the scarf on her head, but take it off as soon as she was out of view of her home. The scarf remained stuffed in her bag all day until she was near home again in the afternoon. But Ruby blamed me for her predicament and taunted me with insults at school. I learned to disappear into corners whenever I saw her approaching, afraid of her snide remarks about me and my religious parents.

As the children of a local Salafi scholar, my siblings and I spent our teenage years knowing that our actions were being scrutinized by the community. We were careful not to put a step wrong in case we became subjects of gossip. But one can't keep temptation in check all the time. And temptation came my way one day in the form of a sausage. At school I would often buy snacks from an ice cream van that parked near the playground. Apart from the usual cornets and crisps, it also sold hot dogs. Initially I was shocked that my countrymen ate the meat of dogs. Pork was bad enough, but dogs as well! Thankfully a friend explained that the meat in the sausage was either lamb or pork. So lamb was OK; but was it halal? The Qur'an permits Muslims to eat the meat of Jews and Christians. The Jews eat kosher, following dietary rules similar to Muslims, so that seemed fine. But Christians do not practice any kind of religious ritual when killing animals for consumption, so this permission caused some controversy among Muslim scholars. Some scholars permit the eating of 'western' meat based on this Qur'anic ruling. Others refuse, saying that the early Christians slaughtered animals according to religious ritual just as the Jews did. Their meat was therefore halal to Muslims. Now that Christians no longer practice religious slaughter, their meat is no longer permissible. This debate was being conducted fervently in Saudi scholarly circles and, as a twelve-year-old, I attempted to follow it as best as I could. One day as I walked to the ice cream van to buy a bag of crisps, the smell of frying onions filled my nostrils. I suddenly made the decision that the liberal scholars were right and that this was permissible Christian meat. I had already ascertained that the sausages were made of lamb. So I bought my first (and last) hot dog. The bread and onions were nice and hot but the sausage was too salty and rubbery. I was not impressed and decided to stick with chips in the future. The next day I was summoned by my parents. They had heard about my act of rebellion. I suspected the ice cream vendor. Perhaps he was a spy for all the Asian mums. But all was soon explained. Ruby, whose dislike of me was almost tangible, had spotted me eating the offensive meal in the playground. Her mother had chastised my mother at the next afternoon's tea party, much to the embarrassment of my poor mother. And that evening her father rang my father to complain. 'What sort of Islam are you preaching if your wayward daughter is eating haram meat?' he asked. 'It may only be a hot dog today, but tomorrow it will be pork and perhaps even alcohol.' A public enquiry was called and the offending sinner was required to repent. I was mortified.

My unhappiness at having to wear the hijab finally disappeared when I was seventeen and studying for my 'A' levels. My parents decided our whole family should go to Mecca that year for the annual pilgrimage, the Hajj. I was used to travelling to Saudi Arabia every summer to visit my grandparents, but this particular visit changed my life forever. For two weeks we lived in isolation from the world in Makkah and Madina, the two holy cities of Islam. There was no television, no music, and no worldly life. We spent our days praying, taking part in rituals associated with Prophet Abraham and Prophet Muhammad (the peace of God be upon them both), reciting the Qur'an, and contemplating our faults and weaknesses. We were totally immersed in spirituality and remembrance of God. I had bought a black Arabian-styled gown (called an *abaya*) for the journey and had planned to discard it on returning home. But when I walked out of Jeddah airport after two weeks of worship, I experienced a sense of joy, inner contentment and pride in my faith that was totally new.

Since the age of twelve, I had seen my headscarf as a burden. It had made me look odd when I had wanted to look like everyone else. It had made me stand out, when I had wanted to blend in. But during the Hajj I began to feel an explosive sense of pride in my *hijab*. The women who performed the Hajj with me were like my mother. They were not timid creatures, ashamed and persecuted because of their headscarves. They were bright, confident and cheerful, equal to the men with whom they performed the pilgrimage. When I spoke to them, I was delighted to find that one was a lawyer from Libya, one was a doctor from Palestine and one was a journalist from Pakistan. And yet they all wore the *hijab* as if it was the most normal thing in the world. A new sense of confidence and belonging surged through me.

For two weeks I was surrounded by millions of people from every single country of this globe. They wore different outfits, spoke different languages, ate different foods, and had different customs. Yet we all shared a bond of faith that was stronger than any worldly bond. I felt humble to be in such a precious community, and felt great pride in my *hijab*, the symbol of my faith. I was no longer an oddity, a weirdly-dressed foreigner, but a Muslim among three million Muslims, all worshipping God in unison in the desert around Mecca. I saw *hijabs* of different styles and colours: the black burkas of the Pakistanis, the chadors of the Iranians, the georgette scarves of the Egyptians, the bright fabrics piled and knotted high on the heads of African women, the pretty chiffons of the Europeans and the white smocks of the Indonesians. I came back to London floating on a light cloud, and for the first time was able to walk to school with my head held high, my scarf fluttering confidently in the breeze. I would never, ever walk alone again.

I had fallen in love with my *hijab*.

PAKISTAN
A New History

Ian Talbot

9781849042031 / November 2012
£24.99 / Hardback / 224pp

If Pakistan is to preserve all that is good about its country—the generosity and hospitality of its people, the dynamism of its youth—it must face the deterioration of its social and political institutions. Sidestepping easy headlines to identify Pakistan's true dangers, this volume revisits the major turning points and trends of Pakistani history over the past six decades, focusing on the increasing entrenchment of Pakistan's army in its political and economic arenas; the complex role of Islam in public life; the tensions between central and local identities and democratic impulses; and the effect of geopolitical influences on domestic policy and development.

While Ian Talbot's study centres on Pakistan's many failures—the collapse of stable governance, the drop in positive political and economic development, and, most of all, the unrealised goal of securing a separate Muslim state—his book unequivocally affirms the country's potential for a positive reawakening. These failures were not preordained, Talbot argues, and such a fatalistic reading does not respect the complexity of historical events, individual actors, and the state's own rich resources. While he acknowledges grave crises still lie ahead for Pakistan, Talbot's sensitive historical approach makes it clear that favourable opportunities still remain for Pakistan, in which the state has a chance to reclaim its priorities and institutions and reestablish political and economic sustainability.

www.hurstpublishers.com/book/pakistan

HURST

41 GREAT RUSSELL ST, LONDON WC1
WWW.HURSTPUBLISHERS.COM
WWW.FBOOK.COM/HURSTPUBLISHE
020 7255 2201

SUB-CONTINENTAL LOVERS

*Sabita Manian**

A poster on a Facebook page of a friend declared: 'PAKISTAN Lovers before doing any *Bakwas* in the name of *Aman ki Asha*... read about this hero first'. The reference to 'Pakistan lovers' alludes to those in India who believe that it is possible for India and Pakistan to have much better relations. The term *bakwas* is a Hindi, Urdu and Punjabi word that is synonymous with speaking nonsense or rubbish. As for *Aman ki Asha*, it refers to a 2010 cross-border initiative promoted by two media groups, one from Pakistan and another from India, to highlight cross-border peace efforts. *Aman ki Asha*, means hope for peace, using words from both Urdu and Hindi, the respective national languages of Pakistan and India. The 'hero' in question is Captain Saurabh Kalia of the Indian Army, who was allegedly tortured and killed by the Pakistani military during the 1999 Kargil conflict.

Aman ki Asha is the brainchild of *Jang*, one of the biggest media groups in Pakistan. *Jang* approached the *Times of India* with the idea in 2008. Within two years the two media groups had decided on a joint plan of action to advance dialogue and collaboration with various actors in civil society, including business groups, religious leaders, students, scholars, artists, artisans, professionals, as well as the respective governments. The initiative was launched formally on 1 January 2010 with a joint editorial on the front page of both the *Times* and *Jang* newspapers. The campaign has been widely promoted through print, online and social media such as YouTube, Facebook, and Twitter. A YouTube video message announced: '*Aman Ki Asha* is a brave, new people-to-people initiative by *The Times of India* and Pakistan's *Jang* Group to bring the people of two fine nations closer together. Culturally, emotionally and peacefully'.

---

* This article is dedicated to my father and his aspiration for peace between Pakistan and India

In less than two weeks, a counter-response to the *Aman ki Asha* video was uploaded with the caption: '*Aman Ki Asha* is nothing more than a deception which [sic] purpose is to infiltrate the minds of innocent and less knoledge-able [sic] Pakistanis who are not aware of the history of the Subcontinent and not aware of the Hindu war doctrine of Hug & Backstab'. And by spring 2012, critics of *Aman ki Asha*, a group which described itself as 'the Youth Campaign Against JEW TV' had added another video titled, 'A final Blow to *Aman Ki Asha*'. It castigated cross-border cultural exchanges and Bollywood style music and dance, posing the question: 'Cultural fusion or compromise on Islamic Values? Islamic Culture?' This criticism was compounded by images of bloody violence in Kashmir and the 1947 Partition with a message that followed on the screen: 'Remember Sipahi Maqbool Hussain? His tongue was cut off because [sic] he didn't say "Jai Hind"'; and 'Opting for *Aman ki Asha* is like spitting on the graves of our martyrs'. That was just on the Pakistan side.

Having followed the efforts of the *Aman ki Asha* campaign, I would argue, after the opening line of the *Tale of Two Cities*, that it is the best of times and surely not the worst of times in Pakistan-India relations. Indeed, the first quarter of 2012 should be acknowledged as nurturing the initial shoots of the South Asian Spring, given the unprecedented thaw and shift in Pakistan-India relations. My optimism is based on current events as well as discussions and coverage on both print and social media regarding the two Asian neighbors. While there is no crystal ball that can predict the final outcome of Pakistan-India relations, a glimpse into news coverage of these relations in early 2012 provides clues for what may lie ahead for New Delhi and Islamabad.

On 4 January, Pakistan's Foreign Minister, the suave Hina Rabbani Khar, told the National Assembly that 'Pakistan was committed to a constructive, sustained and result-oriented process of engagement with India'. I rolled my eyes expecting to see both Pakistani and Indian news media in subsequent weeks and months excoriating the other according to the tradition of the last few decades. My expectations appeared to be confirmed by an editorial in the *Daily Times* that discussed the stagnancy following the eighth round of bilateral talks over water issues between the two South Asian neighbours; the seventh occurred had in 1997! The hiatus between the seventh and the eighth had been a consequence of the 1999 Kargil conflict. The failure of the water summit seemed to be a harbinger of yet another year of bickering, hostility and rivalry between the two neighbours.

Then two incidents appeared to indicate a change in bilateral relations. The first was the shift towards implementation of a previous 2008 agreement on consular access for Pakistani prisoners in Indian jails, which was the springboard for furthering other consular access efforts like the repatriation of captured Pakistani and Indian fishermen to their respective countries. The second was the removal of non-tariff barriers (NTBs) to trade, starting with some agricultural and industrial items. This indicated a potential for stronger bilateral trade that cemented the 'Most Favoured Nation' (MFN) status accorded to India by the Pakistani administration just the previous year. By mid-spring, *Dawn*, the Pakistani newspaper, was reporting that 'business ties between India and Pakistan looked set to deepen' following India's invitation to Pakistan for foreign direct investments (FDI). This FDI initiative complemented the opening of the second 'Integrated Check-post Gate' on the Attari-Wagah border between Pakistan and India, which 'would ease the road traffic and provide upgraded infrastructure for both traders and ordinary travellers using the land route'. This signalled the movement of not only goods, labour and services but also people across the borders with the intent to establish an India-Pakistan Business Council, largely because of the forecast for bilateral trade between the two neighbours increasing from US$2.6 billion to nearly US$8 billion by 2014. A perfect formula for what is described in the field of international relations as 'liberal internationalism'.

While news on the economic front seemed to indicate progress in bilateral interactions, one could presume that on the security front, the most vulnerable of areas between Pakistan and India, the news would not be so positive. The terror attacks on Mumbai, on 26 November 2011, led by the Pakistan-based Lashkar-i-Taiba that left 165 dead and more than 300 seriously injured, had already soured relations between Islamabad and New Delhi. In early spring 2012, this sore was scratched open by intense media coverage of the sole survivor among the ten terrorists, Ajmal Kasab's appeal against his death sentence. The scab continued to be picked at, not only with the continuous appeal hearings in the Supreme Court, but also by the arrival of a Pakistani judicial commission in India to conduct its own investigation into the Mumbai attack. But the Indian authorities did not give the Pakistanis permission to cross-examine Kasab on the grounds that the

Supreme Court appeal hearings had not yet concluded. The court case re-
stirred memories of 26/11 and brought all the animosity between the two
neighbours to the fore. Then, as in the case of trade relations, two events turned the tide. The
Indian government agreed to share with Pakistan the 700-page investigative
dossier about the Mumbai attacks that included not only Kasab's confessions
but also other details such as post-mortem reports of slain terrorists and
case reports of the incident that had been hitherto described as sensitive
security matters. In April 2012, Pakistan President Asif Ali Zardari decided
to go on a pilgrimage to the shrine of Sufi mystic Khwaja Moinuddin
Chishti in Ajmer. After much speculation whether this was going to be a state
visit or not, President Zardari's pilgrimage to Ajmer included a forty-minute
meeting with Prime Minister Manmohan Singh, which laid the groundwork
for a potential bilateral discussion over the disputed Siachen Glacier region
in Kashmir. The Kashmir and Siachen issues are a bone of contention that is
not going to be resolved overnight. However, the fragile trust that had been
broken in the aftermath of the Mumbai attacks was being mended.

On the civil society level, something even more profound was happening.
A report in Pakistan's *The News* caught my eye:

'I'll be a doctor when I grow up.... Abbu says when I come back from India I can
be whatever I want to be, I can even play as much as I want,' she [little Faiqa]
said.... 'Whenever you replace hatred with love, you save lives and that is what
fostering love through *Aman Ki Asha* has done by giving my seven-year-old daughter
a chance to live', said Asif Javed, shopkeeper.

Faiqa, the seven-year old daughter of Asif Javed, a shopkeeper from Gojra
village in Pakistan, was referring to her life after her free life-saving surgery
for a damaged heart in India. The surgery was part of the 'heart-to-heart'
initiative sponsored by *Aman ki Asha*, for about 200 economically underprivi-
leged Pakistani children and funded in each country by the Rotary Club.

Since its inception in 2010, *Aman ki Asha* has devoted much energy to
promoting people to people contacts between India and Pakistan. Its actions
have included not only the initiative where Indian cardiologists treat Pakistani children with congenital heart issues, but also sponsoring cultural and
literary festivals where Pakistani and Indian artists perform jointly. An

example is the Kashmir-born Indian classical music singer Seema Sehgal's Lahore concert.

Accompanied by Pakistani musicians Mohammed Aslam on the harmonium, Haroon Samuel on the tabla, Zohaib Hassan on the *sarangi* and Ustad Akmal Qadri on the flute, Sagal entertained a packed audience with *ghazals* and *geets*. Common television forums, such as the 'Let's Talk' conference in Karachi, have been launched to bring together senior editors and television anchors from both countries. Then there is the *Milne Do* (let them meet) campaign, following the loosening of visa restrictions by both countries and supplemented by the cross-border prisoner release campaign, 'In Humanity's Name'. Both campaigns belong to the civic society domains that have contributed favourably to this South Asian Spring.

Facebook and YouTube have also served as useful devices to promote inter-border civilian cooperation, especially among youth. Young people in both India and Pakistan are 'Tweeting for Peace'. The *Aman ki Asha* Facebook site regales its visitors with a daily account of cross-border developments that foster friendship between Pakistan and India – a constant reminder that the 'hope for peace' can be sustained despite the naysayers. Both the *Aman ki Asha* web and Facebook pages spread the word about the South Asian University (SAU), a nascent regional educational collaboration, whose campus in New Delhi is set to attract and educate students from the eight SAARC (South Asian Association for Regional Cooperation) countries. The idea was first articulated at a 2005 SAARC meeting, which has come to fruition – an idea not dissimilar from the Erasmus University concept that gained momentum as the 'international knowledge workshop' in the European Union. The educational ethos of SAU underscores another effort by *Aman ki Asha's* Education Committee to bring education specialists from Pakistan and India to discuss collaboration on educational reforms. To capture the imagination of the younger generation, this civic society-focused objective has also led *Aman ki Asha* to champion programs for schoolchildren, adding muscle to their trade and investment conferences.

Most importantly, the two media groups that founded the *Aman ki Asha* campaign have resolved to actively moderate themselves and not fan the flames of Indo-Pak animosity. As the campaign's homepage notes: The 'Times of India Group and the Jang Group commit to using their print and electronic media to aggressively promote the benefits of peace in terms of economic development, uniting families, tourism, developing trade, and removing the obstacles to peace'. The two groups have also committed to mutually respecting one another's views without forsaking 'an honest and exhaustive debate on all contentious issues between the two countries, such as Kashmir, water, terrorism, Siachin, Sir Creek etc.'

But these cooperation-boosting efforts have also spawned a counter-campaign from conservative right-wing groups in India and Pakistan. India has its fair share of its neo-nationalist conservative detractors who are no different from their Pakistani counterparts in their perceived insecurities and get agitated if a change in the status quo is detected. In the neo-nationalists' (Pakistani or Indian) zero-sum perception, a step forward toward cooperation is a step back towards submission to the 'other' that in their parochial view diminishes the 'honour' of the nation. It also diminishes the valour and sacrifice of soldiers who have fought the 'other' in previous wars and conflicts. Add to that the context of ever-potent and ever-present seven-decades-long animosity constructed around the national and religious identity of Pakistan and India. Thus the values of *Aman ki Asha* are antithetical to everything the neo-conservatives believe including constructed nationalist identities.

The Facebook poster on the Indian site (described on the first page) was a reflection of and a response to this very dynamic – the horror of their perceived reality (the constant enemy that is Pakistan), turned upside down. At the footer of the poster, emblazoned in the colours of the Indian flag, another warning is given: 'a nation that forgets its martyrs will itself soon be forgotten' (a slight variation of the Calvin Coolidge quote which reads: 'the nation which forgets its defenders will be itself forgotten'). This statement precedes the last line of the same poster: 'our Media and so called human right activist [sic] are sleeping... they are only for terrorists and traitors not for *shaheed* [martyrs]'. By specifically juxtaposing the 'Media', with a capital M, and human rights activists, a connection is made between the supporters of *Aman ki Asha* and the terrorists. And as supporters of terrorists they must be traitors who are disrespectful of martyrs.

Wars and conflicts are catalysts that only accentuate nationalism. Even the nuclear tests by both India and Pakistan have often stimulated such sentiments. Thus emotions ran high in India during the 1999 Kargil conflict, especially when the body of squadron leader Ajay Ahuja, an Indian pilot of a MIG21 downed by the Pakistani army over Pakistan controlled Kashmir, was returned with two fatal bullet wounds, implying as the BBC News noted in its headlines that he had been 'killed in cold blood'. The Indian Facebook poster, *'Pakistan Lovers – Bakwas in the name of Aman ki Asha'* was attempting to revive the memories of that 1999 conflict with its portrayal of the killing by the Pakistani forces of another Indian military man, Captain Kalia. Clearly, the intent of the Facebook poster was to incite mistrust and hatred of Pakistan while simultaneously disparaging the recent efforts of *Aman ki Asha* toward peaceful cooperation. Hence the supporters of *Aman ki Asha* are derisively labelled as 'Pakistan Lovers' and the campaign itself is described as *bakwas* or nonsense.

In a 2005 autobiographical essay, Zubeida Mustafa, Pakistani journalist and former assistant editor of *Dawn*, describes Pakistani perceptions of India following Partition. There was so much hatred in the air, she writes, that 'I grew up believing that all the Indians were bad guys and not to be trusted, ever. They wanted to destroy Pakistan at the first opportunity - that is what we were told and that is what we firmly believed. And that was the general belief in Pakistan.... A whole generation grew up in the painful shadow of the bloody partition experience and consequently perceived India as an implacable enemy. The new government only encouraged this black and white perception. The radio - in those days there was no television - and the newspapers over poured with anti-Indian rhetoric and it was taken for granted that we could never reconcile with Indians'. Mustafa's childhood memories in Pakistan are a mirror image of Indian perceptions of Pakistan. India, in turn, nurtured the image of Pakistan being out to destroy it; a Muslim Pakistan that was never going to reconcile to the idea of co-existing with a Hindu India. This image is hyper-articulated in the media and opportunistically advanced by politicians of various hues.

Consider a recent example. A headline in *India Today,* one of the most highly circulating political periodicals, described India's win over Pakistan in the 2012 Asia Cup cricket as follows: 'Kohli Pounds Pakistan into Submission'. The choice of words here implies a supercilious nationalist pride in a tone of one-uppance. Contrast this with another political periodical, *Outlook India*, whose headline on the same topic was, 'With Kohli's 183, India Beats Pakistan' – the latter, clearly more innocuous headline does not take away from an accurate portrayal of the same news.

The Pakistani and Indian media groups that constitute *Aman ki Asha* have decided to shun incendiary coverage of news. It will take time before the 'habits of cooperation' fomented through increased interaction between Pakistan and India re-shape the coverage of the media into one that portrays friendly rivalry rather than acerbic competition. But given that we are talking about two of the biggest media groups in the Subcontinent, it is clear that from war and death, we are slowly moving towards the spring buds of love. As a 22 April 2012 editorial in *Times of India* announced, 'trade for peace' is the new catchphrase defining the emerging relationship between India and Pakistan – a relationship historically so troubled that, when not actually at war, they have been engaged in a virtual cold war'. The sentiment was reflected by Beena Sarwar, a leading journalist and filmmaker from Pakistan, in an 'op-ed' article also in *Times of India*: 'there is a growing realisation that war between the two nuclear-armed neighbours is not an option. Countries that engage in mutual trade and investment don't go to war'.

Now this is more than wishful thinking; and there are historical parallels that suggest that love and peace can be restored between two hitherto antagonistic neighbours. Take the example of trade and cooperation between the French and the Germans since the early 1950s. Until then, these two European neighbours had gone through centuries of violence and bloodshed not only in their competition to assert dominance in the region but also to assert singular control over the territory of Alsace-Lorraine along the Franco-German border – Lorraine being the territory that was home to Joan of Arc, a fifteenth-century national hero and 'martyr' of France who was later beatified as a saint for her valiant heroics against the English.

Alsace-Lorraine, not dissimilar from Kashmir, was a bone of contention between the French and the Germans especially after its annexation by the Germans in 1871 following the Franco-Prussian War. The glory and spirit of Joan was evoked during every French clash with the Germans since then. Through the first half of the twentieth century, it was considered prize territory, land for which much blood was spilled on both the German and the French soils. Yet today, the French and the Germans, despite the current financial crisis, are deeply intertwined through their economies and other common policies as part of a supranational entity, the European Union, so much so that war or conflict between them is unimaginable. This state of affairs between former enemies is a consequence of nearly six decades of building 'habits of cooperation', ever since the Coal and Steel Community was formed in the 1950s. And as for the contentious Alsace-Lorraine: Strasbourg, in Alsace (France), a German speaking French city, is also the city that houses the European Parliament, the European Council and the European Court of Human Rights – the legislative, executive and judicial branches of the European Union (EU).

The EU has thus been a success story for the centuries' old rivals, France and Germany, who through their 'habits of cooperation' on various economic fronts have sustained their peaceful interaction through interdependence. The fortunes of one are tied to the fortunes of the other within the European community. By pooling resources and integrating more and more economic sectors at every stage (along with other European member states), the political and social interdependence between Paris and Berlin is effectively made permanent.

Meanwhile, Joan of Arc's deification, even in contemporary times, neither takes away from her valour nor does it actualise a sustained hatred by the French of the British or of the Germans. The peaceful coexistence of France and Germany has not led to the 'forgetting' of their martyrs. Similarly, in the context of Pakistan and India, 'trade for peace' may indeed bear fruit, notwithstanding their history or the valour of their martyrs.

Of course, ambitious politicians on both sides will continue to pander to the least common denominator by drumming up nationalism. A recent example is provided by Mullapally Ramachandran, a union Minister of State for Home Affairs from the Congress Party. In spring 2012, Ramachandran declared in an upper house (Rajya Sabha) session that Persons of Indian Origin (PIOs, expatriate Indians) sympathetic towards Pakistan will not be granted Indian citizenship. The declaration was clearly an assertion of nationalist zeal at a time when cooperation between the two countries was gaining the limelight. However, a quick investigation of the Indian Home Ministry's criteria for citizenship, even for PIOs, revealed that there was no formal criterion that prevented those 'sympathetic towards Pakistan' from acquiring Indian citizenship. It was mere sabre-rattling on the part of the minister, perhaps as an effort to pre-empt criticism of cross-border cooperation from the conservative right. Incidentally, Ramachandran's antics were not reported by the mainstream news media, except for *India Today*. The *India*

Today report found its way to the Pakistani online news portal, OnePakistan. com, which has Urdu and English coverage, and a virulently anti-India blog. Such muscle-flexing pomposity will persist among right wing politicians and groups. Europe too, despite its unification, continues to see its fair share of right-wing neo-nationalist groups who have managed to sway even the discourse of mainstream political parties. However, this anti-India or anti-Pakistan rhetoric appeals largely to a generation that is on its way out. It is only a matter of time before the younger generation, no longer haunted by the memories of partition or naked nationalist sentiments, or willing to put up with the feudal vestiges of the draconian older structures of power, decides to resolve the Kashmir issue, until it is no longer an issue between New Delhi and Islamabad, just as in the case of Alsace-Lorraine last century. Cross-border discussions on counter-terrorism coordination and the Siachen issue have already begun to be facilitated by *Aman Ki Asha*. Once cross-border trade takes off, it will enhance not just mutual trust but the internal dynamics of India and Pakistan will also become conducive to more peaceful and less violent domestic order. An Indian can thus be proud to be a 'Pakistan Lover' just as a Pakistani need not see it as a slight to be labelled an 'Indian Lover'. The winds of change and the will of the people, I detect, are certainly headed in the direction of love.

THE RESTING PLACE

Irna Qureshi

I always thought mum would want to be buried in Pakistan. I understood the appeal of being buried in one's ancestral graveyard. There's a romance in being laid to rest in the company of your loved ones. Our graveyard is situated in Nila, the family village near Chakwal in the Punjab. It is reached soon after we enter the village, and it's always felt to me like a special place, a pilgrimage of sorts. On arrival, mum likes to stop there first to pay respect to her parents who lie here, side by side, surrounded by the children that died too young, and ancestors that led full lives.

Leaving the car under the cool canopy of an old banyan tree, I respectfully wrap the diaphanous *dupatta* around my head as I trail behind mum into the main burial ground, cautiously and courteously keeping to the well-trodden narrow path, to avoid treading on the modest mounds which signify resting places. In accordance with Islam, the graves are simple, mostly unassuming, their unremarkable appearance making their residents indistinguishable by their achievements in life. Men and women, young and old, rich and poor, all lie here awaiting judgement, as equals before God.

A few graves are affectionately adorned with sweet-scented strings of deep red rose or pure white, elegant jasmine, while other graves have been damped down this morning with a reviving splash of water. Purposefully we make our way to a low walled section to one side, uttering only *assalamu alaikum ya ahlal qaboor* (peace be upon you O people of the grave) under our breaths, to formally announce our arrival to the residents. Voiceless they may be, but they can hear visitors, mum explains. I imagine mum commanding their full attention today because it's been a few years since she was last in Pakistan. Few of the graves have any markings at all so it's as if mum's feet are being guided by some force to her favourite spot. Stopping beside her parents' final resting place, mum's face and shoulders seem to relax as she bends down dutifully to place a tender finger on her mother's grave. "That's how they know it's you," she tells me before losing herself in prayer and contemplation for the mother she lost some thirty years ago.

Having spent most of our lives in Bradford, alas with no network of uncles, aunts and grandparents within reach, and only mum to look up to, it seems strange to be reminded that she was once someone's daughter too. Her mother could barely read anything other than the Qur'an when she married my grandfather in her teenage years. She was barely literate since the total sum of her formal education was the memorisation of large passages of the Quran, which put her in the meritorious position of being able to invoke God's name without having to break off from her chores. Theirs was a formidable partnership, with respect for each other's values at its core. Given her devout nature, grandma asked her husband to recite Surat Yasin (chapter thirty-six of the Qur'an), such commanding verses with benefits manifold that it's often referred to as the 'heart of the Qur'an'. It is said to be particularly valuable in easing the path that lies ahead and is therefore recited to the dying. They say my grandfather was unable to recite so his bride insisted that he commit the verse to memory. It would be enriching for him, she reasoned. He'd have the benefit of carrying the verse with him at all times, being able to call upon it at a moment's notice.

For his part, my grandfather insisted that his wife learn to write Urdu. He was a clerk in the British Indian Army and would spend most of his married life posted out of town. What he conveyed in letters to his wife, he didn't want to share with a third party. Accepting her challenge, my grandmother would hide the old fashioned child's chalkboard she practised on, lest the women in the village mock her for writing love letters to her dashing husband. For as long as they lived, grandfather's letters addressed to his wife were always neatly written to make them more legible. Grandma had trained her eye to read her husband's letters to such an extent that she actually couldn't read anyone else's handwriting.

Mum is now introducing me to the graves of aunts and great aunts, maternal and paternal, who lie nearby. There are uncles and great uncles, as well as other members of the extended family, interwoven by a complicated web of cousin marriages, making it impossible for me to keep track of the entire network. Like the banyan tree at the entrance, our family's robust roots are mapped out beneath our feet. It's an arresting sight – a century's worth of bonds which began life above ground, cemented after death into the earth below. I am in awe of their enduring strength which continues to prop up the fledgling branches of our family to this day.

I always imagined mum would want to be buried in Pakistan. She might have spent fifty of her seventy-five years living in Bradford, but Pakistan has always been her first love. The soil of the homeland is sweeter and more inviting, she says. She still remembers the scent. But then, Pakistan is where she was born, where she grew up, where her roots were. That's where her inspiration came from. She didn't belong here. It was initially my father's work that brought her, and then circumstance. It was my father and his father who settled in Bradford in the 1950s to work in the textile mills. After her marriage was arranged, mum bid farewell to her entire clan in the early 1960s to begin a new life in Yorkshire. In the days leading up to mum's departure, grandma would repeat a sobering Punjabi saying: 'Off you go, my beloved daughter, to the other side of the River Ravi, to where no-one goes and from where no-one returns'. Grandma no doubt sensed it would be years before she would see her daughter again.

Perhaps mum's relationship with Britain would have started differently, were it not for my father's attitude. To be fair, this attitude was shared by the vast majority of male Pakistani migrants scrambling to British shores to relieve the labour shortage during the post war industrial boom. My father had already been living and working here for the best part of ten years, but he wasn't interested in building a relationship with the place. Residence was purely and utterly a financial arrangement, and a temporary one at that. A British wage and exchange rate meant that men like my father could send more rupees each month to their extended families than they could dream of earning in a whole year back home. The men hoped that working in the mills for a few years would give the family in Pakistan a leg up; clear debts, build a house, and perhaps start a business. The aim was to earn as much as they could whilst living as cheaply as possible.

If ever there was a man dedicated to finding his pot of gold, it was my father. If the work was available, he'd happily do double shifts all week, the equivalent of sixteen hours on the trot. And what was the point of spending Saturday resting when he could earn time and a half at the mill! Being an entrepreneurial chap, dad bought 1 Alpha Street, furnishing the modest terrace with several beds in the two bedrooms and two attics, as well as the lounge, and taking in about fifteen lodgers. A rota system determined who slept when. If you finished work early, you might have to wait for a housemate to get up for his shift before you could use the bed. We might call it overcrowding now, but this was the norm among the migrant workers living in group houses, and of course it made things cheaper. They were probably awake for no more than an hour or so at either end of a shift, which was probably a blessing - there wasn't much personal space to be found.

The men didn't have much time to socialise. Any time off tended to get taken up with births, deaths and marriages among the new settlers. Seriously, people waited until the weekend to bury the dead because the concept of taking a day off didn't exist. Unbelievable as it sounds, dad didn't even attend his own wedding. The family had taken on debt to buy land in Pakistan. It didn't make sense for him to lose money by taking time off and incur the expense of flying back to Pakistan. So with mum dressed in her bridal finery in Pakistan and dad at home in Bradford, the couple took their marriage vows down the phone in 1964. A few months later, the last lodger at Alpha Street was just moving out as mum landed at Heathrow Airport. Thankfully it was a weekend, so her arrival didn't interfere with dad's shifts.

Even after mum joined him in Keighley, dad still regarded his stay here as temporary. Neither was being a homeowner enough to make him feel settled. He didn't buy the house because he was swayed by the area's aesthetic values. It was because he knew it would make him money – what you might call a buy-to-let I suppose, crucially located within a few minutes' walk of several mills. When mum grew tired of using the mismatched crockery she'd inherited from dad's lodgers and decided to buy a dinner set, dad chided her for wasting money on things they'd one day have to leave behind.

Ironically, it was my father who returned to Pakistan after my parents divorced a few years later. Mum, meanwhile, decided to stay in Bradford to raise her children, holding down three jobs to keep a roof over our heads. Christian Housing Aid kindly sent a truck to furnish our rented council home. They also supplied our kitchenware – but rest assured, mum diligently recited the *Shahada* (the Muslim declaration of belief) to ritually cleanse the pots and pans whilst rinsing them three times with Fairy Liquid, just in case they'd been tainted in a previous life by un-Islamic substances.

But it still felt like mum's heart was beating in Nila. Here was her dilemma. Pakistan was the ideal and we were leading second best lives in Bradford, yet mum knew it was easier to make a life for herself and her children in Britain.

It's less judgmental and more forgiving. And the distance allowed mum to pretend to her family that life here was much better than it actually was. It also meant she could indulge us in a love affair with her homeland. It became the place where everything was good, where the sun shone brighter and where the mangoes were sweeter.

Our finances made it impossible, yet mum planned an interim trip back home with a suitcase filled with nothing but anticipation gathering dust under her bed. If mum could just get through the next thirty years of employment in Bradford and raise her children, then she could look forward to retiring to Pakistan with a handsome pension, awarded in pounds sterling, to be spent in rupees at a substantially profitable exchange rate. The day finally came when she did pack up and move to Pakistan to make up for lost time, to be with her nearest and dearest. Poignantly, it was only after she got there that she realised that the people she yearned for had all passed away or moved on. Her parents were no more, and the group of cousins she'd grown up with had scattered. So, after a year or two, she reluctantly returned, having reconciled herself to the idea of living out her remaining years on the soil that doesn't smell as sweet but which her children regard as their permanent home.

I always thought mum would want to be buried in Pakistan. But maybe she didn't want to settle for the arrangement she had with her parents' final resting place. Perhaps it was the thought of only hearing from her children if they happened to be in the country which changed her mind. Perhaps she liked the idea of her children stopping by whenever they feel like it, as they do now. Or perhaps because mum understands all too well the sacrifice involved in living seven seas away from loved ones. The devastating news of her mother's passing was cruelly conveyed to her by a solitary phone call in the middle of the night. The nightmare recurred a few years later, when she was given the crushing news of her father's departure from this world. The burial had already taken place by the time she got the news, not that mum had the financial means to make the trip for a proper farewell. And anyway, we would never have got there in time because Muslims are buried as soon as possible, preferably before nightfall on the day of death. Once more, mum was left to lament her loss alone, without ceremony or cold hard proof to help bring closure, nor even the comfort of family to help ease the pain. Perhaps that's what she doesn't want for her children.

ART AND LETTERS

DEAD STONES AND LIVING WORDS

Boyd Tonkin

For there is no eternal city
And there is no pity
And there is nothing underneath the sky
No rainbow and no guarantee –
There is no covenant between your God and me.
James Fenton, '*Jerusalem*'

Alona Frankel is talking about 'the most horrible event of my life'. A much-loved Israeli children's writer, with a late-blooming career as an autobiographer, she survived the Lvov ghetto in Poland. One of a handful of Jews who escaped transportation to the death camps, Frankel came as a child to the new state in 1949. She sits, genial and youthful, in the conference hall at Mishkenot Sha'ananim just outside the old city of Jerusalem.

Here the postcard-perfect views run along the golden Ottoman walls from Mount Zion to the Jaffa Gate. Built with postwar West German funding (the hall carries the name of Chancellor Konrad Adenauer), the arts centre and writers' retreat perches above the incongruous Victorian cottage-garden charm of Yemin Moshe. This suburb for local Jews was planted with the blessing of the Ottoman pasha outside the (then) squalid old city by the philanthropist Sir Moses Montefiore in 1860. Suleiman the Magnificent's walls and towers may stare at us from across the valley, but here it feels as if the Cotswolds have come to Judaea.

In sultry, still mid May, the hillsides frothing with flowers, Mishkenot Sha'ananim is hosting the third Jerusalem International Writers Festival.

171

Alona Frankel talks with Esther David, an Indian Jewish writer whose left-wing, secular, father in Ahmedabad, a disciple of Darwin and Tagore, nonetheless treasured his family prayer-shawls and Hebrew scriptures, and gave instructions for a Jewish funeral. After the war, Frankel recalls, she had to revisit the family apartment in Lvov. The Holocaust had swallowed her relatives. She found shoeboxes full of old photos. The dead looked at her and, at that moment, 'I realised that I am the only person in the world who can name some of these people.'

'The sheer fact of being alive,' she confessed, 'makes you feel guilty in some way. After what I went through, I thought that I should hide under a bed and only put my hand out for some food.' As a mother, she never told her story of survival to her sons. Then, late in her career, came three volumes of testimony in quick succession, an avalanche of pent-up memory: 'I tried to avoid cliche and not be sentimental. I couldn't write with my blood. So I took a step back and tried to observe that little girl.'

What kind of stories do the dead, or the lost and exiled, require? And who will heed them? In the cool of the evening, on a rooftop terrace, the Palestinian Israeli writer Sayed Kashua discussed literature as mourning, as memorial, with Aleksander Hemon - the Bosnian prodigy stranded in Chicago when Serbian forces attacked his Sarajevo home in 1992. Refugees, says Hemon, enjoy better social prospects and more robust health when they are able to tell their stories. 'Storytelling becomes a mode of survival. It also becomes a means of regaining agency.' Thanks to the shocks of war and flight, Hemon's own narratives of survival found their voice in an acquired language, English.

Sayed Kashua, as an Arabic speaker in Israel, had to make a similar move across the borders of the tongue. With his family's recollections of the nakba of 1948 at painful odds with the official history that surrounded him, he went to an almost entirely Jewish school in Jerusalem. 'I was totally a stranger. I looked different, I talked different, to the other kids. But I knew that language was the key'. That language, modern Hebrew, belonged to the state, not to the heart. Frankel too revealed that she still feels more comfortable in the mother tongue: for her, Polish. 'I remember how scared I was,' said Kashua, 'when I finally had the chutzpah to write in Hebrew.' There is, he says, a 'typically Israeli question' that often arises when he speaks in public: 'In what language do you dream?'

Early in his career, Kashua imagined that the stories of the Palestinian people laid out in the majority tongue of his fellow-Israelis would somehow change minds by themselves. 'I thought that all it needs is to tell the truth, to open their eyes. I don't any more think that I'm writing novels to make a change.' That 'painful journey into another language' still takes its toll. 'Sometimes I feel sick from being here,' Kashua said, 'and I would like to go away for a while.' Hemon: 'Have some honey. My father always says, honey can cure everything.' Kashua: 'Is your father an Arab refugee?' 'Hemon: 'No, he's a Bosnian refugee.' Later, as Hemon raised the hope that the testament of exiles may somehow, like that soothing honey, comfort and even heal, Kashua offered a bleak reply. 'Can you imagine when a refugee tells a story of a trauma, and someone says to him, "You're lying?"' The question hung in the scented night air.

In Israel's brief history as an independent state, not only Palestinians have found that their stories of the lost and the past may struggle to find a hearing. Shortly before my visit to the festival I talked to Aharon Appelfeld. The great Israeli novelist – born in the old Jewish heartland of Czernowitz, now in Romania – improbably lived through the Holocaust. Hiding as a wild child in the woods, his family snatched away, he sheltered with a village prostitute and acted as a servant to a bandit gang before arriving, aged thirteen, in British-Mandate Palestine in 1946.

Illiterate, almost feral, he went to a farm school, where 'they trained us to be peasants... There were some basic lessons, but otherwise I was a peasant boy.' When he learned the renovated Hebrew of the infant state, 'it was a struggle to gain the language. I used the dictionary, and I copied out parts of the Bible... I started with Genesis, and I went from chapter to chapter, book to book.' His literary vocation began with a simple chronicle of his murdered family, nurtured in a time of solitude and forsakenness. 'It was the middle of the 1950s. I was alone, in the fields of the Judaean Hills. I thought, is this my landscape? Is this my language? This was a moment of despair.'

Out of Appelfeld's desolation came a story, then another, then more. His hard-won tongue let the vanished speak. Even though home-grown writers such as SY Agnon served as inspiration, 'Most of the Hebrew writers were born in Israel. I'm actually the only one who adopted Hebrew as my language... My task was to combine the Hebrew language with my horrible experience.'

In fledgling Israel, that 'idealistic, socialistic country', memories of the genocide were almost taboo. 'No one wanted to hear about such terrible experiences... The slogan was, "Forget it! You should begin again."' Appelfeld was asked, 'Why are you writing about the Holocaust? Why are you so Jewish, and not Hebrew?' At first, publishers told him that 'You should write about the kibbutzim, the army. You should be a positive writer.' He persisted. In novel after novel, Appelfeld remembers, honours, transforms the lost, in fictions that alchemise autobiography and history into a kind of myth. As in a painting by Chagall, he gives the dead wings, and lets them fly.

For the novelist David Grossman, a story of personal trauma has taken more than five years to find its form. In August 2006, before he completed his epic novel of a nation in shock and in crisis *To the End of the Land*, his son Uri – a sergeant in a tank unit - died in the second Lebanon war. Two days prior to Uri's death, Grossman had, along with Amos Oz and AB Yehoshua, put his name to a public appeal for an end to the fighting. Now, as he explained on another fragrant evening, the winding path of grief has issued in a book of mourning and renewal: *Falling Out of Time*. Writing, however agonising at times, cleared a way beyond the blockage of bereavement: 'I knew that I had to find a way of being inside my own life, when it had suddenly changed so sharply. Everything had been turned upside down.' The book seeks a passage into that dangerous borderland where 'life touches death in the most barrier-free way. It became the place where I wanted to be most.' But this shadowy frontier, where the dead may speak to the living, held him for too long: 'It was very difficult to come back out of there into the mundane, like a diver who can't come back up to the surface at once.'

A novelist, whatever the cost, must return to that zone of pain. 'I couldn't accept that the writer within me could be beaten. It's like an internal uprising. The only freedom that's left for someone who has suffered such a tragedy is the freedom to describe it in their own words. Writing gave me the ability to take back the life that had been taken from me... What have the drumming of words got to do with is death? Yet this is all humans have left – to say what they feel in the most nuanced way.'

In Jerusalem, the dead so often seem to outrank, to outvote, simply to outnumber, the living. Lined up in massed battalions in the cemeteries, enshrined in the stones of church, mosque, synagogue, they tell over their sacred stories of anointment and appointment in a vast cacophony. These rival histories can collide in a maddening white noise. James Fenton wrote his poem '*Jerusalem*' in 1988, but not a word of it has dated:

It is superb in the air
Suffering is everywhere
And each man wears his suffering like a skin.
My history is proud.
Mine is not allowed.
This is the cistern where all wars begin.

Or, more bleakly and in a single line: 'There is no covenant between your God and me.'

Here all the sons and daughters of Abraham scrap not only with their neighbours' faiths but among themselves. I visited the epicentre of this hubbub: the Church of the Holy Sepulchre, where for a millennium half a dozen Christian denominations have fought so bitterly for preeminence at the site of Jesus's crucifixion and entombment that none trusts the others even to lock and unlock the doors. The church keys are held by a local Muslim dynasty, the Nusseibehs.

Then, in the upstairs chapels, where Orthodox and Catholic altars compete among the tourist and pilgrim hordes, I watched a young Asian woman – dressed in the white blouse and plain skirt favoured by Christians from the Subcontinent, or perhaps Malaysia – silently praying alone in a patch of quietness that she had found or made. No longer a huge mausoleum peopled by loud but deaf zealots, Jerusalem for a few moments shrank to the scale of one biography.

Perhaps I had misread, and wrongly blamed, the dead. Perhaps they too crave liberation from their enlistment in the wars of faith and identity. As the experience of Appelfeld, or Kashua, shows, the powers-that-be above the earth may silence or ignore the stories of the departed if they let slip too much inconvenient truth. If so, then the writers in and of Jerusalem owe the dead another sort of narrative. David Grossman said, in relation to his lost Uri, that 'When a person dies in a war in Israel, their death becomes nationalised. For me it was very important to reclaim the private, intimate person, and to release him from the "national"'.

But it might be that, in this city, the stones of the past and the walls of the present simply weigh too heavily for any such emancipation. At Mishkenot Sha'ananim, I drank coffee on the terrace with the young Israeli writer Nir Baram. He comes from a family settled in Jerusalem for seven generations, but caused a stir at this festival in 2010 when his opening speech denounced all the 'walls', material and political, that the Israeli state had chosen to build. Literally, figuratively, he turns his back on the holy stones. For Baram, secular, hedonistic Tel Aviv is 'the greatest monument of Zionism'. Jerusalem he now finds 'a more religious, less open, more racist city' than in his childhood. 'When I was a kid we went to East Jerusalem every week. We met Palestinian kids all the time. That doesn't happen now.'

'I like Israel,' Baram affirms. 'I believe in Israel. I just want a different future' rather than the combat-ready present in which 'we have basically racist ministers, racist propaganda in the newspapers, racist laws in the Knesset.' He asks, 'do my generation want to go on living this way, with one ethnic group in a superior position to other groups?... I don't want to live in a racist society. I want to see the day when Jewish and Palestinian children attend the same schools.'

As a writer, Baram yearns to tell stories that float free of the bloodstained rocks around us. He has little patience for the anguished introspection and social interrogation of many of his peers. 'There is this notion in Israel that everything you write about should relate to your experience. This is not literature... We are not limited to current affairs. It's not the right way to use the freedom of literature. We expect too much of this culture of "shooting and crying". I don't like it.' His recent novel, *Good People*, returns to Weimar Berlin to consider how and why an ordinary, unbigoted German might have become a Nazi. Baram also likes fantasy, science fiction, satire: tales that displace or reframe the woes of the present, escape from 'shooting and crying', and so may help to set free the living and the dead.

The shooting and crying continues. Jerusalem, now girdled by one more historic barrier in the form of the Separation Wall that snakes across the surrounding hills, may itself be at an uneasy peace. But wars of words have no ceasefire. In the mid-afternoon heat, I walked for half an hour unhindered along the empty sun-strafed roads from the jasmine-scented elegance of the German Colony in West Jerusalem to the Palestinian village of Silwan. Its densely clustered blocks rise sheer up the Biblical slopes of the

Valley of Kidron. Where Silwan meets the old city, just outside the 'Dung Gate', lies the disputed archaeological site of the so-called 'City of David'. Funded by a private foundation but protected by state security, the excavations here have set rival histories, rival narratives, on a collision course. Did King David hold court here, and do the remains prove the primacy of Jewish settlement on these hills? Or has a miscellany of Roman and Byzantine ruins been pressed into the service of expansionary nationalism? As so often in Jerusalem, the dead – like the entombed terracotta warriors of a Chinese emperor – must stand up and fight the battles of today.

This city, in thrall to several competing cults of ancestor-worship, at the same time refuses to let its dead lie at rest. For excavation, for settlement, for development, the earth is disturbed, transferred, reshaped. Every time a digger punches into soil or shatters rock, it becomes an avowal of belief, a historical assertion - or even an act of war. Over a section of the ancient Muslim cemetery of Mamilla, already long-neglected, the Simon Wiesenthal Centre of Los Angeles plans to build a 'Museum of Tolerance'. For years the arguments alleging desecration have bounced around the media, and lawsuits to halt the excavators have dragged through Israel's courts. The Centre brandishes a dusty fatwa supposedly showing that Muslim authorities long ago agreed to the site's deconsecration. Protestors challenge its validity and call in aid the legions of gravestones, and unmapped layers of human remains, that the bulldozers will erase in the name of Tolerance.

At twilight, I visited Mamilla – or rather, the dusty park in downtown West Jerusalem where you may still wander among its crumbling and forgotten stones. Fine domed tombs (Ottoman, even Mamluk?) stand forlorn. Broken slabs and markers lie strewn across the scrubby grass. The souls laid to rest here over more than a millennium do seem unloved, untended. But I remember that the demographic upheavals of the city – 1948, 1967, and now the burgeoning growth of its Jewish population – has to a great extent severed these dead from their living heirs. Few of those who might tell their story can live around here now.

Ten minutes' walk took me to the open-air cafes tucked away down pretty Ottoman lanes off the Jaffa Road and around Zion Square. Drink a glass of wine; watch the football on the big screen that every bar boasts. An ordinary spring night in a Levantine city: can all those unquiet dead stop their murmuring? Not quite. Suicide bombers targeted these streets many times during the two intifadas; in one pizza joint, fifteen people died. To many of these revellers, the Wall has at last wrapped them in safety and normality. But even the televised soccer won't let us forget the past. Chelsea plays Bayern Munich in the Champions League final (and wins, on penalties). Café crowds lustily cheer on Roman Abramovich's team against the Germans. As for the raucous American kids, let off the parental leash for an uplifting sojourn in the Holy Land, the football fails to hold them. Instead they sing Bob Marley, in the middle of Zion Square: 'One love! One heart! Let's get together and feel all right.'

One morning I took a taxi into the occupied West Bank: so near, and so far. I had arranged to meet the writer and lawyer Raja Shehadeh at his home in Ramallah. His books have, via journals, memoirs, reflections and the rambles of *Palestinian Walks*, charted the erasure of memory and denial of history that military occupation – and now settlement-at-gunpoint – has brought. He sent, to pick me up, a local driver who is also a friend. Hani, I found out later, had a brother who was murdered by an American settler; the killer was, eventually, arrested and brought to trial.

In a taxi with Israeli plates, we drive without stops or blocks into East Jerusalem and through the various lettered zones (A, B, C) that designate degrees of Israeli control – military and civil – or Palestinian autonomy. From the inner suburbs onwards, Hani points out the spread of the settlements. The rooftop furniture of apartment blocks will often act as a flag. Palestinian homes sprout black water-barrels; incomers enjoy a mains connection, and so no giveaway tanks. For a stretch along the road, the Separation Wall has halved the width of the carriageway, provoking delays even without the erratic attentions of soldiers and police. But borders, as always, make markets. Where Israel ends, you may while away the queueing-time by buying apricots and okra, cushions and sunglasses, from roadside stalls.

On the breezy heights of Ramallah, once a summer resort before the accidents of conflict thrust upon it the role of de facto Palestinian capital, a building boom is in progress. International aid money, and finance from the Gulf, has sprinkled cranes over the spring hillsides. Land within the municipality, as Shehadeh tells me at his home, can cost more than in Manhattan. Meanwhile, the chain of Israeli settlements that surrounds the city is now almost complete. 'There's a circle around Ramallah,' he notes. 'Even so, Ramallah is fortunate because it's a wider circle than elsewhere. There is still some land left for expansion.' His house overlooks this vista of endless change, driven onwards by the imperative to entrench the occupation.

Dapper, courteous, his precise, rather lawyerly English a relief from the rhetorical frenzy that Jerusalem can breed, Shehadeh sits and talks in this cool and airy shelter not from, but in, the storm. He oversaw the building of this house, with its panoramic outlook over a history in flux, as an antidote to his sadness and confusion after the disappointment of the Oslo accords in the 1990s. 'I couldn't exist with the chaos without and the chaos within. So I decided to build a house. It was one of the best things I ever did.' In the garden he grows roses and delphiniums; raises Swiss chard and tomatoes. They still thrive on these heights.

Throughout the years of the military and now demographic stranglehold in Ramallah, he has written for the sake of memory, of sanity, of survival. 'I started to keep a diary as soon as the occupation began. It became a kind of refuge for me.' His books (the latest entitled simply *Occupation Diaries*) not only register the progress of the conflict but give a voice and a shape to the harrowed landscape around us.

And, of course, they record his walks. Shehadeh still rambles over the hills where, year by year, residential settlements and army installations have flattened or fragmented features of the terrain that bore witness to past lives. The ground itself told its stories of belonging, over many generations. Now the force of arms has stopped them in their tracks. 'It's not so safe anymore,' he says, 'but there are still walks nearby. It's more advisable to walk with others now, but I like to walk alone. It's something that I miss.'

We have lunch in a first-class restaurant owned by a family from Gaza: fine dining on a front-line. Then we drive out through these long-memoried hills. Shehadeh gestures to the settlements, gleaming in the afternoon sunlight, that now punctuate nearly every slope and summit, and the lattice of army-controlled highways between them. After the first large-scale projects of the 1980s, 'the settlers decided there was safety in numbers,' and so smaller satellites sprang up on the adjacent hills. 'They're quite illegal, built on land with clear titles,' he says. The Israeli judicial system often agrees. 'The courts will grant eviction orders, but the army can't enforce them'.

Shehadeh drives me to a spot with glorious views over the undulating wave-formation of the hills. 'I used to walk here for many years, until I had a bad encounter with a settler.' It was 'nasty but telling'. The man, an

American migrant, at first took Shehadeh for a fellow-incomer and addressed him in Hebrew (which he speaks fluently). Having grasped that he had run across a Palestinian, the settler said, 'Show me your ID.' I was taken aback. I didn't know what to answer. I thought, who are you to ask for my ID?' Later in their stand-off, the American said, 'Unlike you, I'm from here.' Did he really believe in that re-writing of the past, I wonder? 'Yes. He did.' His antagonist blocked the exit route, and eventually called in the army. Scrupulous as ever, Shehadeh takes care to tell me that the soldiers did not side with the settler.

One side of Shehadeh's family had lived in Ramallah for many generations, although they arrived here from east of the Jordan. But their home prior to 1948 lay in Jaffa, where his father practised as a lawyer among Jewish colleagues and friends. After the nakba, his father – like so many – could not accept that the story of their life in that place had simply come to a full stop. 'He thought that we would have to move for a while, not that we would never return.' In the wake of the 1967 war, this idealistic peace-maker, a visionary pioneer of the ever-elusive 'two-state solution', negotiated with David Kimche: the fabled Israeli undercover diplomat and intelligence chief. Hostile leaks and spin scuppered their plans.

Shehadeh tells me about a recent trip to Poland, where he attended a literary conference in Krakow. 'Because of its history, my image of Poland was very dark. But the countryside around Krakow is beautiful, and that brightened my view.' Even now, many first-time visitors to the West Bank might say something very similar. During the conference, delegates had the option of a trip to Auschwitz. Shehadeh declined. For him, the camp's remains demanded more than a charabanc outing. 'I couldn't go to Auschwitz in a group. In such a place, I would need to be alone.'

As we talk, he reflects on the historic losses that individuals and whole peoples have endured in the past century. Every catastrophe is immeasurable, incommensurable. Each of the lost has a unique story. 'In terms of numbers, what happened here was child's play. We lost, in comparison, very few. But there was a crucial difference. We lost a country, an identity.'

Shehadeh recommends that, on the way back into Israel, and Jerusalem, I should leave the safe space of the car at the border and pass through the Qalandiya checkpoint as a pedestrian. It will be an experience I should not miss; and a story to tell. Hani tells me that the passage through this notorious flashpoint can take up to five or six hours. Local families, split by the wire and concrete from relatives, schools and markets, will often need to make the crossing several times a week. A baffling regime of permissions and certificates governs Palestinian rights of passage here. Frustration has often boiled over into riots and demonstrations, with shootings and beatings in reply. But I have the good luck to travel on a quiet Saturday afternoon.

This bleak architecture of division and separation, for all its global renown or even infamy, feels merely shabby, scuffed, run-down. Littered with fag-ends, the tall wire fences and graffiti-strewn waiting area remind me of a municipal bus-station in a depressed English town of the 1970s, or a lower-division football stadium of the same era. I become confused about which narrow cattle-pen walkway I should take, but then stand in line in front of the turnstiles for just under half an hour.

While I wait, only one person is turned back. A young woman in a leather jacket stomps irritably back down the wire defile, her story – and its documentation – having failed some crucial test. 'This is us and that is them' – James Fenton again – 'This is Jerusalem.' At last, the tall turnstiles click and spin me through, and my belongings pass through a battered scanner. Finally, I can see the guards: three young women soldiers, national-service age, in a cramped office. One inspects my passport when I place it on a reader. No questions, except to confirm my nationality and when I entered Israel. As I walk to the exit, she calls out to me: 'Have a nice day!'

AKHIT JADOO

Fahmida Riaz

Crossing the dense opaque haze of three thousand years appears the figure of a woman whose name was Akhit Jadoo.

She is mentioned in early Sassanid stories, but that does not necessarily place her in that era. Just as in the writings of any period of history, characters and stories of an earlier age may appear, she could have been there in the Achaeminid age, or perhaps she existed even further in the past.

She arrived in the city of Susa in Mesopotamia, but from where? It is difficult to answer that with any certainty. The only thing that is clear from ancient Iranian literature is that she had the power of inflicting death, and the palms of her hands could emit rays of fatality and annihilation.

Had she come from Samra, on the other side of the Euphrates? Or was she a daughter of the Jadav or Yadav tribe? Did she use to milk their cows and had arrived in Susa riding a bull? Or had she come to the fertile valleys of Iran on the back of a bedecked camel, crossing in a year the immense desert? Did she belong to some Shaman tribe dancing on the shores of the Caspian Sea, absorbed in meditation and worship of the unknown, their activities dictated by the spinning of the stars?

In any case, in Susa and its environs she was seen travelling on a white horse.

Akhit Jadoo was always clad in a red cloak. She was a tall woman of about thirty, her lithe limbs moulded by hard labour. The pupils of her eyes were dark green and her long black hair fell to her waist. Around her head she wore a wreath of red flowers. Wherever it was that she came from, Akhit Jadoo was without doubt descended from learned men who set store by wisdom and a ready wit. This can be presumed because she was wise and quick witted to an extraordinary degree and was well versed in the various branches of knowledge extant in her day.

The lower parts of her pelvis and thighs were marked with slanting white stretch marks which looked like beams of the rising sun and were evidence of the fact that she had given birth to healthy children. She filled these with silver colour. Her breasts had shrunk a little after she weaned her children and she kept them tied with a soft, silken cloth under her red vestments. She rode upright on horseback and an early acquired habit of deep reflection had made her indifferent to life and its extinction.

She had arrived in Susa on her clever, fleet footed horse, crossing hills and valleys where large, black eyed deer with tall, erect antlers hid themselves in the cedar woods startled by the tramping of hoofs. On the way she passed rows of laborers carrying mining tools wrapped in rags, headed for the mountains, where under the watchful eyes of the ruler's soldiers metals were being separated from mud in large bronze cauldrons and smelted in furnaces of different sizes. Unfolding in the distance could be seen fields, where the business of life was going on. On both sides of the path birds twittered in the pine trees, and waving its plume in the air a woodpecker pecked the bark of a tree.

With Akhit Jadoo was a leather bag which she had filled on the way with water from a lake. The only other object she had was a quiver of small arrows which hung on one side of the horse. Very rarely, she would fit an arrow to the bow and shoot a wild duck or some other bird. She would then roast her quarry and eat it. A leather cask full of buttermilk which somebody had given her in the city where she had last stopped, had long been empty. In the many days that she had been travelling she had filled her stomach mostly with wild pomegranates and quince. So she was hungry and exhausted when she reached the environs of the city.

She dismounted at an inn which stood on a lush green plane. Tying the horse to a tree she knocked at the door of the inn.

The innkeeper was a short statured man. He hailed from Khata, from where his ancestors had migrated and come to live in this land. Even before they came, many of their compatriots were settled here, and so it happened that many of the innkeeper's employees were from the same race as he. He was among all of them the most prosperous, and was a cheerful, businesslike person.

He regarded Akhit Jadoo with interest and noticed that she had no goods to sell. Few women ever stayed in his inn all by themselves, though on rare occasions this did happen, so he wasn't too surprised. He asked her, 'Where is your luggage?'

'I have no luggage,' Akhit Jadoo replied. My horse is in the garden, please tell your servants to take him to the stable. I will stay in your inn for a day and a night.'

'I have a suitable room for you. But can you afford to pay for it?' the innkeeper asked her.

'At present I don't have the money, but I'll have it by tomorrow evening.' She replied.

The innkeeper asked her with a smile, 'How will you find the money by tomorrow evening?'

Akhit Jadoo replied, 'I will make a bet with the wise men and intellectuals of the city and challenge them. Then I will win the bet and take the money.'

The innkeeper pondered this for a while and said, 'But what if you don't win the bet?'

'I won't lose. You can be sure of that.'

The innkeeper hesitated no more. After all, the woman before him, clad all in red, wished to stay for just one night. By evening the next day everything would be clear. So why not let her stay?

'Come in,' he said to her, and when she had entered he asked her, 'Tell us what you need.'

'Three good meals,' she told him, 'and hot water to bathe in. I also want a servant to wait on me.'

The innkeeper showed her to a large room with a comfortable bed. He then sent a hardworking young man to serve her. The young man filled an enormous stone basin in the hammam with warm water and offered her an assortment of fragrant herbs to rub on her body. Akhit Jadoo unfastened a simple leather belt that she was wearing round her waist, and went to take her bath.

When she returned, refreshed by her bath, the servant had spread a cloth and laid out a meal for her. He offered her a cup of excellent red wine, after which he served her a meal of Aash chicken, roasted venison, fresh raw vegetables from the inn's garden, and chilled water. At the end of the meal the servant brought her a basin of hot water with rose petals floating on it and a fine cotton cloth to dry her hands on.

Then Akhit Jadoo addressed him, 'O thoughtful servant, I am pleased with your service. What is your name?'

The servant told her his name, Hoshi Aang.

Then Akhit Jadoo said to him, 'I am going to rest now. I give you the task of announcing in the city that tomorrow Akhit Jadoo is going to give the citizens some riddles to solve. Whosoever wishes can participate in solving the riddles, but if he fails to solve them he will have to die. However if somebody does solve them it is Akhit Jadoo who will die.'

Hoshi Aang's eyes widened but he said not a word. He was leaving silently when Akhit Jadoo ordered him, 'Draw the curtains.'

'The window opens into the garden. It is night now and insects will come in from the garden if the curtains are drawn.'

'Hang up a fine cloth to stop them.'

Hoshi Aang complied. Then he said, 'The moon is not out yet. There's only darkness outside.'

Akhit Jadoo stretched out on the bed. 'Yes, let the darkness come in,' she said with the trace of a smile. 'The darkness of the sky enters the body, Hoshi Aang. It brings peace to the blood and the flesh. . . Put out the light before you go.'

Hoshi Aang put out the fat flame of the candle with one sweep of his kerchief.

He entered the city of Susa on foot. Night had just fallen and in the middle of the crossroads lamps had been lit around pavilions. The city elite were drinking wine, and surrounded by musicians they were listening to songs. On some of the pavilions the rich were playing the game of dice on a checked cloth. Elamite slaves, alert and respectful, were diligently serving them.

Hoshi Aang announced Akhit Jadoo's message at several of these junctions. There was some agitation among the citizens on hearing the message, but blended in the agitation was anticipation, and so, the message was soon conveyed to some select intellectuals and scholars of the city.

The following day Akhit Jadoo asked Hoshi Aang to take her to the central intersection of the city. The servant held the reins of the horse and led her into the city.

A carpet had been spread on a large pavilion at the central crossroads of the city and bolsters had been placed on the carpet. Akhit Jadoo took her place on the pavilion, sitting down with the dignity of a queen. When she raised her hand motioning for silence, the noise at the intersection stopped at once.

'Citizens of Susa,' she began, 'you know my conditions. Is there among you one so sagacious and learned that he can find the answer to my riddle?'

At these words there was dead silence in the crowd. Then, gradually, a wave of murmurs arose. Akhit Jadoo's condition, that those who could not find the solution to her riddle would be exterminated, was not new. In fact it was an old tradition. They had heard stories that came to them over long distances; stories that told them that stalwarts guarding some cities hid every part of their body except their face in lion skin. They would ask people who entered the city to solve their riddle. If the new arrivals managed to solve the riddle they would be allowed to enter the city but if they failed to do so they would be killed there and then at the threshold to the city gates. The world and the universe were unsolved. To unravel them, to build cities, to win wars, to find food, to enjoy oneself, everything had to be resolved. Those who could put their intelligence, their wisdom, their curiosity, their quick wittedness, their logic to work, they alone were entitled to respect and importance. Radiant cities needed intelligent people and there was no room in them for fools.

Who does not love his life? Yet rugged young men have travelled far and wide, carrying their weapons, fighting wars, putting their lives on stake to gain wealth and distinction. Riled at the challenge to their intelligence, some of the wise men of the city came forward and agreed to take up the dare.

Akhit Jadoo had them sit facing her on the pavilion. They were altogether twenty people. She then addressed them, 'If you are killed everything that you own now will be mine. Do you agree to that?' The twenty wise men agreed to this condition.

'And now I present all my belongings to you,' said Akhit Jadoo as she untied her simple leather belt from her waist and laid it on one side of the carpet. 'For after we are dead nobody will be able to touch our unholy bodies.'

Among the crowd assembled there Akhit Jadoo spotted the inn's servant and signaled to him. He came to the pavilion and began to empty the wise men's pockets of their cash. In no time there was a pile of coins on the carpet. Another, glittering pile came up as the combatants' jeweled belts, gold and silver ornaments, buttons, bracelets and rings were heaped.

Akhit Jadoo said, 'I give you until sundown to solve the riddle.'

And then she gave them the riddle: 'Honorable wise men, what is it that has ten feet, three heads, six eyes, six ears, two tails, three male organs, two hands, three noses, four horns and three backs, and it bestows life and strength on the world?'

The wise men and the throngs surrounding the pavilion were listening attentively to the riddle. The wise men thought hard but no amount of thinking yielded the solution. Finally they started asking her for clues.

'Is it something that is living?'

'Part of it is living and part of it is not.'

At this the people were even more perplexed. All they knew was that something could either be living or dead.

'What colour is it?'

'White, black, dark and light brown.'

'What does it smell like?'

'Like the earth when it is in the earth. Like water when it is in the water.'

'It must be an animal. Can we eat it?'

'One part of it is desirable, one part is undesirable, and one part is inedible.'

The wise men went deeper into thought. Time was passing, and the horizon began to turn rosy as the sun prepared to set.

Akhit Jadoo announced to the waiting crowd, 'Sirs, the time is over. The wise men of Susa have lost the bet they had entered into with you as witnesses'.

The crowd around the pavilion was frozen, their eyes aghast with shock and fear.

Akhit Jadoo raised her hands and turned her palms towards the wise men. In a flash they were all dead.

Akhit Jadoo gathered all the money and jewels, and stood up to leave with Hoshi Aang.

Sounds of wailing and sobbing rose from the crowd at the death of the wise men. But the citizens knew that it had all happened as per the terms of the bet and consequently they could not punish Akhit Jadoo. Gradually the low caste corpse bearers arrived on the pavilion. The bodies had to be first taken to their homes.

Akhit Jadoo returned to the inn with all the goods. She sold them to the innkeeper and traders who were the guests of the inn. She paid the inn-keeper the asking price for her stay and told him that she would leave the following day.

At night the servant prepared her bath water and the paraphernalia that went with it. After dinner when Akhit Jadoo indicated that she wished to sleep, the servant came and stood by her bed and said to her: 'Oh woman clad in red, a plough to which two oxen are tethered and of which the tiller is a man.'

Akhit Jadoo froze on hearing the right answer to her riddle. With difficulty she brought out the question, 'How did you know?'

Hoshi Aang replied, 'I was a farmer before I was employed by the inn. I had two white oxen. I sold them and paid off my father's debt. Then I took up employment at this inn.'

Akhit Jadoo thought for some time, then said, 'No wonder you were able to guess. The wise men of the city don't go to the fields. They could never find the answer, of this I was sure. But if you had solved the riddle why didn't you say so during the contest?'

Hoshi Aang replied, 'I didn't want to kill you.'

For a while Akhit Jadoo observed him. Wafts of fragrance came from an earthenware burner in a corner of the room, and the room was drenched in a pleasant scent.

'Well, so what do you want of me now?' she asked him.

'Nothing', he answered dejectedly. Maybe I would have liked to sleep with you . . . but not anymore.'

'Intercourse!' Akhit Jadoo repeated softly. If the truth were told, with her very first glance of him a fleeting thought of sex with this handsome, sprightly male had entered her head. But her mind had been preoccupied then and till the end of the contest with other thoughts. It had been ponder-ing on problems which were extremely serious—payment of her rent, acquiring the money. She wanted to collect the money and return to her homeland. She had been successful in her mission that day and her success had filled her with confidence and generosity.

She got up from her bed and came to the arched window in the room. Pushing away the thin screen she looked at the yellow quarter moon melting in the dark blue sky, with the waxing and waning of which she kept an account of her menstrual cycle.

Satisfied, she turned to Hoshi Aang. Yes gladly, intercourse! Handsome Hoshi Aang, you are wise and intelligent. As for me, I have just these few nights when I can savor pleasure without fear of pregnancy. For I do not want to give birth to more children.'

'Yes' said Hoshi Aang, his voice wilting, 'I know that women are familiar with this kind of sinister magic and can overcome pregnancy by intriguing with the moon and their dirty blood.'

Akhit Jadoo gazed at him with her unfathomable eyes, her green pupils glimmering in the candlelight.

Hoshi Aang said to her, 'With your harsh conditions for the riddle you have killed twenty wise men of the city.' He pressed the two sides of his head. 'I have a dreadful headache—taking you in my arms would be like embracing death'.

Akhit Jadoo spoke gravely, 'Had I not done what I did, the phony wise men of this city would have certainly killed me, though the thought does not frighten me. When I gamble it is always death for the loser—on whichever side. O handsome servant, I am just! It is what goes on in this city that is unjust. On the way here there are hills where along with the dead are thrown old people who are still alive—all food for the hovering birds.'

'They are not able to walk', Hoshi Aang said, 'They are so old that most of them can neither see nor hear. They are like the dead.'

'Like the dead!' Akhit Jadoo repeated sarcastically. 'But they were alive. It is not just a matter of the five senses, if there is desire in the heart one is alive. Day and night you people kill your parents. Isn't that true?'

'Perhaps,' replied Hoshi Aang, and blowing out the flame in the lamp he left the room. As instructed he stood at the door all night, guarding it—and shedding tears. Hoshi Aang's family venerated their old more than she could imagine. Where his ancestors came from old people, living or dead, were worshipped. If anyone asked them who their creator was they would without hesitation name their father and grandfather. Those were their creators and their gods. It was for them that Hoshi Aang's ancestors prepared sumptuous food every year, burned incense over it and then distributed it among the poor.

Akhit Jadoo kept gazing at the sliver of moon through the window. She was missing her children and her parents. She would try to return home soon. She had however earned so much in this her last expedition that her family would be able to live a life of ease and comfort. She thought of the innkeeper's handsome servant who had caused her blood to race, and smiled in the darkness. But far more powerful bonds, those of blood, were drawing her to them. She closed her eyes and fell into a deep sleep.

The next morning Akhit Jadoo came into the inn's garden to take her leave. Before he brought her horse to her Hoshi Aang said to her, 'O woman in red, why don't you adopt a profession different from peddling riddles that end in death? Among the wise men you killed there was one who knew the game of numbers. He counted a certain number of goods and as he counted them he described their qualities. The people who gathered to hear him were pleased, and filled with contentment at sharing his insights and wisdom they made offerings to him.'

Akhit Jadoo looked at Hoshi Aang's swollen eyes and understood that he had been weeping all night. She was deeply moved. What had made him weep? Was he weeping for the people she had killed or were his tears for her? She sighed, and wanted to place a hand on Hoshi Aang's shoulder but demurred. She went and sat under a shady tree and motioned Hoshi Aang to sit facing her. Halfheartedly, he sat down and began to gaze at her.

Akhit Jadoo regarded him attentively, then said, 'The basis of man's being is the figure 25. Initially it is divided into five parts: One's destiny, deeds, disposition, personal proclivities, and what one inherits from one's parents. Five things are associated with destiny: One's husband or wife, children, longevity, wealth, and power. Associated with one's destiny are: Man's spirituality, military expeditions, agricultural products, goodness, and evil. Resulting from his disposition are: sexuality, quality of his work, his food and drink, physical activity, and sleep. Linked to his personal proclivities are: his love, hate, honesty, falsehood, and degree of self regard. And as for what he inherits, it is: his body, mind, awareness, intelligence and physical strength.'

Hoshi Aang had been listening to her wide-eyed. At last he spoke, 'If all that is true we are powerless!'

Akhit Jadoo laughed. 'You are free in your actions—well a little helpless, but mainly free. And so goes on the warp and waft of life. Have you ever seen a loom?'

Finally, astonished and bewildered, Hoshi Aang asked her, 'If you are so skilled with numbers, why do you not make them your profession?'

Cornered, Akhit Jadoo replied, 'Because, Hoshi Aang, I have the power to kill. You are a man and your physical prowess and weapons give you the power to kill. You are a servant of the inn. You have forgotten that to live in safety on this earth one needs to be able to kill. I live by my wits. As for taking life, the two—life and death—are twins, and both are present in God. And this is in keeping with His scheme.'

Then with a laugh she said, 'Has not the new game of dice reached your city? It is known as chosar and it is being developed in lands that lie at the foot of snow-covered mountains. Its rule is that a riddle must be provided for every riddle that is asked.'

'I am not as learned as you,' replied Hoshi Aang.

'But you are acquainted with Yazdan (the Zoroastrian deity)? Riddles are made from Him.'

Hoshi Aang had been living here for three generations and was acquainted with Yazdan. In his ancestral land they called him Yasa.

Akhit Jadoo stood up. A yellow leaf fell on her head and was caught in her black hair. It prompted Hoshi Aang to pick up a garland of red roses from a wicker basket and wrap it round her hair.

Akhit Jadoo smiled and said, 'Thank you.'

But Hoshi Aang's face did not shed its sadness.

He said, 'Bu Yasa is only one, a single force.'

'What!' Akhit Jadoo exclaimed. 'Don't say that, lest the earth and the sky are displeased with you and wage a war within you; for they are inside us too.'

'Listen Hoshi Aang,' she said tenderly. She imagined putting her hand under his chin. In reality she could not do that. Just a look of love and no more. More would have been impudent. It would have been impolite to touch him, for the inn's servant seemed not in the mood for amour.

She spoke patiently, 'the answer to my first riddle was "tilling the earth". The agents were not one but three—the bull, the plough and the farmer. Similarly the yazdat—they are numerous. And though they are pitted against one another, at times they also work together. Only then can there be the appearance of oneness. But it is just an appearance, not reality.' Akhit Jadoo sighed and thought, 'How much simpler it is for the artless common people to believe in the oneness of Yazd!'

She mounted the horse, then bent down to say to Hoshi Aang, 'And now show me the way to the town of Karkha.'

For a while Hoshi Aang gazed at her, then he replied: 'Outside the city walls, ride along the river Karkha with your back to the zaggorat . You will pass some hillocks. Some distance beyond those and across the river is the town. A large bazaar is held there today.'

For a long time Hoshi Aang watched the woman ride away, until she disappeared behind the tall city walls. Finally he returned to the inn, sadly, and began to dig out edible roots from the garden. He hated slaughter; so did his father and his grandfather. His grandfather had fled the country of Khatta with his family one night in order to escape conscription. They had sought the path through narrow valleys through which horses sped, their manes waving, headed for new pastures, and migrating from Katta beyond which lay the vast, boundless planes of their home.

Hoshi Aang's people had settled in the fertile valleys. They worked as farmers and servants, blacksmiths and potters; and when they could escape conscription they were people who lived happily with their crops and their children. Yes, but from the seeds sometimes arose magnificent revolutionaries and prophets. There were upheavals in the world and the order of life changed, until calm prevailed once again.

Akhit Jadoo rode along the river. There were clusters of orange trees on the way and the air was scented with the fragrance of their blossoms. Fishermen sat in their boats or on the river bank, catching fish. Seven boats with water mills in them stood along the bank of the river. The water mills were working and flour from the grain moved through the troughs to fall into great basins. The steady garr garr of the water mills calmed Akhit Jadoo's nerves. She brought her horse to the edge of the river and let him drink the water.

She resumed her journey under a clear blue sky. In a little while she spotted a trading caravan on its way to the town of Karkha. Spurring her horse forward she soon joined it.

This was how Akhit Jadoo wandered from town to town posing her riddles. It is said that Jadoo never returned home, for in one town her own insight and acumen were challenged by a man called Faraz Farzana, who laid down the terms she herself used to dictate.

Akhit Jadoo told this man, 'I'll ask you thirty riddles, but only one on each day.' Faraz Farzana consented to this. So every day she gave him a riddle to solve, and he solved it correctly, until the end of the thirtieth day when the sun had turned one full circle on its axis.

Then Faraz Farzana said to Akhit Jadoo, 'Now under your own terms I will ask you a riddle and you will have until sundown to solve it.' She agreed to take up the challenge.

And this was the riddle that he posed: 'What is the name of the tree on which man grows and then wilts? A tree, half of whose leaves remain in sunlight while the other half are in the dark; a tree that is always fresh and green; that is always seen moving in circles but never steps on its own footprints, and actually its movement is horizontal; whose volume remains the same but it is constantly growing?'

Akhit Jadoo was not able to solve this riddle, the answer for which was 'Time'. She was therefore killed. Perhaps she had given her possessions to someone to take to her home, or maybe along with her life she had staked her possessions on winning, and lost. For, this venture was a gambling venture with its own sanctity, in which victory and defeat were ineluctable. All that can be said with any certainty is that the people of Iran, both the highborn and the lowly, remembered Akhit Jadoo and her riddles for thousands of years, and with time they renounced the practice of tossing aged living human beings on some hill where they would become food for carnivorous birds.

But was her name really Akhit Jadoo? Or was that a moniker people had given her which became famous as her name? In ancient Egyptian 'Akhit' was what they called the sphinx and other similar smaller statues, which are images of those who used to pose riddles.

Do practices that gain currency despite being forgotten live amongst us for thousands of years? In my childhood whenever there was an exhibition in town or if a circus arrived, it always figured in one of its entertainment stalls a heavily made up woman half of whose body was cleverly camouflaged in tiger or leopard skin. Believing her to be half woman and half beast, we used to regard her with fear and astonishment.

I want to dedicate this story to a woman whose name I do not know— maybe it was Akhit Jadoo. I met her on an aeroplane. She came from some village in Karnatak and she was riding not a horse but a plane. She had left her village for the first time and was riding a plane for the first time too. She was on her way to Dubai to work as a domestic servant in some shaikh's household, for her children's sake—she had three children. She told me about her children in sign language for she knew not a word of Hindi or English. I had filled her landing card too, and that too gave me information about her.

How many such Akhit Jadoos there are in the world today—magical women! They travel from distant villages of Burma, the Philippines, India, Bangladesh, riding the fleet-footed steed of our age. Many will go back to their homes, but perhaps some, like their prototype Akhit Jadoo, will never return.

(Translated from Urdu by Amna Azfar)

FOUR POEMS

Sabrina Mahfouz

If freedom had a colour what would it be?
The Egyptian flag has three:
red; black; white –
none of these seem quite right.
Black is the colour of asphalt
which no longer keeps
just feet on the ground.
White is the flash of flesh caught
in headlights, face scarf-less,
body undressed by eyes regardless
of how many layers it does or doesn't wear.
Red is for virginity tests, the blood that
might or might not flow,
just so that you know that she knew
she'd never be free
whatever the result might be.
There is an eagle on the flag too,
suspended in the middle,
wings clipped, dipped in wax.
If it makes it up to the light
and lets the wax melt –
unafraid of what lies underneath,
what then?
Will it find it is just one layer,
a sheath?

With the last drip will
the feathers shine and
the sky no longer seem
so high?

In the Revolutionary Smoking Room

Open the window. Isn't it –
despicable deplorable disgraceful suspicious untenable untouchable delightful delicious unbelievable unstoppable grateful curious
tweetable filmable this is fucking serious
debatable inflatable never ever tedious
remarkable reliable spiteful pretentious
responsible blameable beautiful ferocious
– Yes. Can I have another cigarette please?

Stolen time

Where does it go?
Whose pocket does it fill?
Will it spill out one day
from storage barrels?
Will it be aged and vintage,
with a smoother,
more sophisticated taste?
Will who gets to sip it be based
on social status or wealth
or health or race or gender?
Or will it just be free for whoever
finds the cellar where it's been stored?
Do they turn it to ensure it doesn't go bad?
I can imagine that stolen time could
let off quite a whiff if they don't take care
of it properly, with professional services
contracted out to the best in the field.
Maybe it is at a digital-detox spa?
Enjoying growing tall and fat and not being
spat at with each new email.

Eating nutritious meals in preparation
for being the very best time it can be
when it gets back to the real world.
I just hope it didn't find itself
in a pocket with a hole in it –
and so many pockets have holes don't they!? –
spilling down into the hem of a coat
or jeans or jacket – machine washed
or dry-cleaned – never to be seen again.
Anything but that and I'm almost sure
it will come back.

Dating in Cairo

Tree trunks so huge
you could hug
and not touch hands -
which would certainly
suit some people's plans.

AN INDIA AGO

Michael Wolf

Among the most travelled Hajj routes over the last five centuries are those between India and Mecca. The details in this poem are based on conversation with an Indian friend who described the Hajj his father and grandfather made in 1939. Like so much else to do with the Hajj, the journey described here, which took place a mere 70 years ago, would be unrecognisable today. This is why I have entitled the poem *An India Ago*. In it, very old pilgrims say goodbye to those they suspect they may never see again as they set out for Mecca.

Weighed down
With autumn garlands,
The pilgrims guide their horses door to door,
Bidding the neighborhood good-bye,
Cool tears brimming on their eyelids.

The old ones under parasols
Have made their wills.
Some won't be coming back.
They're bound for Mecca, to greet the shrine
And keep a date with Allah.

Trumpets,
Roses, rice grains
Rain down on their saddles as they pass.

Beyond the gates the cheering fades.
A sun-baked plain takes over.

They'll board a train tonight
On the Bombay road.
They won't mind hard wood seats in a third-class carriage.
They've known each other since childhood.
Wed young to distant kin

They have each other,
As silver limbs
Have leaves on trees, in those Mogul paintings
Small as playing cards
Where sultans picnicked centuries ago.

Though fortunate in this
And feeling blessed,
Some will meet their end before they get there,
Breathing their last on choppy seas
In a freighter bound for Jeddah,

Or slake their thirst
From stagnant streams
And, reaching Mecca fevered, lie at dawn
In a stranger's tent, faint breath clouding
A small mirror.

Or later come to grief on the way home.
It doesn't matter.
Made glad by what may sadden us
They take their leave together,
Departing in a way that makes them glad.

SYRIAN SCENARIOS

Manhal al-Sarraj

1. A person suffering from autism stands in front of the camera and makes us witness the scars of the whipping and electrocution on his chest, legs and arms. His eyes are swollen, his cheeks black and blue, his lips split, yet he continues to smile. He is happy to be filmed and to soak up the attention.

2. The little girl lost her mother. Everyone was preoccupied with escorting the martyr to her final resting place, with the revolution, with the slogans. The girl closed the door behind her and drew an image of her mother with chalk on the floor of the room. Beside it she wrote 'Mummy'. She fell asleep embracing her drawing.

3. One wounded ankle is bleeding, the other is covered by a sock adorned with a red ball. A girl, four years of age, with a shoe size of 27, was not rushed to hospital. They treated her in the same way that they treated all the patient revolutionaries – at home, in hiding, and without anaesthetic. As the bullet was removed from her ankle, she screamed in pain. The doctor tried to calm her: 'Soon the pain will be gone!'

4. A three-year-old child knew his faith and his Lord, knew his friend from his foe, knew his path from the moment they killed his mother. He led protests every day, chanting 'Allahu Akbar, takbeer! Allahu Akbar, takbeer! The President will fall!' And he would repeat, 'Allahu Akbar, the People Want the Execution of the President!' He looks in anger from the corner of his eye and inspires those present to follow his lead and to also call: 'Takbeer! Takbeer!'

5. Hiding in underground passages, sitting on a ragged rug and shifting their weight from side to side, drinking maté, dreaming of freedom and justice,

and talking in quiet and quivering voices. They discuss politics and sing; yet at every moment they are under threat of being raided and attacked, tortured, killed, and cut up into pieces.

6. The family wrapped up their martyred son, laid him on two wooden ledges, and tied the corpse with rope. They said, 'Bismillah ur-rahman ur-rahim, In the name of the Most Gracious, the Most Merciful.' They threw the rope to the neighbouring alleyway; the people of the alleyway pulled him along, and then they in turn threw the rope to the next alleyway. Passing in this way from neighbourhood to neighbourhood, their murdered son, shot by gunfire, tied to two ledges, and under continuous gunfire, arrived safely at his grave. In one voice all the alleyways repeated: 'Alhumdulillah! Alhumdulillah! Thank God! thank God!'

7. Her father arrived home dead. The sound of the mother's, aunts' and the whole family's wailing could be heard everywhere. A girl amongst them screamed: 'But this isn't my dad! My dad is more beautiful than this.'

8. Two young men remained for months in the city of wonders. One wrote lyrics and the other sang. The first would randomly write word after word without rhythm or care and the second would happily sing, both of them in harmony and mutual understanding. Hearing them, the residents of the sad city became happy. They would meet every day and gather around these young men calling for the fall of the tyrant and they clapped as they sang. One day the television announced that the singer had been killed. The people were shocked. Then they disregarded this news which did not concern them. So no-one knows how the two voices survived; one would write lyrics and the other would sing and warble. The residents of the city, whose number grew steadily less as they were killed, continued to protest and to call their slogans unceasingly.

9. When the lover was informed, she came at great speed. Pouncing without any thought, she began kissing the face and cheek of her husband's corpse. Her tears fell; she lifted his head and buried it in her chest. Tilting her head and scolding him fiercely, then kissing his face and cheeks and stroking his skin softly. Her headscarf and coat were coming undone. Her

sister called: 'Come here!' The woman did not hear; she was entirely unaware of her lack of modesty.

10. The young man leaping up from between the protestors, the veins on his neck bulging, his index finger raised, shouts: 'I am not an animal.'

11. The man's palm caresses the corpse of his murdered son. He tries to swallow his tears so that he can clearly and in a manly fashion describe the manner in which his son was killed at the protest. Yet the piercing camera sees through his attempts to compose himself. The lens does not turn a blind eye to the man's condition as he had hoped; in fact it exposes all the tenderness in his voice, his weakness and his pain.

12. The mother looks in bewilderment on the moving casket which is carrying her son away, her eyes unbelieving, yet she continues to repeat, reassuring herself and those who hear her, from the Lord in the heavens to His creatures on earth, that her son is a martyr.

13. Exiled, far away, alone, he follows his motherland's revolutions, wishing, craving, laughing, crying, screaming, praying – and when his loved ones are killed, he kneels down in prayer. He screams aloud with his hand covering his mouth. No one hears or sees him in this state. When he is done wailing, he washes his face and returns to his seat in front of the computer. He follows the news, wishing, laughing, screaming, praying – and when his loved ones are killed, he kneels down in prayer.

14. The person, who doesn't understand anything of what is happening except his pain, rushes to the frontline, threatens and promises, then reprimands the world for its negligence – and when he calms down he states an opinion.

15. In his grief the distant citizen yearns to shackle the hands of the aggressors who are fiercely beating their victims, while he watches via the television screen.

16. Pupils at school are chanting with the revolutionaries as if they were adults. Their mothers are waiting at home. These pupils, or at least some of them, may not return, even though their mothers are awaiting their return so that they may bathe, have supper and sleep.

17. He abstained from international festivities. He crouched in the corner replaying all that had happened. He was overcome with sorrow. He thought he'd be able to strap himself with bombs and blow up the world. Later on, with a trembling heart, he was on the verge of surrendering to tears. By the time Valentine's Day arrived his heart was numb and the criminals were victorious.

NIGHT OF DESTINY

Alev Adil

We who speak with the sky, we, covered with dew, the mineral dancers feared by the nights, we the tamers of breezes, the charmers of birds, the guardians of silence.

Louis Aragon, *Paris Peasant* (1926)

It was my last night in that city. I'd been looking for her all day, dodging the traffic, the beggars, the rumours of war. Life is beautiful but cheap there. Even the poor buy flowers, they are a necessity. How cruelly the powerful reason need, the poverty of their imaginations. I slipped from the throng, the stormy heat into the cool, calm, security-guarded luxury of the hotel. The concierge had a package for me. It was from her. There was a notebook, a sporadic diary, many pages made illegible with drawings and scribbles, newspaper cuttings and photographs pasted over her barely legible hand. She had attached a note in her spidery script:

You won't find me. I've already gone. What do you want? Evidence I presume. Here is my life, if you have learnt to love me. If you haven't it will mean nothing. Burn this. Burn everything.

First through ramshackle, forgotten, often purely imaginary libraries in Üsküp, Istanbul and Etropole, then through misty, muddy ghosts of battle-fields, I had followed her from the westernmost border at Vienna to the Field of Crows, where murders still circle in ragged dusty black geometries over-head; then onto the lands of the fire worshippers, where flames burst out of the mountainside. I distinctly heard her name on the wind at Hala Sultan Tekke by the Salt Lake. I had almost caught her shadow at Sarkej Roza, but this is not my story. You don't need to know why I was, I admit it, still am searching for her. Is it hopeless, naïve, misguided, this furtive compulsion of mine? You don't need to answer that either. My sister, my sister of the eclipse, this is her story.

This is all she has given me. I took her at her word, I took it for an autobi-ography, a night journey through a veiled self, marked by a bunch of dog-eared photographs, an expired passport under an assumed identity and these fragments in a slim brown leather notebook. As I read her words I'm writing my story.

I am drunk on thirst, drunk on hunger, drunk on loneliness, here at the edge of the desert, in a Palace of Mirrors, writing as the twilight reaches for the dusty red horizon of Jaipur, waiting for the night of destiny, waiting for the night of power. As though such fragments were prayers. Believe nothing.

Burn this, burn everything.

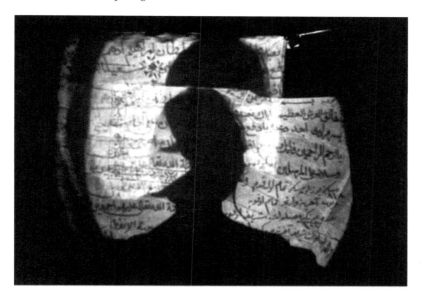

3.03.2003: Kohl

'How did you live in those days?' I ask myself in the mirror. There is no little girl to ask me 'Mummy, what did you do in the war?' If there was what could I say? 'I waited darling, I waited like Penelope. I wove stories and waited for it all to be over'. The build-up to war drags on, so dreaded it's a torture to wait, so inevitable I almost wish for it to be over. The Prime Minister, no longer in his prime, an elfish man with his thinning dry hair arranged sparsely in a stylist's approximation of casual youthfulness, his face glowing with right-eousness and heavy bronze foundation, assures us there are excellent reasons to invade Iraq. Reasons that might not be clear to us, true, but he promises on his integrity, that there are Good Reasons.

A lot of us hate the idea of the war. Millions of us marched, county ladies in fur coats, ancient decrepit Socialists, fashion victims in stilettoes, people in wheelchairs, Christians, Islamic fundamentalists, New Age hippies, pop

stars, journalists, academics, trade unionists, school children. We all marched
to Hyde Park and stood optimistically waiting in the churned mud. We knew
it was not in our power to conjure up peace, but at least we could speak out
against this war.

'What will you do in the war?' I ask myself in the mirror. My reflection
does not answer as I line my eyes with kohl. The 'Today' programme on BBC
Radio 4 chants away in the background. John Humphreys, the presenter, tries
to wring more than platitudes out of some lackey minister. The dossier. As
the build-up to war drags on, so dreaded, so inevitable, everyday becomes a
re-enactment of the day before. I wake up to rumours of war, go to work,
come home, more on the war, dinner, war again and so on. I line my eyes
more and more heavily with kohl. I noticed this because by February I had
sharpened all my eye pencils down to stubs and had to buy five more from
the Body Shop. I keep one in all my handbags. I had always lined my eyes but
now I find myself reapplying my eyeliner as often as I moisturise my lips with
balm in winter. My look has transformed from a contemporary naturalism to
a sooty oriental glare – part *Arabian Nights*, part Dusty Springfield in her
Memphis years.

13.03.2003: The Lines Resemble a Mask

I line my eyes with kohl. I am not the only one. I started to notice a newly
emerging 'we'. We line our eyes with kohl. In my 'Writing the Self' undergraduate seminar I noticed them, Surreyya, Davina, Mia, Ayesha, Amina, Dilan
and others – I don't know all their names. I noticed their eyes too were heavily
lined. And week by week our eyes seem to grow blacker and blacker. This new
'we' I discerned are a disparate bunch: the Mauritian girl who wants to write
chick-lit; the Kurdish girl who wants to be a journalist; the half Egyptian-half
Italian would-be pop star who models herself on Dalida; the rich Iranian girl
killing time and poisoning herself with self-pity; the angry Sudanese girl with
her headscarf tied tight around her head and the circumspect Bengali girl with
a much larger, more modest headscarf, a huge black silky thing with a Calvin
Klein logo brocaded on it, who refuses to read her work out in the class.

It seems to me that as the build-up to war continues we have become a 'we'
despite the disparity in our ages, ambitions, tastes, cultural references. And
we mark this new belonging with more and more kohl. Mia blackens her eyes

so lavishly that the lines resemble a mask. We never speak of the war in class. If I mention it the conversation dies down. I can sense their disapproval, or reticence, if I raise the issue. Perhaps by bringing it up I'm stealing the safe space of the seminar, a respite from the war, from them. Perhaps they want to disown any connection to the wider world. I don't know.

15.05.2003: The Tracks of a Tiny Bird

The eyeliner issue came up in conversation with Mia. She came to the office I share with Professor Cooper on Wednesday to ask for an extension for her assignment. She complained that she was tired all the time, that she couldn't focus. She'd split up with her boyfriend. She wasn't sleeping. 'I line my eyes more and more heavily' she said, 'like I'm going into battle.'

'Have you noticed, a lot of us, more and more of us, are lining our eyes?' I replied, letting the 'us' hung in air tentatively. This new 'we' is an unspoken collective, too disparate to articulate.

'Yes, it hides fear and fatigue,' she said matter of factly, 'and it is quite in fashion too'. Then after the small silence that ensued, perhaps in acknowledgment of the things we did not speak of, 'I know I do it too much,' she said 'but I don't recognise my naked face as me anymore. It looks too ...'

'Undefended?'

'Boring.'

'Boring?'

'Like everyone else.'

Perhaps our reasons differ but I have begun to feel that we are a tribe, a tribe of women with blackened eyes. We mark ourselves out. Whether we wear Playboy bunny t-shirts or headscarves or both (as Amina did last week), we are not like everyone else. Our eyes grow blacker and blacker. We have become an 'us', not bounded by anything as concrete as religion, culture or language but out of the empty space delineated by exclusion. We have become an 'us' because of a feeling that 'they' are making a 'them' of 'us'. Perhaps it's all in the imagination. Perhaps our eyes grow blacker and blacker principally because 'it is quite in fashion'. I blacken my eyes with kohl, drawing a line around the upper eyelids then passing the soft pencil around the inner rims. I darken the outer line further with Guerlein liquid liner, rich and inky black. However thoroughly I try to clean my eyes before bed, I wake to find little black eye prints, like the tracks of a tiny bird, across the pillow case. I wake to hear John Humphreys grilling the latest government stooge and after I fill the battered stove top espresso maker until it gurgles hot bitter coffee, I line my eyes with kohl.

7.07. 2008: Another Blood Wedding

The eclipse begins.
The moon covers the sun, the ghost of the shadow.
   'Who are you?'
   'Is that you?'
It's so dark.
   'I am the bride of Dih Bala.'
Her dowry is blood, is flesh, is the golden light of the horizon.
Facts are more easily forgotten than feelings.
Rage soon replaces guilt.
We bury desire.
An eternal return of the destiny written on your forehead,
an unreadable heritage,
the mystic writing pad of history.

Memory causes vertigo, a vortex of feelings: desire, altitude sickness, inherited amnesia. We mourn the inability to forget. You remember something has been forgotten. A crystal image of time destroys the past, a full moon of forgetting, to save the future. I'm waiting for the future, *l'avenir*, the one whose arrival cannot be predicted. They are ruined maps, the languages that speak us, your head on my shoulder, your hand in mine. The moon covers the sun again.

25.11.2008: 99 Names

Where is the one who could read the writing on my forehead? The one some suppose me to be, whom others fear I will become. Why do I evade her? I need not fear her scrutiny. I will write my own fate. My grandmother believed that her destiny was written on her forehead. There is Botox to take care of that illegible eternal return now. I can erase my secrets if I need to. Although I know destiny still waits at Samarkand. Death is an absolute silence, a disinterested bureaucrat, however much you dress him up as a lover.

Instead of Names, I speak no Word. I take photographs of all the empty beds I've slept in, the rented rooms in strange towns where in the mornings I'd drink hotel coffee and breakfast alone. The empty beds where I practised stopping waiting for a sign, they're something between a habit and a vocation.

Today I walked the Queen's Necklace, past raggedy unlovely beaches. I did not rest, demons on my heels I continued right up to the greener calm of Malabar Hill. I sat in the park. A murder of crows circled the Well of Silence, guests at a sky burial.

The last time we met you asked me, 'Will you always remember?'

'Let the bury dead bury their dead' was all I could say.

12.01.2009: Nineveh

Girl-becoming-Yunus in the heart of Nineveh, whoever you are, I haven't met you yet. Let me be the whale to carry you away from the carnage. Become an imaginary boy-swallowed-whole, the 'I' being a mouth as well as an eye.

There is a space inside that expands, becomes an empty stadium echoing dread. The ground beneath my feet evaporates.

Falling feeling, feeling falling.

How to map and chart this territory,

its quantic laws, barbaric desires, childish rituals,

the way it shifts from an embrace that marks the lineaments of self

to an infinity or crushing gravity.

The country becomes a cage.

The state becomes a stage.

The home becomes a graveyard.

The school is now a hospital ward.

Yunus-as-a-girl perhaps I can encompass and keep you safe in the emptiness that expands within me, brave half-mad prophet-girl under the jurisdiction of capricious, sometimes bloodthirsty, merciless gods armed with uranium enhanced artillery.

She's wailing on the TV, everyone dear to her suddenly dead. Waiting for a ship to carry her away, a whale to shelter her from the drones, the bombs, for a space of becoming more than a stained flag for love and death.

She is calling 'Throw me into the sea.'

Even a rebellious prophet is cared for by her god.

05.04.2010: There is a War on Love. No One will Win

They loved each other limitlessly, untested by time or habit. She was seventeen when she was made a widow, a black widow in a chador with a Kalashnikov and every revenge sura on her lips. Young enough to relish death, high on her funereal ecstasy, death-minded, drunk on lies about a bloody paradise. She was stabbed in a heart that was broken; shot in a head full of explosion. There is a war on love. No one will win. A sacred heart for a sacred heart. Sacred things too are subject to retaliation.

16.08.2012: A MinuteTaker at the Conference of Birds

My sister, my sister of the eclipse, this is her story. This is all she has given me. I took her at her word, I took it for an autobiography, a night journey through fragments in a slim brown leather notebook. There are some empty pages at the end of the little book. I fill them with my story, waiting for the night of destiny, waiting for the night of power. As though such fragments were prayers. Believe nothing.

Burn this, burn everything.

Something that A wrote reminded me of a time I haven't lived, a place I haven't seen, under an open slate grey sky. I came to the tower (the blue plaque read 'Rapunzel cried here') at dusk, in the autumn. Don't ask me when, I can't remember whether we wore our trousers tight or flared that year, whether we dressed like gypsies, soldiers or porn stars, whose song played everywhere, leaked out in every café and bar. It was in the time of forty days – the measure of time they mark you out with when you are born, when you give birth, when you are lost in the wilderness, after you die. It was that kind of time, which is all the time in the world; is no time: the time you measure when everything no longer makes sense.

I could see the entire world from the tower. All the world I could see was empty. There was no one but me. I sang and the echoes orchestrated me, the wind carried me across the desert. No one heard me. I waited. I waited for the one who tracks my invisible footprints. I waited for the one who knows my name, who comes to find me. Whoever you are, I kept watch for you, a tiny figure on the horizon. Believe me it was a cinematic moment. No one filmed it. No one disturbed the elegant line of the horizon but the great flocks of birds that filled the sky. That winter they flew south at a distance: geese, flamingos, little birds whose names I didn't know. I'd come well prepared for solitude and lots of walking but my knowledge of ornithology was, still is, nil.

I shared the tower with birds. My room was filled with ravens and doves. They cooed. They clawed. They crowded me. I remembered what A wrote, that the Sufi sage had said the doves were our nobler feelings, the ravens our anger, our fear, our doubt. The Sufi said I must free the doves, let them fly free; but should keep the ravens locked in or they'd only return with their malevolence redoubled, to shatter the windows, demolish the tower.

In truth I wanted them all gone. They blurred my vision, got caught in my hair. They deafened me. I tried. I did as he said. But the doves (oh, in my darker moments I see only albino pigeons) kept coming back to roost, breeding in the eaves enthusiastically, back in the overcrowded room again. The ravens grew thin, grew restive, they pecked at me, ate the doves' eggs, hatched conspiracies in the darker corners of the room. I lived in a flurry of feathers: birds battering to get out, birds battering to get back in. And a lot of shit.

Let them all fly. I gave up. I left the tower, climbed down Rapunzel's dead plait, avoiding the thorns that blinded her lover. I set out across the sand. The horizon was a shifting curve ahead, the tower an inky black landmark behind me. I walked my words across the desert, letting the wind delete each phrase easefully with sibilant breaths before a sentence could reach any conclusion. I did not mind. It was a kind of mercy. I walked to find a story, to draw a line and mark a path to the sea. It was a journey. It was a map, a map of forgetting.

The birds were my compass. I knew I'd smell the salt, scent the open sea long before I reached the shore. I'd hear the scream of seagulls. I'd know I had arrived. A vulture kept me company. We shared the same dry sense of humour (useful in a desert). When I despaired he'd reassure me that he'd always stick with me until the end. Then further. When the time came he'd polish my bones, make them pretty. I was grateful. We must strive to keep up appearances, to maintain certain aesthetic standards. We must look our best irrespective of circumstance, despite the puzzling absence of a camera crew or paparazzi. After weeks of waiting we doubted we'd ever find the coast and he tried to comfort me. 'Maybe you should give up on the ocean thing. Maybe that's too excessive an ambition for the season. Why don't we see if we can make it to the Salt Lake for the annual Conference of Birds?' A good idea, surely someone in that mirage of flamingos and nightingales, of eagles and swans, surely one of the delegates would have news? They'd know if there was Someone, the Someone who was waiting not knowing I'd been delayed and lost my way, the One who had set out to find me.

Back in the tower the ravens and the doves flourished and mated. A new species, a sleek grey ghost raven was born. Invisible at dusk and dawn, on a grey winter's afternoon, nameless equivocal creatures, they sang all of happiness, all of sadness, violence and tenderness; all of it and all at once. What is there to say of these mercury spun creatures with the habitual stealth of London's December afternoons, who steal the day from you before you are properly awake, who invade your dreams masquerading as presentiments and omens? They cannot be caged. They cannot be trained and tamed. They'll only sing when they feel like it.

Put your hands on this cage of bone. Feel them beating to escape from my ribs, a burst of wings, of feathered wildness, a beautiful terrible song. Send for the hawk to hunt them. Let it swoop and circle its prey mercilessly: a gorgeous symmetry.

REVIEWS

NIHILISTIC HISTORY

S Parvez Manzoor

'History', roars Tom Holland in a moment of cognitive elation, 'is not built upon sand'. To this we may add: 'No, not on sand but upon quicksand!' For, the deeper one probes the notion of 'history', the more intractable it gets. At best, it proffers an obscure, if not a totally opaque, vision of the human condition. Whether conceived as a record of the human past or perceived as the matrix of human existence, history, like science and as philosophy, reveals the unfathomable ends of Man. As science, it collapses before the question of meaning; as philosophy it exhausts itself overcoming the antinomies of reason. While to be human and to strive for meaningful existence is to impose on the infinity of the world a structure and a form, to bestow it a finitude and a temporality, the paradox is that such a partial world of history and society can only be posited from some premonition of the whole. It can only be derived from a totality that is greater than the sum of its parts. Only an imagination that transcends historical, i.e. temporal consciousness renders it intelligible. History, in other words, acquires meaning from a perspective which itself is meta-historical.

Tom Holland, *In the Shadow of the Sword: The Battle for the Global Empire and the End of the Ancient World*, London: Atlantic Books, 2012

Only in modernity is this insight about the transcendence beyond the finitude of human existence turned upon its head. Only modernity seeks to create meaning by refusing to scan beyond the horizons of history. The meaning of human existence, it claims, is inscribed in the process of 'history' itself and is revealed by the story of 'Civilisation' (of which the West is the para-digm-incarnate). The radical conception of 'history' as pure immanence, however, belongs properly to the modern theory of politics; it proclaims the authority of the modern regime and sanctions its claims to imperial destiny and civilisational mission. Eric Voegelin, a perceptive analyst of modernity, for instance, starts his reflection on *The New Science of Politics* by unceremoni-ously confessing to the identity of history and politics in these words: 'The existence of man in political society is historical existence; and a theory of politics, if it penetrates to principles, must at the same time be a theory of history.' Despite the seemingly innocuous allusion to the universal 'man', this is as parochial an insight, and as provincial a theory, as any. It relates only to the modern age. For, what is novel about the modern scheme of things is not the reciprocity of discourse and power, which may be attributed to every regime, ancient or modern, but the specificity of the conception of 'history' and 'politics' that underpins its imperialist world-order. For the pre-modern man, history is not identical with human existence, nor may the latter be equated with mere historical existence. Further, history as pure temporality, as phenomena without teleology, as events without structure and form, signi-fies nothing. The 'history' that imparts meaning to the modern discourse, on the other hand, is a supremely narcissistic form of self-reflection that articu-lates the ends of the modern, quintessentially western, man. The meaning of history thus lies not in the ebb and flow of time in which every civilisation participates but in its march towards the modern utopia. The human quotient of history, in plainer words, is made subservient to its western component.

Tom Holland's book follows a beaten track of western historical imagina-tion: it rejects Muslim accounts of Islam's 'origin' and assigns the Muslim enterprise no place in the meta-narrative of Civilisation. There is nothing in Islam that is *sui generis*, nor has it any role in the future of humanity. The rejection of Islam, a post-Christian faith that does not fit into a divine scheme of salvation that culminates in the crucifixion and resurrection of Jesus, is implicit in the Christian confession and requires no debate. What must nev-ertheless be underlined is the fact that the secular imagination's belittling of the role of Islamic enterprise, its denial to Islam of any signification in the redemptive history of mankind, does not devolve from a study of history: it is a dogmatic necessity for the ideology of the West. For a sampling of the Orientalist reflection regarding 'Islam as a Problem' (of Western imagination and discourse), we may merely reiterate some earlier statements by Carl Becker, a prominent scholar and Prussian minister of culture and education who institutionalised Islamic Studies in Germany. Some of his insights read:

Islamic civilisation is woven of Western elements, and is, as such, a mixed product; … in spite of its affinity with the Greek world, it is in character entirely different from Western civilisation. Islamic civilisation is Asiatised Hellenism.' … 'The Arabs, the Persians, and the Turks evolved Islamic civilisation from Christian Hellenism… Islam did not take into account the fundamental sociological characteristics of the Arab people… Islam was not the creation of the Arabs…' … 'In scorn of and in gratitude to Arabism, the Prophet preached a Hellenised culture-religion, with a tinge of Hellenistic city-life. It is a matter of indifference whether you trace the inspiration to Judaism or to Christianity. The fact remains that the preaching of Mohamed only attained its full significance when, away from the religious-indifferent, booty-loving tribes of the desert, it was reduced to a system under Judeo-Christian clash and cooperation and was substituted by people, entirely unlike the Arabs in matters religious, in the place of their inherited state-church.' … 'And, with justice, it bears the name of Islam; for, when the fabric of the State fell to pieces, religion, as a spiritual framework, linked with the State, held together the entire cultural inheritance of Islam, and transmitted it far beyond.

Even Arnold Toynbee, the erudite though eccentric theologian of history, had his own take on the 'origin' of Islam, 'the parent society of which the Abbasid State marked the final stage': 'The cataclysmic conquests of the primitive Muslim Arabs seem to respond antistrophically, in the rhythms of history, to the cataclysmic conquests of Alexander. Like these they changed the face of the world in half a dozen years; but instead of changing it out of recognition, more Macedonio, they changed it back to a recognisable likeness of what it had once been before.' Seen in this light, Islam is a response to Hellenism; religiously a rejection of the Hellenised monotheism of Christianity and politically the restoration of 'the genuine Irano-Semitic empire of the Achaemenids'. The 'ultimate source of the Muslim Empire' according to Toynbee's panoramic vision, however, is not to be sought in its Mesopotamian heritage but in the North-Semitic one. Hence, the historian could identify the parent of the Muslim culture and name it 'the Syriac society'. Eventually, however, he has to admit, these roles were reversed, for Islam engendered a ecumenical state which 'endowed the Syriac society with a universal church, and thereby enabled it, after centuries of suspended animation, to give up the ghost in the reassurance that it would not now pass away without leaving offspring; for the Islamic Church became the chrysalis out of which the new Arabic and Iranian civilisations were in due course to emerge'. Or, in plainer language and without the hocus-pocus of redemptive history, Toynbee claims that whatever is original to Islam derives from its Biblical (Syriac) component and its North-Semitic (Umayyad) Empire. The Abbasid (Irano-Semitic) synthesis is of little consequence, historically or ideologically. Needless to say, for all his fidelity to the historian's vocation, Toynbee's pronouncement does not impress us as a feat of historical imagination, for it merely restates the theological claims and prejudices of his religious convictions. (Significantly, contemporary revisionist scholarship is equally obsessed with these twin sources of Islam's formative discourse, Hellenised theology and Umayyad politics, and refuses to negotiate with the Abbasid sources. In this regards, it has hardly progressed beyond Toynbee's speculative theo-history.)

The striking fact is that the above statements suffice as a fair summary of Holland's book, testifying not only to the persistence of the Orientalist diatribe, the re-deployment of its imagery, tropes and invective in the service of neo-imperialism, but also to the unoriginality of Holland's effort. For, whatever the validity of these statements, the uncanny fact remains that only within 'the ideology of the West' can these claims be assessed, indeed comprehended. Only within the story of the West's triumphal march towards 'civilisation', which allows her to reduce all history to a single narrative, her own, can these be made intelligible. What remains unexamined in this imperial tale is the centrality of the egocentric vision that regards all human past as the booty of the current victors, that, say, conscripts ancient Egypt but discards the modern one, that empowers classical Greece but dispossesses her modern offspring. Only a retroactive appropriation of the human past, only a perception of the future as given, only a faith in the arbitration of force, is what makes this intellectual imperialism possible. Holland's book, putatively a study of nascent Islam, remains totally committed to this ideological worldview which reduces everything pre-modern or non-Western to a Western coefficient.

The most revealing sign that Holland's historical vision has been commissioned in the service of Western triumphalism, that its ostensible concern with the past directly addresses contemporary sensitivities, comes from his telling description of the sixth century as 'looking back to the world of classical civilisation and looking forward to the world of the Crusades'! (p.18/986 of the iPad edition.) Needless to say, as a historical insight, it is facile and self-serving: recycling of the past for jingoist politics. Ironically, then, by reducing Islam to an interregnum between Rome and the Crusades, between dark ages and the modern light, between the 'loss' of the Mediterranean world and its *reconquista* by the rightful owners, it refuses to engage with the testimony of history, seeking a verdict on history but conducting no real historical inquiry. For those who shun such preconceived notions, prejudices really, Holland's book then has very little to offer: it is an ill-conceived effort to conceal political rhetoric as historiography.

Curiously, the ultimate thrust of Holland's ostensibly historical inquiry, by no means lacking an impressive lineage, is towards nihilism. In accordance with the postmodern move towards detranscendentalisation, it simply reverses the order, chronologically if not ideologically, of 'truth' and 'power' in human affairs. It is not the discovery of a novel truth that paves the way for the foundation of a new power structure, an 'ecumenical church transforming itself into an 'ecumenical empire', as for instance is the case in Toynbee's universal history which recognises a plurality of civilisations; rather, it is power that creates its own 'truth', a comprehensive narrative of ends and beginnings, a teleology and a genealogy of historical existence that legitimises political order. Rather than power being the fruit of truth, the spirit acquiring a body as it were, truth, according to the transcendence-denying metaphysics of nihilism, is merely the 'myth' of power. Accordingly, Islam as faith did not create Muslim empire; rather, it was the establishment of the Arab Empire that produced the Islamic metanarrative, and by so doing radically metamorphosed the primitive faith. The body-politic was the midwife of body-Islamic rather than the reverse as is the claim of the traditional narrative. That Muslim accounts portray Muhammad as Prophet, Lawgiver and State-builder appears to modern sceptics as the fusion of the personalities of Jesus, Paul and Constantine, just as the logical corollary of this claim, namely that what took Christianity three centuries to accomplish happened in the Islamic case within one lifetime, and that too largely through the efforts of a single individual, the Prophet, merely rouses their incredulity and sharpens their critical faculties. Their hunch is that the evolution of Islam as a theo-political discourse has as protracted a history as that of Christianity. Indeed, the formation of Islam as faith, creed as well as law, took shape in a 'sectarian milieu' where monotheism was the staple of all religious nourishment and to which Arabia, a cultural and religious desert, contributed nothing. Similarly, the historical insight regarding the intimate ideological marriage between Christianity and Roman Empire (all the distinctive attributes of Jesus, the Lord (*kyrios*), the Saviour (*Soter*), God's Son (*fili divinus*) were also the official titles of Roman emperors, indeed of the Caesar Augustus who was the contemporary of Jesus), has been accepted as the template for the complicity of monotheism's universalism and imperialism. In fact, the Umayyad caliph 'Abd-al-Malik is now cast in the role of a Muslim Constantine, just as it is to him that Islam's 'declaration of independence' from other Biblical faiths, paralleling Christianity's cutting of the umbilical cord with Judaism, is attributed. In short, Islam as a 'finished product', the jurists', theologians', even mystics' Islam, is a collective enterprise, stretching far beyond the righteous rule in Arabia.

We may also note that since the secular construction of the universal category of 'religion', the more radical reinterpretations of Islamic history follow the better-known but still not properly deciphered patterns of Christianity's transformation from a local cult to an imperial church. While such parallels corroborate the sociological postulates of structuralism and may even provide better insight into the power-ideology nexus, their polemical intent cannot be overlooked. We cannot easily dispense with the misgivings that the Christian parallels are being stretched too far, that the phenomenological insights into the nature of 'religion' (of which Christianity provides the paradigm) are now determining the course of historical inquiry, if not cannibalising historic consciousness altogether. We must also remind ourselves that in dealing with the Islamic tradition, the Western response is constantly to oscillate between positivism and Christian apology, between a historical narrative with no Islamic meaning and a phenomenological claim with no historical legs to stand on. We need not go into the story of 'how the West was won', an imperialist account which sanctioned the obscene lies and murderous politics of both Orientalism and anti-Semitism, nor may we dwell on the perennial racism, from Aristotle to our days, with regard to anything that has to do with the Orient, in order to remain vigilant against the self-serving ideology of an enlightened, tolerant and peaceful modernity. For

Islamophobia is now writ large in every single discourse of politics and morality; it is as equally at home in the academy as it thrives in the corridors of power. Indeed, it is the drone that always supplies the background hum to all the musical harmonies of current global politics and imperial wars. It is hardly accidental, though immensely painful, then, that the drone has become the emblem of our times.

A graphic illustration of its role as the pivot of the political theology of our times comes from Ahmed Rashid, who recounts an early instance of its deployment as such: 'On August 5, Baitullah Mehsud, the all-powerful and utterly ruthless commander of the Pakistani Taliban, was killed in a US missile strike in South Waziristan. At the time of the strike, he was undergoing intravenous treatment for a kidney ailment, and was lying on the roof of his father-in-law's house with his young second wife. At about one o'clock that morning, a missile fired by an unmanned CIA drone tore through the house, splitting his body in two and killing his wife, her parents, and seven body-guards.' Even for those who would hail this action and agree with Rashid that Mehsud's 'death marked the first major breakthrough in the war against extremist leaders in Pakistan', the legitimacy of causing so much 'collateral damage', the wife, parents-in-law and seven body-guards of the dreaded terrorist, must remain questionable. The allusion to the drone attack in this discussion, it must be underlined, is neither gratuitous nor carries any polemical intent. It serves as a suggestive image of the revisionist technology in the field of nihilistic historiography. Like the modern, remotely controlled machine, it may track some 'legitimate' target in an uncharted landscape of ancient history, but for every hit that it scores, it causes massive devastation of other historical landmarks.

Far more grievous than the moral affinity of drone technologies and post-modern methodologies is the incompatibility of the notions of history that distinguish the hierarchical episteme of modernism from the nihilistic one of postmodernism. Despite Marx's insight that by the irreverent gaze of modernity, all that is solid melts into air and all that is holy is profaned, early modernists staked their claim to self-legitimacy on the putative cognitive solidity of the historical truth. In the landscape of religious myth and fantasy, they argued, the task of enlightened reason was to identify, preserve and, wherever possible, restore the landmarks of history. History was the sole pathway to truth and the accessibility, intelligibility and certainty of historical knowledge was, for these champions of modernity, an epistemological axiom. Time however takes its toll and not even this formidable bastion of modern metaphysics has withstood its onslaught. For postmodernists, truth is but a linguistic construct which has no claim beyond the reality of the discourse of which it is a part. Indeed, the truth of history is no longer a radically different epistemological breed than the unicorn of fable.

All this is quite evident in the case of the Biblical tradition which, for better or worse, has borne the brunt of the onslaught of modern methodologies which were most passionately, indeed fanatically, committed to the ideal of the historical truth. The outcome of almost two centuries' intense intellectual labour, however, is a far greater cognitive uncertainty, if not downright nihilism. Today, the recovery of the historical truth is no longer regarded as a scientific enterprise. It is no longer contended that the discipline of history requires no leap of the creative imagination; that it simply aims to uncover the original meaning of ancient texts. Historiography as science, it is now conceded, is little different from the art of story-telling, for it too seeks to create a plausible or meaningful narrative out of a jumble of inchoate facts. The failure of the modern project to redeem its promise of sifting historical fact from fiction, or as in this case, of distinguishing the Jesus of history from the Christ of faith, has been instrumental in the growth of a form of skepticism that, at its most drastic, despairs of the possibility of obtaining any objective historical knowledge at all.

To appreciate the consequences of the modern quest for historical certainty, we can do no better than listen to Thomas Thompson, an expatriate American professor of Old Testament Studies at the University of Copenhagen and a leading spokesman of the 'minimalist school' of biblical scholars. This is what, in his opinion, these critical-historical methodologies have revealed of the Biblical tradition: 'Today we no longer have a history of Israel. Not only have Adam and Eve and the flood story passed over to mythology, but we no longer can talk about the time of the patriarchs. There never was a "United Monarchy" in history and it is meaningless to speak of pre-exilic prophets and their writings. The history of Iron Age Palestine today knows of Israel only as a small highland patronate lying north of Jerusalem and south of Jezreel valley. Nor has Yahweh, the deity dominant in the cult of that Israel's people, much to do with the Bible's understanding of God. Any history we write of this people would hardly resemble the Israel we thought we knew so much about only a few years ago. And even that little will hardly open to us the Bible's origins in history. Our history of the biblical tradition has come topsy-turvy. It is only a Hellenistic Bible that we know..... We can now say with considerable confidence that the Bible is not a history of anyone's past. The story of the chosen and rejected Israel that it presents is a philosophical metaphor of a mankind that has lost its way.' Thompson's assessment of the historicity of the Gospels is little different. The quest for the historical Jesus, for instance, he pronounces, 'is beside the point, since the Jesus of the Gospels never existed. There is thus nothing to the story of Jesus but the power and fascination of a very ancient and very enduring Messiah myth'. Jesus of the Gospels belongs not to history but to the religious imagination of the ancient Near East; he is as real as the reality of the discourse that sustains him, but no more.

Holland merely extends the reign of scepticism and nihilism that ensued from a critical study of the Biblical texts to the history of early Islam, except that in his courtship with revisionist scholarship he is far too deferential and obsequious. Straddling both modern hubris and postmodern despair, he cannot resist the polemical temptation, rejecting Muslim accounts when it suits his purpose, but relying on them when it is expedient. Nevertheless, for all his ambitions to present a critical history, he adopts a literary structure - seamless narrative - that is inimical to safeguarding even the slimmest distinction between historical fact and fiction. It is also the nemesis of his vulgar historiography. He labours hard to achieve stylistic felicity but, alas, succeeds only in flattening the intriguing subtlety of the academic monographs he has chosen to approach without deep scholarly roots. Little wonder, instead of mastering the material at his disposal, he seems to have been mastered by it. Cognitive certainty, even plausibility, that he so often feigns is nothing but the wilful elimination of all logical caveats. Nor is he embarrassed by the colonial or missionary passions that his text gives full vent to, often for no other reason than his own pleasure. From the slanderous title to the ever copious flow of sarcasms, not to mention the ubiquitous presence of unsavoury slurs against Arabs, Holland's book reminds us that whatever decency, courtesy and humanity that has become de rigueur in public discourse can be reversed by a single nasty ambush.

In short, Holland's work comes across as a manifestly tendentious reading of an ongoing academic debate that is erratic and wayward at best and acrimonious and sterile at worst. All that is conjectural and inconclusive in this forum wears, for Holland, the mask of certainty; everything that can only be discussed in arcane monographs, that does not as yet admit of any synopsis, that is still shrouded in historical haze, that is deliberately deferred to caution, even reticence, has to be sacrificed for the lure of a best-seller. When the very rationale of the revisionist project, its claim of the inadmissibility of the testimony of indigenous sources, remains highly contentious, when the critical vision animating its élan hasn't advanced from deconstruction to reconstruction, when even foreign archives do not contain annals of alternative history, when the only available metanarrative is that of the triumphant West, cognitive discretion that is the better part of the historian's valour is conspicuous by its absence in this account. The ultimate irony however is that for all its adulation for the labour of others, it ends up by trivialising the academic effort. Nothing of the earnestness, rigour, stringency, methodological creativity and sheer patience and forbearance of the researchers that also characterise their project is discernable in Holland's summarisation, just as his outcry against Western scholars who in his view have uncritically endorsed the tendentious accounts of Arabic historiography sounds like an inarticulate howl. Nor does he show any confidence in the ability of the academy to self-correct, to remain committed to its traditions and worldview and yet produce a reasonable, or even plausible synoptic account of early Islamic history. All he can do is to question either the integrity or the intelligence of the academy. Likewise, his presentation of the 'Muslim position' is merely to regurgitate Al-Qaeda bulletins and then gleefully refute them. Indeed, he neither craves nor cares for a meaningful conversation between any Muslim and Western, orthodox or academic, interlocutors. Such unfortunately is also the battle-cry of the current Islamophobic ideology: Islam must be excluded from all discourse and dialogue, just as Muslim presence in the West must also come to an end. Whatever the intent of the author, the champions of this obscene and murderous ideology are likely to use Holland's book for their own ends. And there's no way he can evade this responsibility.

Certainly, Holland cannot be accused of any kind of political correctness, not because of his pathos for historical truth or scholarly objectivity, but because his passions have their own crusading logic. One really wonders if his is a historical study or an incendiary sermon, bigotry devouring all humanity or hatred confounding all rationality. What could, for example, one make of the following comment which provides a clear indication of the theological rancour and intellectual muddle that characterises Holland's effort: 'For a non-believer to claim that the Qur'an might have originated outside of Arabia, or derived from Christian hymns, or been written in Syriac, is liable to be no less shocking to Muslims than has the Muslim denial of Jesus's divinity always been to Christians.' (pp. 84-5/986, iPad edition). If not malicious and deceitful, this remark is downright stupid, and from the canons of logic, dead wrong. Casually, or cavalierly, Holland manages to disown the very concept of 'history' on which the whole edifice of modern knowledge and morality stands and which, putatively, supplies the raison d'être of his own inquiry. For Holland appears to be totally ignorant of the modern claim that theological and historical explanations do not belong to the same order of discourse; that God and history do not cohabit in the same cognitive universe; or, that God is not the *deus ex machina* of historical causation. Nor has he any inkling of the fact that Muslim-Christian differences on the nature of Christ's divinity, whatever that be, belong not to the realm of history but to the nature of transcendence, not to the historicity of an event but to its significance. The distinction is of capital importance in dialogue, between Muslims and Christians or between Monotheists and secularists. For crucifixion may, or may not, have been a historical event, but the promise of salvation through the Cross is a tenant of faith. Historical method may adjudicate the Christ-event; it has nothing to say about its role in the divine scheme of things.

If Holland is searching for real parallels, comparing historical arguments with the historical and theological ones with the theological, apples with apples and oranges with oranges as it were, then he needs to look beyond the Muslim-Christian differences on the nature of the divine, perforce a matter of disagreement among monotheists as the transcendent can never be fully comprehended, neither in discourse nor in narrative. Neither metaphysics nor myth is able to unravel the mystery of the revelation. And yet, he must also realise that the Christian stake in 'history', in the terrestrial event rather than its cosmic significance, is far more stupendous, perhaps non-negotiable. For God and humanity, transcendence and immanence, body and spirit become one in the Christian story and Christian reason renders it doctrinally ineligible. For others, the testimony of history alone may decrypt this narrative. A recent Israeli film *The Body* (2001), for instance, dramatises the Christian paradox through a fictional account in which a crucified body, dating back to the first century AD, and carrying other signs including a gold coin bearing the marks of Pontius Pilate and faint markings around the skull, is unearthed by local archaeologists in Jerusalem. Leaving aside all consequences of this discovery, and the identification of these earthly remains as belonging to Jesus of Nazareth, the crucial fact is that the modern man is able to entertain the possibility of such a scenario and of the ability of modern science to resolve the problem of identity and chronology within the framework of history. For the sceptics, the two millennia long Christian claim that no such body of the historical Jesus can exist because of the Resurrection, counts for nothing. Sadly, such is also the nihilistic tenor of Holland's work. It too is informed by the moral and intellectual spirit of a literary genre that finds all distinction between history and historical fiction redundant. *In the Shadow of the Sword* is shallow theology, not a historical narrative.

For Muslims, revisionist history has nothing to say, as it carries no categorical imperative of any kind. It is all form and no meaning, all method and no truth, all search and no goal, all doubt and no faith! But such is the misery of all historical imagination; in order to discover meaning, it has to scan beyond the horizons of history! We, who have traversed beyond the borders of the theo-political discourse of classical Islam and have outlived the loss of its worldly kingdoms, have still not renounced the goal of a single human community. Nor, as children of Adam, may we shirk our primordial commitment to the creation of Just Order on earth. It is this trans-historical covenant that gives meaning to our existence and defines our mission in history. Nihilistic reason, humbled by the cognitive emptiness of unredeemed history, is unable to fathom this paradox, the ultimate fact of the human condition.

LEGLESS IN GAZA

Naomi Foyle

Out of It is the first ever novel by a British Palestinian, but it is remarkable for far more than this distinction. A compelling family drama set in twenty-first century Gaza and London, the novel skilfully carves its own niche in a genre – Palestinian literature – dominated by poetry and tending in recent diaspora fiction and memoir toward the epic. One can never escape the Nakba in writing about Palestine, but by concentrating on a span of months, and making judicious use of flashbacks, Selma Dabbagh compresses a long painful history into a taut Aristotelian three act drama that sweats intimacy and intrigue. Here *bildungsroman* meets noir detective novel, peppered with sufficient political argument to engage the well-informed reader and introduce the newcomer to the characters' *gestalt*. While her authorial view of the colonial nature of the conflict is never in doubt, Dabbagh also confronts head-on the complex issue of Palestinian violence, both externally and internally directed. While the protagonists' personal relationship to that violence is at times too fleetingly explored, and the obscure temporal setting is frustrating, Dabbagh's lyrical style seduces, and her pacy confidence propels the reader on to her novel's unexpected yet inexorably plotted climax. Like a blast of Mediterranean sea air, *Out of It* is a sultry yet bracing account of a generation growing up in the shadow of their parents' failure.

Selma Dabbagh, *Out of It*, London: Bloomsbury, 2012

The *bildungsroman* traditionally tells a coming-of-age story, but if Dabbagh's three main characters are all long past adolescence, that is because their emotional and sexual development has been arrested by dispossession, exile, war, cultural conservatism and the secretive nature of their own family. Now entering their late twenties, their childhood Swiss educations of little use in Gaza, twins Rashid and Iman are drifting apart: he into a haze of dope smoke and erotic dreams of his English girlfriend Lisa; she into the dangerous orbit of the macho fighters vying for control of the Strip. In contrast, their elder brother Sabri, wheelchair and house-bound since a car bomb took his legs, wife and child, is bitterly focused: stuck in the family's second-floor flat – in a building surrounded by tents after an IDF demolition job on the neighbours – he conducts historical research into the liberation struggle, and keeps a meticulous log of Israeli incursions. The siblings' father, an ex-Organisation member, has quit both family and party for the high-rises and malls of the Gulf, leaving their mother to nurse Sabri's wounds and feed her own grittier political instincts with a regime of newspaper clippings. Not simply the way things are, these family traumas and losses are gradually exposed as mysteries the novel forensically unravels.

Character as much as political circumstances drives Dabbagh's plot, and she draws these difficult people with a deft combination of vivid physical description, nuanced internal monologue, and often heated dialogue. Stoned and jealous of his mother's fierce protective instincts toward his brother, Rashid considers how she must look staring into the sunglasses he's wearing in the kitchen to hide his bloodshot eyes: 'Her face would be as distended as one of her aubergines, her pinched nose ballooning into something broad and squat …' (It would give far too much away to reveal the significance of that description, which, like much of Dabbagh's carefully planted imagery, is only apparent on a second read.) Sabri rejects sympathy, but alone in his room is still haunted by the smell of his wife on their first date, which he has tried to preserve on a shirt he keeps wrapped up a plastic bag. Iman, still a virgin - as demanded of her – silently clings to thoughts of a new infatuation, Raed, although she realises: 'It was emotional distortion by boredom. She could not even remember his features anymore, they seemed to have become worn down by the number of times she had gone over them in her mind.'

Raed's death in an Israeli hospital bombing drives Iman to seek out a group of uncompromising religious militants. But while this impulse may be understandable, it occurs so rapidly in the opening pages of the book that her transformation from dutiful women's committee member to willing sacrifice is not entirely credible. Iman wants to 'act' but seems curiously vague about what the fighters might expect of her; in fact they have been recruiting young women from Organisation families as suicide bombers. This strategy is designed to goad the established Palestinian leadership, and indeed targeting civilians wins no favour with Iman's family. Though Rashid just wants free of politics, Sabri concurs with his mother who, reacting to the news of one bomber's mission in an Israeli playground, spits: 'Deserves to be dead. The twit. Look what they did last night in return for that. The hospital! Bastards.'

But little in this tiny, over-crowded piece of land goes unnoticed, and on her way to meet the fighters' leader – himself under IDF surveillance – Iman is shadowed by the charismatic Organisation man Ziyyad Ayyoubi, who soon parcels her off to the Gulf for her father to deal with. Here Dabbagh portrays Iman's impotent rebellion more convincingly. Strip-searched at the border by Israeli guards who won't let her go to the toilet when her period starts, all she can do at her father's place is refuse to grow up into his and his girlfriend's idea of womanhood. Once more she is put on a plane, this time to join Rashid in London, where he is taking up a scholarship and her virginity at last becomes no-one but hers to decide what to do with.

In Gaza, the characters' frustration and pain is inseparable from their social and physical environment, which Dabbagh documents in powerful, telephoto detail – picking out the carnation seller made destitute by the siege; 'baby fingers slipping over eyes from foreheads, blocking visions of makeshift paths', as a crowd takes to the beach to avoid the targeted roads. This cinematic quality is all the more impressive considering the first time the author visited the Strip was during Palfest 2012, after the novel was published. In the Gulf and London, her descriptions are as vivid, but her tone more often veers into pointed mockery of her characters' self-delusions. Lisa, an aspirational activist who dines with Lords and famous poets after demos, and jauntily describes civilian deaths as 'small fry' in an email requesting data on casualties, takes the brunt of this satire – perhaps a justifiable literary revenge for centuries of Western Orientalism, or maybe simply a case study in how not to approach solidarity work. Several Brits do not come off well in *Out Of It*: as indeed, they often don't in Mike Leigh films. But satire is also employed against Iman's father, and Londoners are redeemed by Rashid's supervisor, who has dedicated his career to the Palestinian narrative and as a result has no office but a cramped flat that smells of wet dog; by a formidable mountain of a duty lawyer who appears when Rashid needs her; and by Eva, an ill-informed medical student who humbly attends a demonstration in London and realises that she is needed in Gaza, where she plays her part in the novel's climax.

The novel starts with Rashid and ends with him, though it would be unfair to reveal in exactly what manner. The penultimate chapter, which swerves into the mind of one of the religious militants, is commanding and moving, though Rashid's own impulsive movement toward violence again requires a touch more authorial attention. His actions are breath-taking, but his emotional reactions too thinly conveyed. This is not a problem elsewhere in the novel, which gives an exceptionally fine portrait of family tensions; it must therefore indicate not a lack of skill in the author, but a conscious choice to sacrifice depth for pace. This, however, is a false economy. As in film, literary action can be presented in slow motion, permitting memories and minute sensations to surface, and complicating the texture of ostensibly split-second decisions. Hopefully in the future Dabbagh (and her editors, if they were behind this emphasis on pace) will trust that her sentences are as gripping as her narrative twists and turns, and allow herself, and the reader, the luxury of dwelling a little more deeply on her characters' psychological growth.

If the novel has one other flaw, it is its peculiar lack of political specificity. Organisations are never named, dates never given, and a West Bank town that comes under heavy bombardment is not identified. Israel itself is barely mentioned. Some of these decisions have explanations – Dabbagh is on record as saying that she wanted to make the Israelis invisible, as they do the Palestinians, and the novel lets drop at one point that Palestinians call the PLO simply the Organisation and the PA the Authority. But I am not convinced that leaving so much else to guesswork was a good idea. While I deduced that the book is set around 2007-8, I am still not sure, and a general readership might easily assume it was set in the present day. While one might argue that things haven't changed much this century in Gaza – hospitals are still being bombed, militants are still being assassinated – surely things have gotten much better recently for Israel, which hasn't suffered a suicide bomb since 2008, and in fact much worse for the Gazans? At the same time, the Boycott, Divestment and Sanctions movement and Palestinian cultural resistance are flourishing, and while this is not something the novel could be expected to address, its lack of dating runs the risk of giving a false impression of the current state of Palestinian resistance. Especially given the fact that many Westerners still blanket associate Palestinians with 'terrorism', isn't it dangerous to write novels about suicide bombers without securely placing these attacks in their historical context? And how in general can Palestinian resistance be accurately assessed if the struggle is presented as atemporal? Perhaps a British-Canadian reviewer of a British-Palestinian novel does not have the right answers to these questions, but they trouble me, and so I raise them here.

Dabbagh does usefully emphasise the role of shopkeepers' strikes in the first Intifada, which is now mostly remembered in the West for its stone-throwing children, and the boycott, which dates from 2005, gets a mention. Development, aid and human rights workers play a central role in the novel's political vision, which – as it has to – includes a running critique of these mop-up small measures. What the Palestinians really need is for their plight to be universally recognised for what it is, and here Dabbagh's imagery makes a striking contribution. Rashid explains to Lisa that the conflict 'was not a war … it was more of a cage fight, where the other side could throw these flying kicks but their side was limbless … and kept getting disqualified for spitting.' But it is Sabri who nails the novel's central metaphor:

'Soldier on guard says that they've identified "someone on two legs a hundred metres from the outpost". The other soldier, in the lookout, says "a girl about ten" but by then they are already shooting. Girl's dead, etcetera, etcetera … The point is this use of code, on two legs, denoting human. It reminded me of that speech by their Prime Minister saying that we were beasts walking on two legs. I thought I could make something of this. The idea that having legs makes you human … My thesis being that the Occupation, the closures, the siege have made amputees of all of us, crawling around in the mud. Legless in Gaza. The lot of us.'

Out of It is an ingeniously plotted, lyrical novel, equally at home with email and ancient Umayyad verse, and attentive to the poetic resonance of the most mundane scenarios. Its existence is testament to the extraordinary resistance of the Palestinians to their planned annihilation. I therefore advise readers to watch out for the novel's feet and shoes – they will not be kicked or thrown at you, but subtly placed at key junctures to remind you of who, in all their multiplicity, the Palestinians are: where they have come from; and where, if there is any justice at all in this world, they are going.

IMPERIAL PROTECTION

Ahmad Khan

'One fact in all this is widely known and beyond dispute', wrote Bartolomé de las Casas, a contemporary of Columbus, 'for even the tyrannical murderers themselves acknowledge the truth of it: the indigenous peoples never did the Europeans any harm whatever… they or their fellow citizens had tasted, at the hands of these oppressors, a diet of robbery, murder, violence, and all other manner of trials and tribulations'. What las Casas said about the Spanish conquests is equally applicable to other victims of European imperialism. The task of ruling indigenous peoples was certainly not unique to the 'long 19th century', and the reign of Queen Victoria witnessed the engagement and annexation of ever-greater territory, and along with it, native populations. How Britain chose to deal with the indigenous peoples of its colonies is a tale bound inextricably with the work of one particular organisation, The Aborigines' Protection Society.

James Heartfield, *The Aborigines' Protection Society: Humanitarian Imperialism in Australia, New Zealand, Fiji, Canada, South Africa, and the Congo, 1836-1909*, London: Hurst, 2011

James Heartfield's history tells the story of a dynamic organisation campaigning between 1836 and 1909 through the midst of highly fluctuating colonial enterprise. As notions of Empire evolved and became engrossed in competing socio-political ideologies, the Aborigines' Protection Society attempted to place humanitarian concern for indigenous populations at the forefront of colonial policy. However, as the book demonstrates, deliberations on the welfare of indigenous populations by this philanthropic society did not necessarily facilitate the 'protection' of native societies located at the fringes of Empire.

The activities of the Society were firmly rooted in the wider contextual history of imperialism. As a product of a particular cultural and social milieu, James Heartfield presents an account of a society intimately connected with the pressing concerns of Empire. The first part of the book examines the Society's ideological genesis in British society, highlighting its links with individuals across the colonial polity; the second part focuses on specific outposts of Empire, assessing the changing and often contradictory advocacy of the Aborigines' Protection Society in these cultures.

In 1837, a Select Committee on Aborigines began hearing evidence on the maltreatment of indigenous populations; and as Heartfield shows, concerns over the welfare of native societies was more than a disinterested anxiety for far-off individuals. It represented both the grander, civilising notion of Empire, as well as emerging disquiet about a white settler population removed from the central authority of British government. The Society formed against a backdrop of class prejudice and romantic notions of the 'noble savage', determined to protect and isolate their adopted charges from the 'dregs' of the settler population. The patrician nature of the society, Heartfield argues, coloured its attitudes towards both natives and settlers; calls for native protection in the form of reservations and protectorates remained an inescapable feature of the society's outlook, and said much about their attitudes to both indigenous populations, as well as their fellow countrymen.

In the rush for Empire, the Committee received evidence documenting the abuse of indigenous populations across the globe. Particularly poignant testimony from Tasmania concerning the Australian Aborigines formed a cornerstone of the report: 'within a very limited period, a few years, those who are most in contact with Europeans will be utterly extinct … an intercourse of nearly half a century with a Christian people has even deteriorated a condition of existence than before our interference, nothing more miserable could easily be conceived'.

The Aboriginal cause became integrated into discussions concerning race and resources that permeated public discourse. The notion of 'Fatal Impact', meaning that indigenous, or in the scientific racialist tradition of the period, 'lesser' races, were destined to die out when confronted by more civilised races, informed the advocacy of the Aborigines' Protection Society. In this sense, as Heartfield convincingly suggests, campaigns for the formation of protectorates and reservations reflected the preoccupations of an expanding colonial establishment: the noble savage, in his pure and original state, required protection from the surplus settler class.

The unease concerning a white settler class proved a powerful political tool. As more and more settlers left British shores to seek their fortunes in distant climes, such movements impelled the hands of a burgeoning colonial apparatus in the form of governors, magistrates, and security forces. The sense of dissonance between a centralised colonial venture on the one hand, and a white settler empire on the other, whether real or imagined, created the kind of spatial fluidity that unsettled upper class sentiment. Locating itself within this spatial discontinuity, the Aborigines' Protection Society fulfilled a useful role for London. The Colonial Office could utilise the perceived concerns of native populations, through the Aborigines' Protection Society, as a counter and check on settler demands. As such, the Society served both an ideological and a practical role in the mission of Empire.

The effects of this tripartite relationship between empire, settler and native, placed the Aborigines' Protection Society at the heart of colonial affairs, and exposed the often fleeting and paradoxical nature of its designs. It could simultaneously critique the annexation of indigenous territory, whilst remaining firmly behind the mission of Empire. Nowhere is this sense of mutability more apparent than in the evolving implications for colonial rule. What began as lobbying to regulate settler activity gradually morphed into applications for extending colonial rule. This shift in momentum from protection per se, to protection through extension, is perhaps not all that surprising. After all, as the book amply highlights, the protection of Aborigines proved a useful policy for justifying the ostensible 'moral' purpose of Empire – it was not imperialism in a pejorative kleptocratic sense, as practised by other European nations, but rather a far nobler mission to regulate and improve lawless territories. The Aborigines' Protection Society helped to extend British rule, but failed to see that almost every location where annexation was advocated, the lives of natives deteriorated.

Heartfield provides a panoramic overview of some of the scientific 'shocks' that formed an indispensible part of the complex theorisations involving race, society, and history throughout the period. Malthusian political economy concerning resources and the struggle for existence resonated throughout the epoch; conceptions of superior races alongside the oft-quoted 'fatal impact' had deep implications for colonial policy. More meaningfully, these debates were to receive an impetus grounded in scientific enquiry when Darwin published his *The Origin Of Species*, followed later by *The Descent Of Man*. The inference behind the subtitle, 'the preservation of favoured races in the struggle for life', would not have been lost on a mid-nineteenth century Victorian audience, with the treatment of indigenous populations riding high on the colonial agenda. The political connotations of Social Darwinism were transformed into the immediacy of Empire. Even Darwin could not fail to note the almost total disappearance of Australian Aborigines from Tasmania: 'I do not know of a more striking instance of the comparative rate of increase of a civilised over a savage people'.

Utilising several case studies in the second section of the book, Heartfield documents the activities and policies of the Aborigines' Protection Society. In an unsettling example of the forms of 'protection' the society advocated, it lauded the removal of native children from their parents in Australia, so that they may be 'early removed from the pernicious influence of their countrymen'. The tendentious undertones of such ideals will not be lost on the modern reader. It was however entirely consistent with the 'philanthropy as discourse', in the Foucauldian sense, that the society internalised; only through the creation of an aboriginal myth of a vulnerable people disenfranchised and extrapolated, could the society exercise its moral mission.

In perhaps the most insightful section of the book, Heartfield shows how the Society did not extend the licence of protection to native peoples when they began to assert their own agency. In Canada, an uprising of the mixed-race Métis community was dismissed by the Society with the incredulous remark that such 'half-breeds', seemingly not really indigenous people, 'claimed the right to elect their own legislature, magistrates and school commissioners'. An emerging dimension of native self-advocacy did not fit neatly with the directives of a society entrenched in the industry of colonialism.

Similarly, in Southern Africa, as more and more native labourers were integrated into the metropolitan centres, the emerging transition from protection to rights created a paradigm that did not complement the Society's work. It remarked that it did not wish to see, 'masses of uncivilized men invested with political rights which they would be unable either to appreciate or understand'. Instead, and somewhat predictably, the Society called for the establishment of a protectorate in the form of a Union of South Africa, overseen by 'responsible imperialism'. Such policies culminated in the Native Lands Act, the infamous precursor to apartheid, and placed the society on a fatal and decisive break with native opinion.

Sol Plaatje, who championed native self-representation and whose opposition tracts went on to form the founding principles of the African National Congress, was openly attacked by members of the Aborigines' Protection Society. Plaatje wrote scathingly of the proposed establishment of 'Basutolands', later known as 'bantustans': 'a carefully prepared, deliberate and premeditated scheme to encompass the partial enslavement of the Natives'. The Aborigines' Protection Society unravelled with the emergence of new nationalist movements that declared that the natives were no longer voiceless, if they ever were, and certainly in no need of 'separation' or 'protection'.

As a 'history' of the Aborigines' Protection Society, there are weaknesses in this book. Heartfield ends his history in 1909. It would have been useful to see how the Society's policies led to more specific forms of domination and discrimination – apartheid in South Africa, or the 'stolen generations' of Australia. The narrative of the book does not always flow in a streamlined fashion. Whilst the case studies of particular locations do enable a thorough picture of events in the colonies to be constructed, it occludes some of the earlier narrative exploring the changing faces of this complex Society. At times the sheer detail of names and events can leave even the most attentive reader overwhelmed. The book's final and weakest chapter on the Congo is somewhat hastily written, and one is given the impression that its content is more ceremonial than insightful.

However, Heartfield succeeds in presenting a deeply personal portrayal of the Aborigines' Protection Society, one which defies any straightforward reading and categorisation. Extensive research, much of it based on the archives of the Society itself as well as other colonial sources, permeates the arguments in the book. The result is an intimate portrait of the Aborigines' Protection Society, the debate and discussions at its meetings, and the often fraught internal proceedings that accompanied such a palpably ambiguous mandate. Furthermore, one is given a definite sense of the context in which the Aborigines' Protection Society operated, including the changing political contexts of British society, the evolving notions of Empire, as well as the challenging relationship between the Crown and its settler communities.

This is a pertinent book for our time. As indigenous and tribal groups across the world suffer marginalisation and disenfranchisement, this history reminds us that we must be weary of casting them as helpless beings devoid of agency. Notions of humanitarian intervention blend seamlessly with a history of humanitarian imperialism. The cultural and social hegemony of the privileged is often translated as intervention, and 'helping' those in distant locations across the world. The society's slogan, *ab uno sanguine* ('of one blood') is a noble idea but as debates concerning race and power continue today, the book is a cautious reminder that 'the road to Empire was paved with good intentions'.

ET CETERA

TOP TEN MUSLIM CHARACTERS IN BOLLYWOOD

Rachel Dwyer

Muslims have long played a major role in the Indian film industry. The industry has given us many iconic Muslim figures such as actor Dilip Kumar (Yusuf Khan, seen as the actor's actor in Hindi cinema), actresses Madhubala (Mumtaz Jehan Dehalvi, for many the greatest beauty to grace Bollywood screens) and Waheeda Rehman (often in roles that cast her as a life- and love-tormented female before she was cast as that most quintessential of all Bollywood characters: the even more long-suffering 'Ma'). There have been great Muslim directors such as Mahboob and Kamal Amrohi. Since the 1990s, its biggest male stars are the three Khans: Shahrukh Khan, Salman Khan and Aamir Khan, who no longer change their names to sound 'modern'. Yet, Muslim characters in Bollywood, as it has been known since the 1990s, are doomed to minor roles fated simply to represent their community and conform to a series of well-established stereotypes. Hindi films usually have lead actors and actresses who are North Indian upper-caste Hindus, who can be seen as 'normal Indians', while characters from other regions or religions are usually typecast, not infrequently in negative roles.

Muslim characters may appear in any genre of Hindi films. But they can be found more specifically in a group of sub-genres called 'Islamicate' – that is films which deal with the cultural, rather than religious, life of India's Muslims. These sub-genres include: the Arabian Nights fantasy, which became less popular after independence but still exists as a B-movie genre; the devotional film, often centred on Garib Nawaz of Ajmer (the twelfth-century Sufi Saint Moinuddin Hasan Chishti), replete with miracles and popular religious practices which also fall into the B-movie type; the historical films which are concerned with India's Muslim past, in particular the Mughal period; the films about the culture of the courtesan (*tawaif*), which are relatively few but include some of the most loved films in Hindi film history; and the 'Muslim social', the name by which all these genres were formerly known but which is now restricted to films set in the contemporary world of India's Muslims. A new genre has also emerged post 9/11 in which Muslims behave just as badly as an Islamophobic worldview suggests they do. These genres usually feature particular forms of music, notably the *qawwali* and the *ghazal*; styles of dress associated with India's Muslims; make generous use of poetic Urdu and create a world of excessive formality.

Here are the top ten archetypal Muslims you will have the pleasure of watching in Bollywood movies.

1.Veiled Beauties

The beauty of actresses such as Madhubala, Waheeda Rehman and Sadhana is legendary. So shrouding them in a veil makes little sense. But the veil serves a useful purpose: it leads to cases of mistaken identity when two friends fall in love with the same woman (*Chaudhvin Ka Chand*, 1961) or where the beloved's identity has to be discovered by the hero (*Mere Mehboob*, 1963). However, it is only the hero who cannot see behind the veil. The audience enjoy time in the *zenana* (womens' quarters) where elaborately dressed beauties languish, speaking flowery Urdu, singing and dreaming of romance.

2.The Tawaif and Nawabs

The dominant image of the Muslim woman in Hindi cinema is the *tawaif* (dancing girl, courtesan). This is not as unfortunate as it sounds as she represents the lost elite culture of the North Indian cities, in particular that of Lucknow. Dressed modestly but in sumptuous costumes and jewellery, she sings and dances for her clients' entertainment but remains 'pure' and desirous of love and marriage. The two most important *tawaif* films are Kamal Amrohi's *Pakeezah* (1971) and Muzaffar Ali's *Umrao Jaan* (1981), starring Meena Kumari (Mahjabeen Bano) and Rekha, respectively. Rekha plays a *tawaif* again in *Muqaddar Ka Sikandar* (1978), where her performance, swinging her hips and rolling on the floor in her pink and silver dress to the famous song 'Salaam-e Ishq', is matched by Amitabh Bachchan's as he looks totally bored with the spectacle and finally takes to the dance floor himself. Courtesans as sisters to the hero (*Mere Mehboob*), or mothers of the heroine (*Mehboob ki Mehndi*,1971) are more of a problem as, however sorrowful the circumstances, no respectable family will marry into such a benighted household.

A respectable *Mujra*, the courtesans' elaborate song and dance session, must be graced by a Nawab, who provides us with much scope to explore Indian Muslim culture. He could be an artistic character unsuited to the modern world such as in Satyajit Ray's *The Chess Players* (1977), but he could also be a decadent drunk, who divorces his wife by saying 'Talaq talaq talaq' during an argument (*Nikaah*, 1982), or a melancholic but refined gentleman, as in *Mere Huzoor* (1968). However badly he might treat his wife and family, he never forgets his manners, is always impeccably dressed in a *sherwani*, speaks with flowery Urdu and demonstrates proper *adab* (etiquette).

3. Emperors
The Mughal Emperor is a stock in trade of the historical film. The favourite is Akbar (1542-1605), who represents composite culture or secularism in the Indian sense, and has equal regard for all religion. In one of the greatest Indian films, *Mughal-e-Azam* (1960), his religious tolerance extends to celebrating the festival of Janmashtami, the Birth of Krishna, with his Hindu wife. *Jodhaa-Akbar* (2008) presents an earlier stage of this Muslim-Hindu romance, with Akbar as a muscular hero, a fighter and a tamer of elephants as well as a lover, a Sufi, a seeker of truth and promoter of religious tolerance. Again, he does not prevent Jodhaa from following her own culture – perhaps because he has seen her skills with a sword – even allowing her to worship Krishna in the palace and to cook him a vegetarian meal. The big song number in the film is, somewhat unusually, about tax cuts. Akbar lifts the *jizya*, the tax levied on non-Muslims by Muslim rulers, resulting in his subjects bursting into song and dance ('Marhaba') at his generosity in what seems to be the first version of the Republic Day Parade.

4. Loyal Sidekick
Although the lead character is usually Hindu, he is usually furnished with a Muslim friend who is willing to die rather than let his *dost* (friend) down. The loyal Pathan was seen earlier in versions of Tagore's story, *Kabuliwala*, and then as the loyal friend of Vijay (Amitabh Bachchan) in *Zanjeer* (1973), who sings,

'Yaari hai imaan mera' (friendship is my faith); while Shahrukh Khan takes on this role in *Hey! Ram* (2000). The late AK Hangal, who played the blind Imam in mega-hit *Sholay* (1975), gave the loyal Muslim archetype the name of his character in the film, Rahim Chacha. Unfortunately, the Chacha, or Uncle, can only prove his love by dying for the sake of the hero, his Hindu friend.

5. Poets and singers

Hindi film lyrics have close links to Urdu poetry and the films celebrate relentlessly the *ghazal* and the *qawwali*. Muslims are taken to be extremely fond of poetry, and as sensitive poets and singers, incorporate songs into the film in a relaxed and appropriate manner. The hero is a poet in *Mere Mehboob*, and a *qawwal* in *Barsaat Ki Raat* (1960), where he performs alongside female *qawwals* in perhaps the most famous *qawwali* of the Indian cinema, 'Na To Caravan'. In *Amar, Akbar, Antony* (1977), the Muslim brother is a *qawwal*, named after a great Urdu poet, Akbar Allahabadi. Akbar's *qawwali*, 'Parda Hai Parda', is about getting his beloved, sitting in the front row with her father, to remove her veil, even though he knows she does not wear a veil in the hospital where she works as a doctor. In Sufi-themed movies, where the lead character is not a Muslim, such as *Dil Se* (1998) and *Rockstar* (2012) the film score still draws on these traditions. So the lyrics of *Dil Se's* 'Chaiya Chaiya' are adapted from Bulleh Shah, a sixteenth-century Punjabi Sufi, and *Rockstar* has a *qawwali* praising Nizamuddin of Delhi.

6. The Intolerant Muslim

The Hindu male is a secular figure, respectful to other religious traditions, especially Muslims. The Muslim male, on the other hand, is the opposite: anything but tolerant. In *Bombay* (1995), when the Muslim heroine declares her wish to marry a Hindu, her father draws a knife on him, though after marriage, her husband allows her to continue her religious practices. In *Gadar Ek Prem Katha* (2001), a Sikh husband rescues a Muslim woman in the Partition riots and allows her to continue her religious practice after their marriage. When she visits her family in Pakistan, they kidnap her but he follows her over the border, and shows his secularism by acceding to all her family's demands until he is told to curse India. That proves a demand too far and results in his single-handedly bashing the entire Pakistani armed forces to show that he may be tolerant but is definitely not weak.

7. The Gangster

Bollywood thrives on gangster films. But it is fascinated most by Haji Mastaan, who rose to dominance in the 1970s, and his protégé, Dawood Ibrahim, now thought to run the mafia from Karachi. The quasi-biopic, *Once Upon a Time in Mumbai* (2010), featured their story until the rise of Dawood, and a sequel is expected. The popular actor Rishi Kapoor played his first deleterious role as Rauf Lala, a butcher and a pimp, a very negative representation of a Muslim, in *Agneepath* (2012). The audiences adored the loverboy's new incarnation, largely because he redeemed himself by singing a *qawwali*.

8. The Pakistani

The Pakistani, by definition, is the enemy. In *Sarfarosh* (1999), a Pakistani spy enters India as a *ghazal* singer, albeit one who bites ears off baby goats, giving a sinister turn to the poetic tradition. Pakistani women have more positive images than the men, at least in films where they fall in love with Indian men. When an Indian Airforce officer, Veer, is imprisoned for years in Pakistan at the hands of the evil husband of his beloved Zaara Haayat Khan, in *Veer Zaara* (2004), the women in her family and her lawyer, Saamiya Siddiqui, reunite the couple, showing love has no boundaries. In *Ek Tha Tiger*, 2012's big hit, Tiger (Salman Khan) a RAW (Indian Intelligence) Agent falls in love with his Pakistani counterpart, Zoya, whose undercover work includes putting on a musical in Dublin before they meet again in Istanbul at a United Nations gathering where the orchestra plays Elgar's 'Pomp and Circumstance' ('Land of Hope and Glory'). No, I didn't get the reference either!

9. The Terrorist

The idea of terrorism within India is often raised in the context of Kashmir in such films as *Mission Kashmir* (1998) and *Fiza* (2000), where Muslims are depicted as terrorists. Earlier films showed Kashmir mostly populated by Hindus (*Kashmir Ki Kali*, 1964; *Jab Jab Phool Khile*, 1965). Two big budget films, *New York* (2009) and *Kurbaan* (2009), argue that American Islamophobia creates terrorists. In the latter, a Hindu academic marries a Muslim without listening to her father's warnings, which are shown to be well-founded: in New York City, he locks her up in what seems to be an Afghan horror film about abused and murdered women, before he blows up the Subway.

10. Modern Muslims

Rarely do Hindi films show a modern, secular Muslim. But there are exceptions: the comedian Mehmood's slapstick Hyderabadi Muslim in *Gumnaam* (1965); Ali in *Dhoom* (2004), Farhan Qureshi in *3 Idiots* (2009); Aslam Khan in *Rang de Basanti* (2006) and Iqbal in the film of the same name (2005). Shahrukh Khan's performances as a Muslim have created new roles: in *Chak De! India* (2007), he redeems himself as a hockey coach after being accused of deliberately losing a hockey match against Pakistan; in *My Name is Khan* (2010), he marries a Hindu (inter-communal marriages in films are usually Hindu man and Muslim woman), and when her son is killed in an Islamophobic attack, sets off to tell the President of the United States, 'My name is Khan and I'm not a terrorist'.

Lastly, Indian cinema's understanding of enlightened, tolerant Islam is best seen in *Coolie* (1983). The coolie of the title is Iqbal, played by Amitabh Bachchan, his girlfriend is a Christian and his best friend is a Hindu. His other ally is an Allah-fearing hawk, Allah Rakha, who wears a necklace saying 'Allah', that glints to advise Iqbal to go on the Hajj. He also helps Iqbal fight his enemies. The film includes miracles such as the survival of Iqbal after a shootout on Hajji Ali's shrine when, covered in the *chador* (covering) of the saint, he recites the *kalma* (declaration of faith) and writes 786 (the numeric equivalent of God's name) in his blood as he faints. Prayers at mosques, temples and churches accompany his operation and recovery. People lose and regain their memories after being hit on the head by framed verses of the Qur'an, and prayers to the 'Lord of Medina' bring lightning strikes to save Iqbal's mother. During the making of the film, Amitabh almost died and it is seen as proof of the miracles shown on screen that he survived.

CITATIONS

Introduction: The Culmination of Love by Aamer Hussein

A number of translators of Sufi works have been consulted, including Gertrude Bell, R.A. Nicholson, David Pendlebury, Victor Kiernan, Adiya Behl, Simon Weighman and Dick Davies. Other works used include Annemarie Schimmel, *As Through a Veil: Mystical Poetry in Islam* (Oxford: OneWorld, 2001) and Eva de Vitray-Meyerovitch, *Le livre de l'eternite* (Paris: Albin Michel, 1962) and *Mystique et poesie en Islam* (Paris: Desclée de Brouwer, 1973). Wherever possible, the Persian and South Asian originals have been consulted.

The best work on al-Hallaj, bar none, is Louis Massignon, *The Passion of al-Hallaj*, translated by Herbert Mason (Princeton University Press, 1982, 2 volumes); a reprint of Rudolf Gelpke's translation of Nizami's *The Story of Layla and Majnun*, is published by Omega Publications (1977). *Rabi'a: The Life and Work of Rabi'a and Other Women Mystics in Islam* by Margaret Smith (Oxford: OneWorld, 1994) provides a good introduction to her life from a Christian point of view, but a highly recommended study from a Muslim perspective is Widad el Sakkakini's *First Among Sufis* (translated from the Arabic by Nabil Safwat; Octagon 1982). For Iqbal see Annemarie Schimmel, *Gabriel's Wing: Study into the Religious Ideas of Sir Muhammad Iqbal* (Lahore: Iqbal Academy, 1989). There are numerous translations of Rumi, all widely available.

The Ghazal by Robert Irwin

The Routledge *Encyclopedia of Arabic Literature*, Julia Scott Meisami and Paul Starkey eds., 2 vols. (London, 1988) is an excellent guide to medieval and modern Arabic literature. *The Penguin Anthology of Classical Arabic Literature*, ed. Robert Irwin offers a wide range of translations (of varying merit) of Arabic poetry and prose. Mahmood Jamal's *Islamic Mystical Poetry: Sufi verse from the Early Mystics to Rumi* (London 2009) covers a wider range of poetry than its title suggests, for the Urdu mystical poets all came later than Rumi. Julie Scott Meisami's *Medieval Persian Court Poetry* contains a penetrating chapter on the *ghazal*. There is also a good chapter on love poetry by A. Hamori in *The Cambridge History of Arabic Literature: 'Abbasid Belles-Lettres*, Julia Ashtiany et al, eds. (Cambridge, 1990)

Sacred Love, Lyrical Death by Christopher Shackle

The following works have been mentioned in this article: Bulleh Shah, *Sufi Lyrics*, trans. Christopher Shackle (Cambridge Mass.: Harvard University Press, forthcoming 2013); Ghulam Farid, *The Message of Diwan-i-Farid*, trans. Shahzad Qaiser. (Lahore: Suhail Academy, 2009); Hasham Shah, *Sassi Punnun*, trans. Christopher Shackle. (Lahore: Vanguard, 1985); Waris Shah, *The Adventures of Hir and Ranjha*, trans. C.F. Usborne. (London: Peter Owen: 1973); Sudhir Kakar and John M. Ross, *Tales of Love, Sex and Danger* (New Delhi: Oxford University Press, 1986); Francesca Orsini, ed. *Love in South Asia: A Cultural History* (Cambridge: Cambridge University Press, 2006); Samina Quraeshi, *Legends of the Indus* (London: Asia Ink, 2004); Lajwanti Rama Krishna. *Panjabi Sufi Poets* (London: Oxford University Press, 1938); Roger Scruton, *Death-Devoted Heart: Sex and the Sacred in Wagner's Tristan and Isolde* (New York: Oxford University Press, 2004); Annemarie Schimmel, *As Through a Veil: Mystical Poetry in Islam* (Oxford: Oneworld, 2001) and Anna Suvorova, *Masnavi: A Study of Urdu Romance* (New Delhi: Oxford University Press, 2000).

The Massacre of Karbala by Imranali Panjwani

For further sources on Karbala, see Abu Mikhnaf, *Maqtal al-Husayn*. Translated by Hamid Mavani. (Middlesex: Shi'a Ithnasheri Community of Middlesex 2001) and al-Tabari, *Tarikh al-Tabari*. (New York: State University of New York Press 1988). There is a full list For a full list and is a useful index of sources in Mohammad Ishtihardi, *Lamentations – Part II: The Tragedy of the Lord of Martyrs*. Translated by Arif Abdulhussain (Birmingham: Al-Mahdi Institute, 2001).

The quote from Abu Mikhnaf is from *Maqtal al-Husayn*, p. 170. The poem appears in Annemarie Schimmel, 'Karbala and the Imam Husayn in Persian and Indo-Muslim literature' in Muhammadi Trust., *Al-Serat: The Imam Husayn Conference, Volume 12* (London: Muhammadi Trust, 1986), p. 29. It is also available online at: http://www.al-islam.org/al-serat/karbala-schimmel.htm. There are also many other articles in this volume which shed light on the poetry associated with Karbala as well as its socio-political dimensions. Al-Husayn's letter appears in Muwwafaq Khwarizmi, *Maqtal al-Husayn*, ed. Muhammad Samawi (Qum: Anwar al-Huda, 2003), vol 1, pp. 188-9; it can also be found in several other places such *al-Futuh* and *Nahj al-Shahadah*. The quote from Ibn Kathir is from *Al-Bidayah wa al-Nihayah* (Cairo: Dar al-Hadith, 1994, vol 8, p. 1169); Al-Saduq's quotation is from his *Uyun Akhbar al-Rida* (The Sources of Narrations on Imam Reza), translated by Ali Peiravi (Qum: Ansariyan Publications, 2006, vol 1, p. 560); and from al-Mufid is from *Kitab Al-Irshad – The Book of Guidance* (London: Muhammadi Trust, 1988, p. 353.)

The Universal Declaration of Human Rights can be accessed at: http://www.un.org/en/documents/udhr/index.shtml

See also: Abdullahi Ahmed an Na'im, 'Shari'a and Basic Human Rights Concerns' in Kurzman (ed.) *Liberal Islam: A Sourcebook* (New York and Oxford: Oxford University Press, 1998, pp. 222-38) and Mohsen Kadivar, 'Human Rights and Intellectual Islam' in Kari Vogt, Lena Larsen & Christian Moe (eds.) *New Directions in Islamic Thought: Exploring Reform and Muslim Tradition* (London: I.B. Tauris, 2009, pp. 47-72); George Hourani, *Reason & Tradition in Islamic Ethics* (Cambridge: Cambridge University Press, 1985); Murtada Mutahhari, *Understanding Islamic Sciences* (London: ICAS Press, 2002), pp. 49-88; William Shepard, *Introducing Islam* (London and New York: Routledge, 2009, p. 33); and Charles Taylor, *A Secular Age* (Harvard University Press, 2007 pp. 299-322).

A Veronica on the Eve of War by Martin Rose

This piece is an adapted chapter from a recently completed memoir of Baghdad 1988-90, for which the author is seeking a publisher.

Prescribing Death by Jalees Rahman

The standard text for studying the role of physicians and human experimentation in the concentration camps of Nazi Germany is *Auschwitz, die NS- Medizin und ihre Opfer* by the German journalist and author Ernst Klee. It is not available in an English translation, but it provides a thorough account of the crimes that were perpetrated by the physicians in Nazi Germany, as well as their ties to the German military and industry. In English, George J. Annas and Michael A. Grodin, *The Nazi Doctors and the Nuremberg Code: Human Rights in Human Experimentation* (New York: OUP, 1995), offers an excellent discussion of the history of the Nuremberg Code in the context of the Nuremberg Doctors' Trial and describes how the Trial revolutionized our understanding of how important it is to protect the rights of the individual in medical experimentation.

Can Malays Kiss by Shanon Shah

Information on the Obedient Wives Club was gathered from the following news sources:
Chong, Debra. 'Obedient Wives Club publishes explicit sex book'. News. *The Malaysian Insider*, October 12, 2011. http://www.themalaysianinsider. com/malaysia/article/obedient-wives-club-publishes-explicit-sex-book/;

Dateline SBS. 'Obedient Wives Club'. Online video streaming. *YouTube*, October 30, 2011. http://www.youtube.com/watch?v=eaoZh7StKIs;
Kuhn, Anthony. "Obedient Wives Club' Irks Some Muslims In Malaysia'. News. *NPR*, January 30, 2012. http://www.npr.org/2012/01/30/146066783/ obedient-wives-club-irks-some-muslims-in-malaysia.

The statistics on urbanisation in Malaysia, Europe and North America are from:
United Nations Department of Economic and Social Affairs/Population Division. (2006). World Urbanization Prospects: The 2005 Revision, [online] New York: United Nations. http://www.un.org/esa/population/ publications/WUP2005/2005WUP_DataTables2.pdf;

Department of Statistics Malaysia. (2010). Population and Housing Census, Malaysia 2010 [online] Putrajaya: Department of Statistics Malaysia. http://www.statistics.gov.my/portal/index.php?option=com_content&view=article&id=1215%3Apopulation-distribution-and-basic-demographic-characteristic-report-population-and-housing-census-malaysia-2010-updated-2972011&catid=130%3Apopulation-distribution-and-basic-demographic-characteristic-report-population-and-housing-census-malaysia-2010&Itemid=154&lang=en

The details for *Perempuan, Isteri dan Jalang* are: U-Wei Haji Shaari (dir). Perempuan, *Isteri Dan...?* Berjaya Fp, 1993.

The discussion on the film also relied on: Khoo Gaik Cheng. 'Recuperating Malay Custom/'Adat' in Female Sexuality in Malaysian Films'. In *Asian Media Studies: Politics of Subjectivities*, edited by John Nguyet Erni and Siew Keng Chua, 207–224. Oxford: Blackwell, 2005.

The discussion on Hikayat Raja Kulawandu and Malay love literature is from:

Muhammad Haji Salleh. 'Finding Love in 'Hikayat Raja Kulawandu''. In *Lost Times and Untold Tales from the Malay World*, edited by Jan van der Putten and Mary Kilcline Cody, 241–256. Singapore: National University of Singapore, 2011.

The discussion on *Faridah Hanom* is from: Christine Campbell. 'The Thread of Eroticism in 'Faridah Hanom', an Early Malay Novel by Syed Sheikh Al-Hadi', in *Lost Times and Untold Tales from the Malay World*, edited by Jan van der Putten and Mary Kilcline Cody, 257–267. Singapore: National University of Singapore, 2011.

The discussion on *Ombak Rindu* relies on a critical review by Rozana Isa (in Malay):

'Ombak Hairan dalam?' News. *The Malaysian Insider*, April 21, 2012. http://www.themalaysianinsider.com/opinion/article/ombak-hairan-dalam/

Sub-continental Lovers by Sabita Manian

Poster from Lachit Borphukan FB site can be found at: https://www.facebook.com/pages/Lachit-Borphukan-The-Forgotten-HERO/202226543165322

Aman ki Asha homepage is at:
http://amankiasha.com/faqs.asp;
and its *YouTube* video is at:
www.youtube.com/watch?v=dz6YylorUGM
Counter-response to Aman Ki Asha are at:
www.youtube.com/watch?v=-LR47DPXhBY&feature=related and
www.youtube.com/watch?v=0Zz81aJwwik

Indian Army Fans, Facebook page poster:
www.facebook.com/permalink.php?story_fbid=230548573693533
&id=148871771858485

Hina Rabbani Khar's statement to the National Assembly was published in
The Daily Times, 5 January 2012; it can be accessed at:
www.dailytimes.com.pk/default.asp?page=2012\01\05\story_5-1-2012_pg7_3

The Daily Times editorial on water issues appeared on 26 January 2012:
http://www.dailytimes.com.pk/default.asp?page=2012\01\26\
story_26-1-2012_pg7_10

The quotes from *Faiqa* are from the News 23 March 2012:
www.thenews.com.pk/Todays-News-13-13361-Girl-leaves-for-India-for
-heart-treatment

For coverage of the Kargil conflict see:
http://news.bbc.co.uk/2/hi/south_asia/387702.stm;
and BBC's 30 May 1999 report, 'Indian pilot 'killed in cold blood' , is available here:
http://news.bbc.co.uk/2/hi/south_asia/356366.stm

For cricket coverage see:
India Today, 18 March 2012: http://indiatoday.intoday.in/story/ind-vs-
pak-asia-cup-2012-report-kohli/1/178310.html;
and *Outlook India*, 18 March 2012:
http://news.outlookindia.com/items.aspx?artid=756175

On Ramachandran see:
India Today, http://indiatoday.intoday.in/story/pro-pakistan-people-of-indian-origin-will-not-get-citizenship/1/178198.html;

Ministry of Home Affairs, Government of India:
http://indiancitizenshiponline.nic.in/acquisition1.htm;
and OnePakistan.com "Pro-Pakistan-People of Indian Origin" (n.d.):
http://pakistan.onepakistan.com/news/pakistan/64010-pro-pakistan-people-of-indian-origin-will-not-get-citizenship-says-home-affairs-ministry.html

Zubeida Mustafa, 'Pakistan's Changing Images of India: A Personal View' appeared in *Logos*, (Vol. 4.1 Winter 2005); it can be accessed from:
http://www.logosjournal.com/issue_4.1/zubeida.htm;
and Nosheen Abbas's blog 'Pakistan: Perceptions vs. reality' is at:
http://blog.dawn.com/2009/06/02/pakistan-perceptions-vs-reality/#totalcomments

Nihilistic History by S Parvez Manzoor

The quote from Eric Voegelin appears in: *The New Science of Politics* (Chicago: The University of Chicago Press, 1952. p 1). For Carl H. Becker., see: *Islamstudien: Vom Werden und Wesen des islamischen Welt*. (Leipzig: Verlag Quelle & Meyer, 1924) 'Der Islam als Problem'. Pp. 1-23. This chapter has also been (loosely) translated by S. Khuda Bukhush, in *Contributions to the History of Islamic Civilization*. *Vol. II*. Reprint by Accurate Printers, Urdu Bazar, Lahore-2, s.a. Arnold Toynbee is cited from: *A Study of History* (OUP, 1947) (Abridgement by D.C. Somervell) pp. 15-6, and 145.

Thomas L. Thompson's two notable works are: *The Mythic Past* (London: Jonathan Cape, 1999, p. xv.); and, *The Messiah Myth* (Cambridge: Basic Books, 2005). The citation is from the inside flap of the cover jacket itself!

'Powerful and important' — Noam Chomsky

REVOLT IN SYRIA

STEPHEN STARR

9781849041973 / June 2012
£14.99 paperback / 240pp

'This searching inquiry is painful reading, but urgent for those who hope to understand what lies behind the shocking events in Syria, what the prospects might be, and what outsiders can – and cannot – do to mitigate the immense suffering as a country so rich in history and promise careens towards disaster.' — **Noam Chomsky**

In January 2011 President Bashar al-Assad told the *Wall Street Journal* that Syria was 'stable' and immune from revolt. In the months that followed, and as regimes fell in Egypt and Tunisia, thousands of Syrians took to the streets calling for freedom, prompting ferocious repression by the authorities.

In *Revolt in Syria: Eye-Witness to the Uprising*, Stephen Starr delves deep into the lives of Syrians whose destiny has been shaped by the state for almost fifty years. In conversations with people from all strata of Syrian society, Starr draws together and makes sense of perspectives illustrating why Syria, with its numerous sects and religions, was so prone to violence and civil strife.

Through his unique access to a country largely cut off from the international media during the unrest, Starr delivers compelling first hand testimony from both those who suffered and benefited most at the hands of the regime.

www.hurstpublishers.com/book/revolt

41 GREAT RUSSELL ST, LONDON WC1B
WWW.HURSTPUBLISHERS.COM
WWW.FBOOK.COM/HURSTPUBLISHERS
020 7255 2201

LOVE AND DEATH AT THE MOVIES

Merryl Wyn Davies

The clock was running down on a lazy Sunday afternoon. It was time. Resolutely, I stifled the sniffles, pulled myself together and phoned home. I knew instantly something was wrong. It was the way my mother lifted the receiver: 'What's wrong, Mum?' I had never heard the like of the wail of utter desolation in which my mother declared: 'Laurie didn't marry Jo — again!' So it was true. We sobbed together, unapologetically.

Love — what is it good for, eh? Clearly spreading cinematic misery far and wide and disturbing the peace of quiet Sunday afternoons! This shared emotional trauma was occasioned by watching a television matinee of *Little Women*. It was the classic 1949 version with the incomparable June Allyson as Jo and Peter Lawford as Laurie giving life to the unendurable conundrum of the love that ought to have been but is never fulfilled.

And no, I'm sorry Louisa M Alcott, your *Little Women* may be a thinly veiled version of your own life, but who can accept with complacency that Laurie ends up with the insufferable Amy, or that Jo is truly happy and reconciled to life with the improbable Prof Bhaer, even when embodied by Rossano Brazzi! As far as my mother and I are concerned it is eternally, perpetually, repeatedly just not on. Except, of course, for the inescapable fact that it is unalterably always just so. That's the movies for you — love fixed and imperishable as death, with death being the other stock in trade of cinematic trauma.

When it comes to the movies the rest is never silence. Captured forever on celluloid are innumerable variations on the manipulation (whether cynical or sincere) of one's heartstrings. Submit to the experience of watching a film, no matter how often, and the outcome can only be calculated in the quantity of tissue boxes required. The mystery is that there are such infinite ways in which we are each seared, wrung dry and emotionally scarred for life by particular instances of love and death in the movies. What we mean by love and how we view death are complicated and compounded by our vicarious encounters with their on-screen expressions.

I know! It took me nearly five hours to watch a badly subtitled video of the 1960 Bollywood classic *Mughal-e-Azam* (running time three hours and 20 minutes). Even my limited understanding of Urdu told me the translations were incorrect. So there were innumerable pauses while the meaning of the dialogue and its poetic flow was explained and discussed, which added to rather than distracted from the intensity of the experience. However, it took a further six hours of argument (heated and vociferous) concerning the nature and meaning of unconditional love, eroticism versus chaste idealism, archetypes and historical verisimilitude, the cinematic requirement for heartbreak balanced by the temptation to placate audiences by mitigating total tragedy and much else besides before my translator and I agreed to disagree about our understanding of the grand passion and fate of Prince Selim and Anarkali.

Frankly, my dears, there are some films where one always gives a damn! At each viewing there is the rising tension of expectation, the grasping for breath as the inevitable emotional climax approaches and one embraces the realisation that what must be will happen all over again. I assure you there are worse things in heaven and earth than waiting with philosophical fortitude for a denouement. Can you conceive of sitting through four hours of a rip-off video of *Gone With the Wind* (1939) only to discover it ends just as Rhett Butler exits the door and turns ... Blank tape sputtering where Rhett should deliver his immortal line. All that emotional energy expended only to be left even more disconsolate than the film in its entirety could manage. Does Rhett really not give a damn in this inconclusive video version? Surely not. I am no Scarlett O'Hara, so it is impossible to find consolation in her perennial mantra: 'I'll think about that tomorrow'. What point would there be in trying to rethink her predicament, how could a return to her one true love, the red earth of Tara, have any poignancy without her final dismissal by the man who really loved her despite all her caprice and wilful emotional blindness? I was mad enough to mount my own civil war against inept video pirates everywhere.

I came to know films, the classic great films of the Golden Age, courtesy of television. So far as I remember, the iconic mythological journey to redemption that is John Ford's epic western *Stagecoach* (1939) was shown every Christmas Eve of my childhood, as regular a visitor as Santa Claus. Another Ford classic staring John Wayne, *She Wore a Yellow Ribbon* (1949) recurred so often that we used to watch just to see if we had forgotten any of the dialogue! These were films so good they transcended the formulaic requirements of their genre. And yet, for all their overt themes of brittle civilisation threatened by the impending menace of savagery and the empowerment of the hero to use violence to secure civilisation as we know it, my conscience was always on the side of the Indians who dropped like flies – unnamed, unnumbered (except there were lots of them), imperiously unconsidered. I am sure that those doomed to die so unconscionably in the maximal era of ubiquitous cinematic and television westerns that was my childhood laid the foundations of the anti-imperialist values of my adulthood.

There were, however, some perverse rules about which films were permitted to enter our household via the cathode ray tube. You will recall that my mother, as I indicated at the outset, was a woman prone to emphatic, nay disturbing emotional empathy. We grew up with the story of what happened when as a young woman she went to see a performance of Madame Butterfly. At the end of the opera she stood up – and drenched the gentleman in the row in front with the not inconsiderable torrent of tears that had accumulated in the folds of her oilskin mackintosh! I had to leave home before I actually got to see *Gone With the Wind* (the complete version). And as for *Brief Encounter* (1945), David Lean's brilliant angst-ridden tale of middle class resignation to marital rectitude in the face of the chaste yet considerable temptation of grand passion – it was totally prohibited entry, end of story.

Mother's susceptibility to the course of true love not running smoothly probably explains why I ended up being emotionally scarred by cinematic war and death in my most impressionable years. I could have done without the traumatising, yet I am beholden to the moral and ethical niceties it bequeathed. At the going down of the sun and in the morning there are experiences I can never forget.

How can cinema sensitise people to the horror, futility and waste of war? Look no further than into the eyes of Vladek Sheybal in the final scene of Andrzej Wajda's film *Kanal* (1957). I know I was much too young for the film when I first saw it on BBC TV, and much older than my years once it had been viewed. The story concerns the last desperate attempt to live to resist another day by the few remaining members of the Warsaw resistance. They take to the sewers, pursued by the enemy. Sheybal plays a musician, though to me his voice whatever he is saying is always a hollow symphony of resonant despair. Eventually he makes it to the outlet of the sewer system only to find it blocked by a grating welded to the pipe. There is no way out – only waiting to be consumed by the inevitability of death. It is an image of desolation captured in art I have seen raw in reality. The image does not lie.

Wajda's Polish classic stood apart from the routine standard fare of westerns and war films one saw in one's youth. Hollywood and British cinema, for reasons which are not hard to grasp, specialised in vindications of righteous victory. However much gunfire, however improbably large the legions of enemies mown down, the reality of war was essentially glossed over for nationalist purposes. Our people did their bit, however grim or dangerous, stoically with right on their side. Death in war is portrayed as a noble and necessary enterprise in which our plucky fellows are sacrificed for the greater good. This is not to say such routine vehicles cannot shock. I well remember the incredulity my brother and I experienced the day we saw John Wayne – yes I said John Wayne – die on the sands of Iwo Jima, in the film of that ilk. I am not sure we stopped to consider what such an enormity might signify – we just never thought it possible for a John Wayne character to expire, not even at the end of a film.

The end of *The Sands of Iwo Jima* sublimates the sacrifice of John Wayne with a re-enactment of that ultimate icon of righteous victory – the raising of the American flag on the summit of Mount Surbachi. The film's credits assure us that the three actual survivors of that famous incident participated in the film, though as in the famed photo which immortalised the moment, you are hard pressed to indentify faces. *The Sands of Iwo Jima* was made in 1949, the survivor's cameo role in that movie is not one of the indignities heaped on them as chronicled in Clint Eastwood's modern reworking of these same events in *The Flags of Our Fathers* (2006). Modern revisionist war films have complicated narratives and can overdose on scale and simulation in documentary style and graphic detail of the sound and gruesome incidents of war. Why is it then, do you suppose, they somehow lose the intensity of emotional engagement in the process? Maybe the craven emotional manipulation and imperious attitude to the first casualty of war – truth – in old fashioned films is precisely what raises the telling questions that linger in the conscience. You sense something is missing and have to ponder the missing ingredients. The more revisionist films attempt to reason with the inchoate nature of reality, the less they satisfy as answers to the necessary questions. Eastwood includes all the right lines in a complex interweaving of storylines. He does some historic justice to the Indian Ira Hayes, one of the survivors of the flag raising. In *The Flags of Our Fathers* Ira Hayes is even played by a First Nations actor, the estimable Adam Beach. Yet if you want to get the moral of Ira's story it is more potent and intense in the Johnny Cash song than in Eastwood's cinema epic. Movies can be tricky things and are funny like that.

Don't get me wrong. I have experienced revisionism and barely escaped with my sanity intact, let alone lived to tell the tale. It was during the time of my final exams at university. I was persuaded that one evening of indulgence would do no harm by one of my flatmates and her boyfriend, neither of whom had exams. Off to the cinema we went in boisterous spirits. *Soldier Blue* (1970), the hot title du jour, was the selected objective for our excursion. Well, I was doing anthropology so a movie about American Indians might even be claimed as work-related.

Why is it that when we flirt with impropriety we so seldom stop to think things through? *Soldier Blue* is a slow moving and entirely innocuous film until it becomes an explicit reconstruction of the Sand Creek Massacre of 1864. I knew all about Sand Creek. I had read numerous histories of the America's 'Indian Wars' and their horrors. I had spent the previous summer holiday working in the Museum of the American Indian in New York. Excuses have I none. It is impossible now to view *Soldier Blue* as it appeared on screen in London in 1971: the most violent film ever made, so they claim. Such mercies as modern censorship requires do nothing for the images of carnage I carry in my head. Sand Creek was a peaceful village, flying the American flag in token of acceptance and honouring of treaty terms when a detachment of Colorado militia swept through intent on slaughter. *Soldier Blue* is a different kind of revisionism because it is not trying to make an argument or weave complexity into its narrative – it just shows what happened. Women's breasts and men's genitalia were, as so often in reality, severed to be made into souvenir tobacco pouches. Women were raped, children smashed to pieces. As the carnage went on and groans ricocheted around the cinema, I felt an urgent need to get out, to be gone, not to be there. But so immobilised were the other watchers there was no way out. I was trapped.

When we left the cinema the sun had gone down and I could only remember. When we got back to the flat I remembered and remembered – and there were no cigarettes left and all the shops were closed. In the morning I was still busy with my remembering. I have no memory of what exam I had to attend or even if I answered any questions. All I know is I was remembering then and for ages after. I was remembering while trying to forget the feeling of actually being inside history. Not thinking about history, you understand, or reasoning with knowns and unknowns of what happened once but the palpable sense of being there in my mind and spirit. It does not have to be a great movie to achieve so much. I am, however, sure that movies cannot achieve this end by just being grotesque and graphic. Take *Catch-22* (1970), for instance, the mediocre film of a wonderful book, which demonstrates it knows that verisimilitude is not enough in and of itself. It builds and builds the tension of Snowden's secret before spilling the realism of his ruptured intestines all over Yossarian. Snowden's secret is the fragility of human life which is not designed for the rigours of warfare. We are ready for the emotional intensity of this simple truth by the time it all comes spilling out.

The design flaw in humanity is our unwillingness to imagine and be tutored by our limitations. The movies are made for us to indulge the creative capacity to feel and experience the thoughts, ideals, aspirations and life traumas of other people. This is why movies specialise in love and death – the eternal imponderables of the human condition. This is why I keep watching movies, not in expectation of answers, just to familiarise myself with the various permutations of the questions.

And yes, I have seen the ultimate question. It is a scene in a television movie called *The Day After* (1983) which the BBC decided to show as part of its week long nuclear holocaust festival. Now don't be coy, such things have their place in public service. This one little scene is a testament to the importance of the creative imagination. What is the worst thing that can happen? To be a housewife in the American Midwest on an ordinary day, just pegging out clothes on the washing line when, suddenly, nuclear missiles launch from their underground silos behind your back. This is an image worth a lifetime of remembering, lest we find ourselves in the day after. Let's pray that experiencing such an image can make thinkers of us all, the kind of people who take counsel with their humane conscience. It's what movies can do, sometimes.

CONTRIBUTORS

Alev Adil is the Head of the Department of Communication and Creative Arts at University of Greenwich, London • **Merryl Wyn Davies** is Director of the Muslim Institute • **Rachel Dwyer** is Professor of Indian Cultures and Cinema at School of Oriental and African Studies, University of London • **Hamza Elahi** is a civil servant based in East London • **Naomi Foyle**, poet and novelist, is the co-founder of British Writers in Support of Palestine • **Khola Hasan** is Director of Albatross Consultancy Ltd., which deals with issues of women's rights in the Muslim community • **Aamer Hussein** is Senior Editor of *Critical Muslim* • **Robert Irwin** is the author or editor of seventeen works of fiction or non-fiction, of which the most recent is *Memoirs of a Dervish* • **Ramin Jahanbegloo**, the Iranian-Canadian philosopher, is Noor-York Chair in Islamic Studies at York University, Toronto. His books include *Beyond Violence* and *The Gandhian Moment* • **Ahmed Wakas Khan** is a freelance journalist and World Editor at 'The Platform' • **Sabrina Mahfouz**, a writer and performer, is currently the Leverhulme Trust Associate Playwright at Bush Theatre, London • **Sabita Manian** is Professor of International Relations, Lynchburg College, Virginia • **S Parvez Manzoor** is a critic based in Stockholm • **Imranali Panjwani** is the editor of *The Shi'a of Samarra: the Heritage and Politics of a Community in Iraq* • **Irna Qureshi** writes about being British, Pakistani, Muslim and female at http://www.bollywoodinbritain.wordpress.com and tweets at @irnaqureshi • **Samia Rahman** is Deputy Director of the Muslim Institute • **Jalees Rehman**, a German scientist and physician, is Associate Professor of Medicine and Pharmacology at the University of Illinois, Chicago • **Fahmida Riaz**, one of Pakistan's foremost literary figures, has published several volumes of poetry, fiction, and criticism, and has also translated Rumi and Forough Farrokhzad (from Persian) and Sheikh Ayaz and Shah Abdul Latif (from Sindhi) into Urdu • **Martin Rose**, a career British Council officer, has served in Baghdad, Europe and North America and is currently Director of the British Council in Morocco. He is writing a book on his time in Baghdad • **Manhal al-Sarraj** is a Syrian novelist based in Sweden. Her first novel, *As the River Must*, considers the Hama massacre of 1982, and is banned in Syria • **Christopher Shackle** is Emeritus Professor of Modern Languages of South Asia, School of Oriental and African Studies, London • **Shanon Shah** is doctoral candidate at the Department of Theology and Religious Studies, King's College, London • **Boyd Tonkin** is the Literary Editor of *The Independent* • **Michael Wolf** is a writer and film producer. His books include *The Hadj: An American's Pilgrimage to Mecca* and *One Thousand Roads to Mecca*.